Peter Edelman is the Carmack Waterhouse Professor of Law and Public Policy and the faculty director of the Center on Poverty and Inequality at Georgetown University Law Center. He is the author of *So Rich, So Poor: Why It's So Hard to End Poverty in America* (The New Press). A top advisor to Senator Robert F. Kennedy from 1964 to 1968, he went on to fill various roles in President Bill Clinton's administration, from which he famously resigned in protest after Clinton signed the 1996 welfare reform legislation. He lives in Washington, D.C.

NOT A CRIME TO BE POOR

ALSO BY PETER EDELMAN

Searching for America's Heart: RFK and the Renewal of Hope

So Rich, So Poor: Why It's So Hard to End Poverty in America

NOT A CRIME TO BE POOR

THE CRIMINALIZATION OF POVERTY IN AMERICA

Peter Edelman

NEW YORK
LONDON

© 2017 by Peter Edelman All rights reserved.
Afterword © 2019 by Peter Edelman
No part of this book may be reproduced, in any form,
without written permission from the publisher.

Requests for permission to reproduce selections from this book should
be made through our website: https://thenewpress.com/contact.

First published in the United States by The New Press, New York, 2017
This paperback edition published by The New Press, 2019
Distributed by Two Rivers Distribution

ISBN 978-1-62097-163-5 (hc)
ISBN 978-1-62097-548-0 (pbk)
ISBN 978-1-62097-553-4 (e-book)

CIP data is available

The New Press publishes books that promote and enrich public discussion and
understanding of the issues vital to our democracy and to a more equitable world.
These books are made possible by the enthusiasm of our readers; the support of
a committed group of donors, large and small; the collaboration of our many
partners in the independent media and the not-for-profit sector; booksellers, who
often hand- sell New Press books; librarians; and above all by our authors.

www.thenewpress.com

Composition by dix!
This book was set in Fairfield LH

Printed in the United States of America

For Ellika, Zoe, Levi, and Elijah

Contents

Introduction

Vera Cheeks, a resident of Bainbridge, Georgia, was pulled over and ticketed for rolling through a stop sign. The judge hit her with a $135 fine and ordered her to pay in full immediately. She told him she was unemployed and caring for her terminally ill father and had no money, so the judge said he would give her three months of "probation" to pay up. He sent her to a room behind the courtroom where, reports Cheeks, who is African American, "there was a real big lady. There were cells on both sides of the room and there was a parade of people paying money to the lady. They were all black. It was like the twilight zone, totally mind-boggling."

The woman said Cheeks now owed $267—the fine plus $105 for the (for-profit) probation people and $27 for the Georgia Victims Emergency Fund. The woman put a paper in front of Cheeks and told her to sign it. Cheeks said she would not. The woman said, "You're refusing to sign the paper. I'm going to tell the judge to put you in jail for five days." Cheeks still refused, and finally the woman demanded $50 or else Cheeks would go to jail. Cheeks's fiancé, who was at the courthouse, raised the money by pawning her engagement ring and a lawn implement. That avoided jail for the moment, but Cheeks remained at risk of being locked up if she was late with even one payment.

Cheeks grew up in New York City and then lived in Orlando, Florida. Romance brought her to Bainbridge ("I met a gentleman") in 2014, although she is "more of a city girl" and "not so happy" in the small town. She had been a vocalist with bands that went on tour and also was a pharmacy technician, which she said was her best job. She went to Morgan State College in Maryland for a year but dropped out when she had her first child. She has two daughters, three grandchildren, and two "granddogs." She used to go to church but is not so impressed by the ministers now, so she prays on her own. Her health isn't great, but she has stopped smoking because she wants to be around as her grandchildren grow up and to be able to travel.

The Bainbridge, Georgia, court system had tangled with the wrong person. Vera Cheeks was furious. She had never seen anything like it. She was "traumatized" by what she saw and just "cried to see what they do to people" there. She thought something was very wrong, but she said the people in the town didn't seem to know it was wrong and were scared to do anything about it anyway. She went home and started looking for a lawyer. She Googled on her computer for three hours until she found Sarah Geraghty of the Southern Center for Human Rights, got in touch with her, and retained her. Cheeks says that Geraghty was ecstatic because, the lawyer told her, she had been looking for a case like that. Geraghty not only resolved Cheeks's problem but also brought to an end the local court's system of making money at the expense of low-income people and people of color.

Cheeks is relieved not to have gone to jail for what amounts to the crime of being poor. And she is glad that she and Geraghty could do some good for the people of Grady County, Georgia.

Mass incarceration has been doing its damage for decades, but Vera Cheeks personifies a newer criminalization—the criminalization of poverty. Cheeks was saved, but millions of others have no such good fortune. And the debtors' prison with which Cheeks was threatened is just one aspect of a larger phenomenon: in America today, it is too often a crime to be poor.

Punishing the poor is as old as the Bible. In England, almshouses showed up as early as the tenth century, and the Elizabethan Poor Laws were enacted at the end of the sixteenth century. The United States had almshouses, workhouses, and poorhouses from its beginning, going on to pauper auctions in the later nineteenth century, and followed by so-called scientific charity.

We still punish the poor, but the contemporary history is more complex. Beginning with the New Deal, federal policy began to reach the poor in positive ways. Social Security, unemployment insurance, and fair labor standards made an enormous difference, even if flawed in their coverage. The sixties saw an explicit focus on reducing poverty, and poverty fell from 22.4 percent in 1959 to 11.1 percent in 1973. African American poverty dropped from 55.1 percent to 31.4 percent over the same period, with the historic civil rights statutes enacted during the sixties playing a significant role.

Beginning in the seventies, progress slowed and public attitudes regressed. Even so, important new policies were adopted over the following decades. Food stamps (now SNAP), housing vouchers, the Earned Income Tax Credit, and the Child Tax Credit, along with Social Security and other existing programs, have made a significant difference; without them, more than ninety million people would be living in poverty, twice the number of people counted as poor today.

Nonetheless, a constellation of factors has held us back: tax, employment, and welfare policies that worsen inequality and poverty; the deindustrialization of our country and the consequent flood of low-wage jobs; the weakening of unions; changes in family structure that have left many women and their children alone to cope with low-paying work; the deterioration of the public education system, which is supposed to be a stepping-stone upward; mass incarceration; a long-standing crisis in affordable housing; and continuing issues of discrimination. All these combine to create, exacerbate, and perpetuate poverty in our very rich nation.

At the same time, negative attitudes toward the poor and public policies to put those attitudes into law have intensified, especially with the Great Recession that overtook us during the George W. Bush years, and now the Trump era. Anger simmered for decades as people struggled with low-wage work, and then it exploded with the recession's sudden blow. Lower-income whites complain vehemently about slackers who they say take government handouts instead of working, and they especially allege that African Americans make use of affirmative action to take away their jobs. Never mind that welfare and affirmative action are close to defunct; the narrative is a stock line practically from coast to coast, and the 2016 election proved its punch.

Despite the gathering forces, we reached the year 2000 with a poverty level of 11.3 percent, almost as low as the historic low in 1973. Especially since then, politics about poverty and much else has soured, and feelings about race in particular have deteriorated. Racism is America's original sin, and it is present in every area of criminalization, whether through out-and-out discrimination, structural and institutional racism, or implicit bias. Joined together, poverty and racism create a toxic mixture that mocks our democratic rhetoric of equal opportunity and equal protection under the law.

Beyond mass incarceration, beginning in the 1990s we adopted a new set of criminal justice strategies that further punish poor people for their poverty. Low-income people are arrested for minor violations that are only annoyances for people with means but are disastrous for the poor and near poor because of the high fines and fees we now almost routinely impose. Poor people are held in jail to await trial when they cannot afford bail, fined excessive amounts, and hit with continuously mounting costs and fees. Failure to pay begets more jail time, more debts from accumulated interest charges, additional fines and fees, and, in a common penalty with significant consequences for those living below or near the poverty line, repeated driver's license suspensions. Poor people lose their liberty and often lose their jobs, are frequently barred from a host of public benefits, may lose custody of their children, and may even lose their right to vote.[1] And immigrants, even some with green cards, can be subject to deportation. Once incarcerated, impoverished inmates with no access to paid work are often charged for their room and board. Many debtors will carry debts to their deaths, often hounded by bill collectors and new prosecutions.[2]

This system of modern peonage—a government-operated loan shark operation—has been going on for years, but it came into public consciousness only in light of revelations from Ferguson, Missouri, in the wake of the killing of Michael Brown.[3] Outsized fees and fines are a big, national business and they occur with regularity. Right now in the United States, ten million people—representing two-thirds of all current and former offenders in the country—owe a total of $50 billion in accumulated fines, costs, fees, charges for room and board in jails and prisons, and other impositions.[4] Community policing has turned into community fleecing.[5]

The problem of "high fines and misdemeanors" exists across the country: throughout much of the South, in states ranging from Washington to Oklahoma to Colorado, and of course in Ferguson. It calls up memories of the sharecropper economy that characterized the South well into the second half of the twentieth century, with families always ending the year owing the plantation more than they had earned from the cotton crop and therefore obligated to continue for another season.

Many states couple jailing with widespread suspension of driver's licenses. Others mainly use license suspension to coerce payment of the debts, heedless of the fact that this makes it much more difficult for the working poor to get to the jobs they need to pay off their debts.

Even without the use of jailing or the wholesale suspension

of driver's licenses, exorbitant fines and fees are now a staple throughout most of the country to make up for the revenue shortfalls that have resulted from tax cuts. Meanwhile, white-collar criminals get slaps on the wrist for financial crimes that ruin millions, and wealthy scofflaws owe a cumulative $450 billion in back taxes, while fines and fees from the justice system hit lower-income people—especially people of color—the hardest.

In addition to being inhumane and destructive, locking up people who are unable to pay fines and fees is wasteful. The people who can afford to pay, and even those who can find the money only by not paying the utility bill or by selling their blood, make money for the authorities. But the cost of actually incarcerating a person for failing to pay a fine or scheduled payment typically exceeds whatever is collected. Some jurisdictions have figured this out and now confine themselves to using driver's license suspensions and heavy-handed collection agencies. Even without incarceration, the weight of criminal debt inflicts major damage.

Mass incarceration, which has disproportionately victimized people of color from its beginning in the 1970s, set the scene for the new criminalization of poverty. But to understand the new impulse to make being poor a crime, one has to follow the trail of tax cuts that began in the Reagan era, which created revenue gaps all over the country. Deep budget cuts ensued, and the onus of paying for our justice system—from courts to law enforcement agencies and even other arms of government—began to shift to the "users" of the courts, including those least equipped to pay. Poor people's inability to pay the bloated fines and fees continues to criminalize their poverty in an unwinnable cycle.

Compounding the problem are the for-profit corporations with their high-pressure lobbyists—prisons, probation companies, and purveyors of medical services and tests. The for-profits promised lower costs, but they fulfilled the promise only by delivering grossly inferior services, treating inmates so sadistically or so negligently that sometimes death was the result.

The anti-tax lobby told voters they would get something for nothing—the state or municipality would tighten its belt a little, it would collect big money from low-level offenders, and everything would be fine. This hurt not only the poor. In state after state the dismantling of the tax base crippled public education and damaged the futures of children across lines of income, hurting many more children than just those who live in poverty.

The anti-tax forces did damage in other areas as well, stripping down mental health services, legal services, and even law enforcement. Budget cuts led to the further deterioration of mental health and addiction treatment services, making the police the first responders and jails and prisons the de facto mental hospitals, again with a special impact on minorities and low-income people.

"Broken windows" law enforcement policy—the idea that mass arrests for minor offenses promote community order—aided and abetted the new criminalization, making the police complicit in the victimization of the poor. Enforcing "quality of life" rules was touted as a way to achieve civic tranquility and prevent more serious crime. What it actually did was fill jails with poor people, especially because those arrested could not pay for bail.

Nor is the new criminalization confined to jailing low-income adults for minor offenses. Poor children also became targets of the new criminalization. Public school children, particularly in poor communities of color, are arrested and sent to juvenile and even adult courts for school behavior that not long ago was handled with a reprimand. The dangerous rhetoric of "superpredators" and the murders at Columbine High School in Colorado led to "zero tolerance" policies and brought an enlarged police presence, called "school resource officers," into public schools, with the ironic result that the murder of white suburban children led to punitive policies that hit poor inner-city children the hardest.

Poor women are targets of the new criminalization, too. Underfunded police departments looking for shortcuts had originally created "chronic nuisance" ordinances as a way to shut down crack houses, but they also began to require landlords to evict people who were calling 911 too often. This phenomenon—bad enough as it was, with its utter lack of procedural due process—turned into a monster when the ordinances were applied to victims of domestic violence: women in some poor communities are now evicted by police order from rental premises for calling 911 too often to seek protection from domestic abuse.

Homeless people, always targets of criminalization, are also experiencing a new wave of punitive laws, including jail terms for public urination and sleeping outdoors. The use of law enforcement both to criminalize homelessness and to drive the homeless entirely out of cities is increasing. Punishing the homeless often reflects underlying prejudice, but municipalities are now enacting even more punitive measures due to shortages of funds for housing, mental health services, drug and alcohol treatment, and basic cash assistance. Low-income people are also deterred from seeking public benefits by threats of sanctions for made-up allegations of benefits fraud. As elected officials have moved to the right, laws designed to keep people from seeking assistance have grown more common.

For at least two decades, the new criminalization of poverty crept into communities large and small, driven by misbegotten law enforcement politics and the search for revenue, but with little public attention. Of course some states and localities did not make excessive use of fines and fees, and most judges applied the law as fairly as they could. And there are certainly cases where community safety requires a response, albeit with appropriate penalties. That said, though, the new criminalization of poverty is a major national problem.

Ferguson opened our eyes. In a promising turn, a movement to fight back is showing signs of developing, with regard to the new criminalization as well as mass incarceration itself. Organizers and some public officials are attacking mass incarceration, lawyers are challenging the constitutionality of debtors' prisons and money bail, judicial leaders are calling for fair fines and fees, policy advocates are seeking repeal of destructive laws, more judges and local officials are applying the law justly, and journalists are covering all of it. The Obama administration's Department of Justice stepped into the fray on a number of fronts. Ferguson was a spark that turned isolated instances of activism into a national conversation and produced numerous examples of partnerships between advocates and decision-makers.

Now we must turn all of that into a movement. The ultimate goal, of course, is the end of poverty itself. But as we pursue that goal, we must get rid of the laws and practices that unjustly incarcerate and otherwise damage the lives of millions who can't fight back. We must fight mass incarceration and criminalization of poverty in every place where they exist, and fight poverty, too. We must organize—in neighborhoods and communities, in cities and states, and nationally. And we must empower people to advocate for themselves as the most fundamental tool for challenge. We need elected leaders, judges and lawyers, and journalists, too, but we will get more done and get it done sooner if it is grounded in the people who demand action.

Robert Kennedy was and is my inspiration. His commitment was to end poverty and racism, and to build that effort on a base of the voices of low-income people of all races. It was my privilege to be at his side as he connected with residents in the Bedford-Stuyvesant neighborhood in Brooklyn, farmworkers in California, and people struggling with severe malnutrition in Mississippi and eastern Kentucky. It was no accident that his presidential campaign in 1968 drew in large numbers of lower-income voters of all races. He had connected with them and they connected with him. For a movement to end poverty as well as mass incarceration and criminalization of poverty, Robert Kennedy is an inspiration.

Our momentum has been slowed since then and in many senses we have lost our way. But we have a new consciousness, and we can see it in the people in the streets of Ferguson and in the work of people across the nation addressing poverty at the grassroots.

It drives a growing push for justice, and Bryan Stevenson reminds us why: "The opposite of poverty is not wealth. It is justice."

And Deuteronomy gives us our charge: "Justice, justice shall you pursue."

NOT A CRIME TO BE POOR

PART ONE

The Criminalization of Poverty

1

Ferguson Is Everywhere: Twenty-First-Century Debtors' Prisons

In New Orleans's Municipal Court, Section A, even when the judge was presiding, not a word was audible to anyone in the audience, and, with multiple negotiations happening simultaneously around the room, no one in the gallery could understand anything that was going on. In the center of the grim circus were the shackled men wearing orange jumpsuits—almost all African American—being held for arraignment, awaiting trial because they could not make bail, or doing time for criminal contempt because they had not appeared in response to a "judicial attachment" or bench warrant for nonpayment of debt owed to the court.

Most of the shackled men, many quite young, were embarking on (or well along in) a long or even endless voyage of debt and incarceration. Unlike other jurisdictions, New Orleans does not jail people at the time they are sentenced and unable to pay a fine. But this is a distinction without a difference: many of the accused are held for days before being arraigned, and more are in for longer times while awaiting trial because they can't afford to post bail. More yet will serve multiple stints in jail for nonpayment of debts to the court, ad infinitum.[1]

In too many cities and small towns across the country, scenes like the one in New Orleans occur every day. The details differ, but high fines and fees are the order of the day in juvenile as well as adult courts.[2] Even in jurisdictions and individual courtrooms where low-income arrestees are not jailed when initially sentenced, the dearth of public defenders, the almost ubiquitous use of money bail (in adult courts), and the ever-mounting payments owed mean repeated time in jail along with unmanageable debt. Ferguson is almost everywhere.

Constitutional violations on the part of the courts are rife, and they go uncorrected largely because of the shortage of public defenders. Police often violate the Fourth Amendment, making stops without reasonable suspicion, making arrests without probable cause, and using excessive force. First Amendment rights are violated when free expression is suppressed, including prohibition of the use of cellphone cameras to film police activity in a public setting. Fourteenth Amendment rights are curtailed when there is racial, economic, and other discrimination by police, judges, and other officials who disregard equal protection and due process.

The very act of jailing an indigent person for a fine-only, low-level offense is unconstitutional, and many of these jailings occur in states that actually have laws explicitly banning debtors' prisons. In 1983 the Supreme Court heard the case of Danny Bearden, an illiterate ninth-grade dropout who was convicted of receiving stolen goods and placed on probation with a fine of $500 and a $250 order of restitution. His parents put up the first $200.

Danny Bearden was going to pay the rest himself but was laid off from his factory job. He tried very hard to find work, but finally had to tell the probation people he had lost his job and could not make the payment then due. His probation was revoked and he was sent to jail. The Supreme Court decided in *Bearden v. Georgia* that "punishing a person for his poverty" violates the equal protection clause and that an indigent defendant cannot be jailed for inability to pay a fine unless he has "willfully refused to pay the fine or restitution when he has the means to pay."[3]

Yes, *Bearden* and state law are flouted every day. The people who hear the low-level cases are often municipal judges or justices of the peace who are not lawyers or are lawyers but serve part-time and practice in completely different areas of the law. Some judges do not know the law, but other judges know it well and apply it harshly nonetheless.

The Supreme Court has not given clear guidance for what "willfully refused" means, and the literature abounds with instances where the judge said the defendant had expensive-looking shoes or the like and therefore must be able to pay. A judge in Illinois asked all defendants if they smoked, and when any said yes, the judge said they have the means to pay.[4] A judge in Michigan found that because the defendant had cable television he was capable of paying.[5]

And the *Bearden* ruling that a defendant's ability to pay must be taken into account does not apply when a person is arrested on a bench warrant for defaulting on a payment plan, because now the debtor has committed a crime that *does* carry a jail sentence. Failure to pay constitutes criminal contempt, which allows incarceration as well as further fines and fees. Because the contempt is a crime that allows jailing, there is no protection for indigence and *Bearden* becomes irrelevant. The right to an attorney that stemmed from *Gideon v. Wainwright* applies (which doesn't mean one is available), but *Bearden* does not apply.

Even the right to an attorney comes with a price tag. The Supreme Court decided in *Fuller v. Oregon* that charging a fee for a public defender can be constitutional if people who would suffer a "manifest hardship" are relieved from paying it (a requirement ignored in some states).[6] In fact, forty-three states charge for having a public defender.[7] Florida does not waive its $50 public defender application fee for the indigent, instead instructing its courts to include it as part of sentencing or as a condition of probation.[8] In North Carolina, defendants have to pay not only the $50 fee but also the full value of the defense services provided, and in Virginia a defendant must pay up to $1,235 for a public defender on each count for certain felonies.[9] South Dakota charges $92 an hour; even a defendant found innocent nonetheless owes $920 for ten hours of representation. If he cannot pay, it is a crime.[10]

Coming into focus now is the highly questionable constitutionality of money bail—the practice of making a defendant put up a large sum of money to ensure that he will appear for trial, regardless of whether he poses a danger to the community or himself. Defendants who cannot come up with bail—in low-level matters as well as in more serious cases—are kept in jail pending trial. The unmistakably different impact of money bail on the rich and poor calls for litigation, which is now under way in a growing number of courts, both on equal protection and due process grounds and the Eighth Amendment's explicit ban on "excessive bail."

"PAY OR STAY"

The days of the $50 or $100 fine for a speeding ticket are long gone. The fine today is $250, $300, or more. Ferguson charged fines of up to $531 for "high grass and weeds" in someone's yard.[11] Fees of one kind or another—for example, $500 toward the cost of running the courthouse gym in one county in Michigan—are then tacked on, with multiple fees totaling much more.[12]

Two interacting trends accelerated in the 1990s: sky-high fines and fees for minor infractions, and a dramatic increase in the number of cases. Justices of the peace and speed traps were facts of my childhood in the 1940s, but relatively speaking they were penny-ante. My father always announced when we went through Hill City, Minnesota, on our way to see my grandmother that he was driving with particular care to avoid being caught in the speed trap. Even so, the fine might be just $25 or $50; an overnight stay in jail would be rare. In the 1990s, though, the need for revenue caused public officials to increase the amounts of their fines and invent new and expensive fees. Police officers were then required to meet new arrest quotas.

"Broken windows" policing produced more fines and fees. And there is the malicious part, too. Jill Webb, a public defender in Tulsa, Oklahoma, told me the police there regularly place a squad car at a stop sign in an African American neighborhood and arrest people for rolling stops. Only in the African American neighborhood. That is neither about revenues nor about broken windows.

Tulsa is representative. At the age of fifty-three, Rosalind Hall of Tulsa, Oklahoma, owed $11,258 in fines and fees stemming from repeated shoplifting connected to three decades of drug addiction and mental health issues. She had served time for the crimes and was now struggling to be clean and sober, but every time she was unable to meet a deadline on a portion of her fines and fees she was slapped with more debt and a new stint in jail. Her mental health issues made steady employment unlikely and her future seemed to hold an unending cycle of periodic jailing and additional debt, until Nicholas Kristof wrote a column about her in the *New York Times.* The court in Tulsa was so embarrassed that it let her out of jail and forgave her debt. Hall wept when she heard the news.

Many others in Tulsa don't fare as well. The *Tulsa World* reported that "about 28 percent of the nearly 23,000 people booked into the Tulsa Jail in 2014 were arrested on court debt-related complaints," up from 8 percent in 2004.[13] The reason? Follow the money. Raising taxes in Oklahoma requires a supermajority in the legislature. The rest unfolds as one might expect. In fiscal year 2015 alone, the court system took a $4 million cut in its state appropriation, and the courts now have to find 70 to 90 percent of their own funding.[14] So it's not surprising that yearly collections from defendants went from $1.6 million in 2008 to $4 million in 2014.[15]

The combined fines and fees for a first-offense misdemeanor DUI conviction have jumped from $498 (not cheap) to $715.50. The fine itself is $166.50 (which is the cheapest traffic ticket), and the fifteen types of possible fees include a law library fee, a charge for the court information system revolving fund, the forensic science improvement assessment, and the child abuse multidisciplinary account fee. This amount does not include other costs mandated by the judge, such as "supervision" fees and drug tests. If the defendant defaults, $80 is added for a bench warrant, and ultimately the debt is referred to a collection agency, an action that adds 30 percent to the total.

Nor is the state letting up. In 2016, the legislature doubled nearly all criminal and many civil fees in the state. Senator Greg Treat, vice chairman of the Senate Appropriations Committee, said tersely, "The courts could not have functioned without raising some of those fees." Trent Baggett, assistant executive coordinator for the District Attorneys Council, added that "offenders should help pay a fee for the prosecution of their cases."[16]

On paper, it looks like Oklahoma complies with *Bearden*. Rule 8 of the regulations that govern the courts requires a judicial inquiry into whether the defendant can pay. No doubt some defendants do avoid incarceration, but when almost 6,900 people in Tulsa County alone are jailed in a single year for not paying court-imposed debts, one has to wonder what is going on. Jill Webb told me that in practice "the judges don't make an inquiry before finding that the defendants are able to pay. The only thing the judges know about our defendants' ability to pay is that they are so poor they can't bond out." The *Tulsa World* reported that "one woman explained [to the presiding judge] she had to choose between having her electricity cut off and paying her court cost." The judge explained that the court's remedies are the same as those of the electric company, only the court's version is sending people to jail. "Nobody wins, I promise you that," the judge concluded.[17]

There are a variety of scenarios around the country, but they all add up to the same thing: prosecuting people for low-level offenses, squeezing them for money, and jailing them if they miss payments, in a cruel game of "pay or stay." In one version, the judge tells the defendant he has a choice—pay now or go to jail and get daily credit against what is owed for as long as it takes. The judge may make the "generous" offer that the defendant can minimize jail time if family or friends help out. Of course, these are low-income people, too, who typically can scrape up money, if at all, only by not paying the rent or a utility bill, or even by selling blood plasma. Some judges allow community service, but community service is not an option for people who have a job. And depending on the jurisdiction, community service is a euphemism for work that more closely resembles the re-enslavement of the post-Reconstruction era than the kind of time spent helping young people or the elderly that most people envision when they hear the words "community service."[18]

Natasha Edet, whom I met in New Orleans, was employed as a security guard and had never been arrested before. She was nonetheless jailed on a misdemeanor charge of simple battery after a fight with a former girlfriend. She spent fifteen days in jail because she could not afford $500 for bail. Jack Muse, the public defender assigned to represent her, finally succeeded in getting her released on her own recognizance. She ultimately agreed to plead guilty to disturbing the peace, but one still wonders why Edet had to be incarcerated for even a minute. Sandra Bland came to the world's attention after committing suicide while jailed in Houston, Texas, for a traffic infraction. She should not have been arrested in the first place, but once arrested, she should have been released on her own recognizance. Natasha Edet must have been just as terrified.

Money bail is key to the whole system of gouging defendants in New Orleans (and elsewhere). Arrestees are held pending trial unless they can pay for bail. If they cannot make bail, they are under pressure to plead guilty so they can get out of jail, while also being sentenced to expensive fines and fees. Public defenders told me that fees in district court routinely include $200 for a transcript fee, $500 for a judicial expense fund, $244 for the usual felony court fee, and at minimum $300 for drug tests and other "services" ordered by the court. Fees in excess of $1,000 are routine.

Jonathan Smith, who served with distinction as head of the Special Litigation Section of the Civil Rights Division of the U.S. Department of Justice, told me, "In New Orleans the bail system is what makes the whole corrupt system work. The bondsmen went to the state legislature and got them to add 3 percent to the regular 10 percent bail fee which is then divvied up among the court, prosecutor, defender, and jailer. Now everyone has skin in the game."

PROBATION AND PAYMENT PLANS

Instead of jailing a defendant at the time of conviction when he cannot pay the fine, a judge—who in all likelihood effectively coerced the defendant to plead guilty in order to get out of jail—may place him on "probation" and release him, but only if he signs a payment plan that adds another $40 a month or more, plus interest on the debt. This is not real probation. It is called "offender-funded probation" or "pay-only probation."[19] The only "service" provided by the "probation" agency is to collect the "supervision" fee that is appended to the already burdensome payment plan.[20] This story is ubiquitous.

Probation can be a racket all in itself. This can be true regardless of whether the agency is public or one of the for-profit companies that exist in thirteen states. Adel Edwards, who lives in Georgia, has a significant intellectual disability and cannot read or write. His infraction was burning leaves without a permit. He was fined $500 and another $528 in probation fees in the Municipal Court of Pelham. He did not have the money on the day he was in court, so he was put on probation for one year. No one asked about his ability to pay. The for-profit probation company, Red Hills, demanded an instant payment of $250, which he could not raise, so he went to jail for several days until a friend came up with the money. He made an additional four installment payments over a year that added up to $138. Even when his probation had expired, the Red Hills people nonetheless threatened him regularly with more jail time if he did not pay what he owed them.

The number of people on probation has skyrocketed, rising from roughly 800,000 adults in 1977 to more than four million in 2010.[21] In forty-four states offenders are charged for the costs of their own probation or parole (up from twenty-six in 1990), and forty-nine (except Hawaii and the District of Columbia) have a fee for electronic bracelets in lieu of detention while waiting for trial.[22] Defendants are also charged for drug testing, vehicle interlocking for those with a DUI, and any court-ordered treatment they receive, as well as interest, late fees, payment plan fees, and collection fees. The charges can be stiff. Home supervision and alcohol monitoring cost between $180 and $360 a month,[23] and drug testing can be $25 per week, or $1,300 a year.[24]

In Boulder, Colorado, probation can cost up to $1,200 a year. A misdemeanor first DUI is about $600. Urine analysis is $8 multiple times a week for a year or two. There are domestic violence classes, driving classes, rehab classes, and more—alcohol classes are $23 each and offenders have to attend fifteen to twenty of them. Electronic home monitoring for a sentence or pretrial release costs $14 a day. For people who fall behind on their payments, the court is quick to "revoke and reinstate," adding to what probationers owe and often suspending their driver's licenses as well. The authorities are mostly uninterested in throwing people in jail, because they want to make money, not spend it. For the same reason, they do not use unsupervised probation; "supervised probation" brings in the money.

The thought may cross one's mind that Boulder is a rich suburb, so no harm, no foul. But a Boulder public defender mentioned to me that she knew of someone who had been arrested for riding a bike without two hands on the handlebars, and she added that it was not a white college student. She said it is the transient population that is getting arrested disproportionately. "It's a pretend liberal community where everyone votes Democrat, then they get on a jury and don't want any crime on the streets of their perfect utopia. The juries are terrible."

Observers in Florida call its surcharges "cash register justice." In 1996, Florida added more than twenty new sets of fees, and it has added even more since.[25] The state repealed most of the exemptions for people unable to pay, and added a mandate that defendants be charged for the costs of their prosecution and public defense regardless of their ability to pay.[26]

Florida allows private debt collection firms to add a surcharge of up to 40 percent on unpaid court debt.[27] Fees are authorized for room and board, medical care, probation supervision, substance abuse treatment, electronic monitoring, and urinalysis. And then there are the fees the state imposes to subsidize other government functions: mandatory fees go to crime prevention programs, the Crime Compensation Trust Fund, the Crime Stoppers Trust fund, and on and on. Minimum fees of $100 for conviction on a felony and $50 on a misdemeanor are charged across the state.

Florida's chief justice, Jorge Labarga, strongly disapproves of what the legislature and governor have done to the judicial system in his state. Labarga participated in a panel of state chief justices on fines and fees at the White House in April 2016 and voiced his displeasure. He observed that filing fees in civil cases are so high—around $400—that people who want to get a divorce simply cannot get one. And he said the fees and fines in the courts are adding more than $1 billion to the state's coffers, most of which is used for purposes unrelated to the courts, while in a recent session the legislature actually cut the budget of the state's trial courts by $2.7 million.

In some courts around the country, the court clerk sets up the payment plan and there is no "probation" at all. It doesn't matter—it's just about money. That is what they do in New Orleans. People who are convicted and are unable to pay the fines and fees get a payment plan, with monthly installments that are backbreaking for the indigent and near indigent. The main purpose is to make money to run the court system, especially traffic court, where the penalties have been jacked up the most, and the state district court, where people likewise are slapped with steep fees.

Nor do the debts stop escalating.[28] When people default on their payments, the court issues a bench warrant (called a judicial attachment in Louisiana). Some of the men in the orange jumpsuits were in court because they were arrested on such a warrant. They were on their way to being held in criminal contempt for failure to pay, and to doing more time and owing more money.

Alana Cain's story is typical: She was convicted of felony theft in the district court and was assessed both a fine and court costs that included $600 in fees for the judges' "judicial expense fund." Even though Cain was destitute, the collections department told her to pay $100 a month. She borrowed from family and friends and paid regularly, but she was late on one payment, an anomaly that triggered an arrest warrant, an eventual arrest, and jail. Jail staff said she would have to call a family member to get a court date, but there was no free phone in the jail that she could use. She finally found an inmate with a phone account and was able to reach her sister, who scheduled a court date for her. By that time she had already been in jail for one week. The judge told her she would do ninety days the next time she missed a payment.[29]

DRIVER'S LICENSE SUSPENSIONS

Very frequently, with or without incarceration, a judge will order the suspension of a debtor's driver's license, a loss that all too often means that the defendant simply drives without a license, because he has to get to work, or take his child to see a doctor, or buy groceries. At least 75 percent of those who have their licenses suspended keep driving.[30] So the debtor may be arrested again for driving without a license, this time to be incarcerated and certainly to be hit with another set of fines and fees.

Damian Stinnie is one of the nearly million people in Virginia who have had their driver's licenses suspended. Despite spending much of his childhood in foster care, Stinnie graduated from high school with a 3.9 grade point average—a great story so far. Entering the world of work, he found a job and lost it and then, seeking work, received four traffic violations and racked up $1,000 in fines and costs. He was unable to pay the full amount within thirty days on his new $300-a-week job, so his driver's license was automatically suspended, meaning that Stinnie was among the 75 percent of those suspended who were sanctioned for not paying, not for the infractions themselves. As is routine in Virginia, no one asked Stinnie if he could afford to pay. At that point he joined the millions who face the dilemma of choosing between getting to work and taking the risk of being penalized for driving without a license. With the expansions of the state's fines and fees in 1998, assessments ballooned from $281.5 million to $618.8 million in 2014, with collections going from $192.2 million to $258.6 million.[31]

California is the leader and all-time champion in taking away driver's licenses. As of 2015, more than four million Californians had lost their driver's licenses for some kind of fine that they did not pay on time, often for an infraction that had nothing to do with driving. That is more than one out of six adult Californians.[32]

Florida suspends driver's licenses with abandon.[33] It does that without any inquiry as to whether the person is able to pay the underlying debt, and it sends people to prison for five years when they have been arrested three times for driving on a suspended license.[34] Needless to say, many people take the risk because they have no choice. Florida's Chief Justice Labarga said at a conference I attended at the White House, "Florida loves to suspend driver's licenses. If you spit on the street you lose your license."

Texas has about 1.2 million residents who have lost their licenses, and Florida has about 700,000.[35] When people in those states have unmanageable debts due to repeated arrests for driving on a suspended license, the next step is jail, whether they are indigent or not. Eight of the fifteen states studied in a landmark 2010 Brennan Center report suspend driver's licenses to punish missed criminal court debt payments.[36]

Nor are suspensions confined to traffic infractions. Montana suspends licenses for unpaid student loans. Iowa suspends for public drunkenness, with no car involved. Other states suspend for writing bad checks, graffiti, and littering.[37] In 2012, Tennessee added a category of suspensions for non-traffic-related offenses and now has 90,000 suspensions in that category to go with its 170,000 suspensions for traffic-related offenses.[38] A study by Robert Eger III of the Naval Post-Graduate School in Monterey, California, reported that at least eighteen states suspend for not paying the fines on non-driving traffic violations, adding up to 40 percent of all license suspensions nationally.[39]

People with means can often forestall suspensions by paying fines and fees, steep as they are, while those without means will be trapped in the vicious circle of repeated suspensions and ever deepening debt. Of course, some who drive under the influence deserve to lose their license, regardless of their income. On the other hand, some suspensions for unrelated behavior are unfair for everyone and should be repealed. So long as those are operative, though, the people with means will be finished with the courts after one suspension, while those without means will most likely join the treadmill of repeated suspensions and further fines and fees.

"PAY TO STAY"

The size of a convicted person's criminal debt continues to mount while she is in prison and on parole—a further criminalization of poverty originating in the omnivorous search for revenue. Outrageous as the destruction wrought by the dark farce of "pay or stay" is, charging the poor for their incarceration—"pay *to* stay"—sinks to even lower depths.

National Public Radio reports that forty-one states charge for room and board in prisons and jails.[40] Riverside County in California charges $142 a day to stay in its jail.[41] Nor is it only room and board. A convicted person is charged for such things as criminal lab fees, administrative fees, fees associated with the emergency response to the crime, funds for prison construction, and even prosecution reimbursement. Inmates are typically charged for medical expenses.[42] This is as true in juvenile courts as it is in adult courts.[43] In Dallas an inmate was found unresponsive in solitary confinement and taken to the hospital, where he was pronounced dead. The City of Dallas sent his father an invoice for more than $1,000 for the ambulance ride.[44]

The charges begin with diversion, the otherwise salutary policy of avoiding a criminal record for a minor offense. Too often, though, diversion is available only at a price and therefore is inaccessible to people with low incomes. In a national *New York Times* survey of two hundred defense lawyers, two-thirds said their clients were effectively barred from diversion programs by the fees. And the price can be steep—up to $5,000 for drunken driving in Dothan, Alabama, for example.[45]

The squeeze goes on through parole. Texas inmates on parole

owe $500 to $2,000 in offense-related debt. County clerks have at least thirty-nine categories of court costs in misdemeanors and thirty-five types in felony cases.[46] If you think the state does not actually try to collect, think again. The Illinois Department of Corrections sued Johnny Melton and won a judgment for almost $20,000 to cover the fifteen months he was in prison for a drug conviction. He had received part of a settlement of a lawsuit over his late mother's will that was supposed to help him upon his release, but instead he was homeless after he was paroled, his money seized by the courts to pay for his imprisonment. Shortly thereafter he died, destitute.[47] Melvin Moore inherited close to $14,000 from his grandmother, which stimulated a lawsuit suing him for $338,650 for his twenty years in prison and a verdict for all but $4,000 of his inheritance, which was protected by law.

It is easy to see how people end up never being able to pay off everything. The oft-heard phrases "school-to-prison pipeline" and "cradle-to-prison pipeline" are in fact too narrow. Along with the many collateral consequences following incarceration and even arrests, we have developed a criminal justice system in America that ensures a "cradle-to-coffin pipeline."

2

Fighting Back: The Advocates and Their Work

Thomas Harvey became aware of the damage being done in St. Louis County's eighty-two municipal courts shortly after he graduated from law school in 2009. Interning at the St. Louis public defender's office while in law school, he had regularly seen African American defendants in court clad in orange jumpsuits, chained together, and charged with low-level misdemeanors "treated like they weren't human beings," in his words, "not criminals, only poor people who were caught in the system and locked up for forty-eight to seventy-two hours before seeing anyone." While trying to get warrants resolved for homeless people, he discovered that the warrants were endemic throughout the county and were applied not only to the homeless.

"The system needs to be abolished," Harvey says. "It's been preying on black people and poor people for fifty years, using the courts as a tool to continue systemic racism." He concluded that the only meaningful reform would be a centralized full-time professional court system for the entire region.

From the point of view of race and poverty, Missouri, like too many places in our country, is in many ways the land that time forgot, according to Jonathan Smith, formerly of the Justice Department. Missouri reminds Smith of the Eastern Shore of Maryland: "It felt for a long time like civil rights had bypassed it. You had that unembarrassed 1950s worldview."

Thomas Harvey and the ArchCity Defenders set up a team to observe courts across the county and wrote a powerful report that documented the hold the municipal courts had on poor people, who individually often had as many as ten open cases around the county. The report became a building block for the monumental report about Ferguson that Smith helped write when he was at the Justice Department.[1]

The Defenders' first major step after Ferguson became infamous was to join with others in suing that city and the city of Jennings, Missouri, to end the injustice of those two courts.[2] In July 2016 they settled with Jennings in an agreement that completely reworked that city's governmental structure and its debtors' prison regime. Co-counsel Alec Karakatsanis, then of Equal Justice Under Law and now with Civil Rights Corps, called the resolution of that case "the most significant ever debtors' prison settlement." It emptied the jail of all the mistreated people still being held, paid a total of $4.75 million to nearly two thousand people who had been locked up for a total of almost 8,300 days, refunded everything they had paid in fines and fees, forgave the entire extant debt, and converted the low-level misdemeanors not repealed into civil violations.[3]

The story with Ferguson is more complicated. While the Defenders pursued their lawsuit, protracted negotiations between the government and the Ferguson officials were under way and in March 2016 finally resulted in a consent decree.[4] The final product is strong, covering an extensive list of agreements on police practices and municipal court reforms geared to reduce the gross use of fines and fees as a piggy bank for the city, but the road to the agreement was hardly smooth.

Christy Lopez, a Department of Justice lawyer then and a key player in the process, says that the local officials in Ferguson "never believed they had a problem," and when they were on the verge of entering into an agreement they pulled out. The federal government had to file a lawsuit against the city before city officials finally believed it was serious and agreed to the settlement. Even after the agreement, the city dragged its heels for months in its compliance.

Ferguson did finally change its modus operandi considerably. It brought in a new city judge and a new clerk, eliminated ten thousand old arrest warrants, reduced the ceiling for city revenue generated through fines and fees from 30 percent of its budget to 12.5 percent, and got rid of some of its most egregious "crimes," such as "manner of walking in roadway." Overall, traffic tickets in Ferguson went down by 85 percent and arrests decreased by 86 percent. But as of March 2017 the Defenders' suit had still not culminated in a binding agreement, which is crucial with regard to damages for the individual victims of the city's overreaching. Lopez says the progress up to that point was an especially good example of synergism among the government and private lawyers, along with the continuing protests and electoral changes in the city government. In a step backward, in April 2017 the incumbent white mayor was reelected against an African American opponent in a city that is 67 percent African American.

Building on their successes in Jennings and Ferguson, Harvey and the Defenders next enlisted the law firm of Arnold & Porter to join in suing the municipality of St. Ann, Missouri. St. Ann has only about thirteen thousand residents, but it has a large jail and contracts with twenty other municipalities to house their ill-gotten inmates. The Defenders' strategy here is to shut off the St. Ann jail to the other municipalities, most of which were still raking in fines and fees from county residents who owed money in multiple places. Many people paid off a debt in one place only to find themselves jailed in another, a practice known as the "muni shuttle."

In another step, the Defenders joined with the law firm Williams & Connolly to sue St. Louis County as a whole to challenge the constitutionality of a warrantless arrest procedure called a "wanted." Purportedly to alert police throughout the county of a police officer's desire to "question" someone, the notice in practice became a request to arrest the individual without a warrant. Further, working with the law firm of Tycko & Zavaree, the Defenders sued the cities of Florissant and Maplewood in the county for jailing people who are unable to pay fines, a brazen flouting of the Supreme Court's decision in *Bearden v. Georgia*.

Through these and other efforts, Harvey and his colleagues have undertaken important legal efforts that can help to undo the criminalization of poor people. Altogether, municipal court revenues in the region dropped from $54 million in 2014 to $29 million in 2016.

PUBLIC DEFENDERS IN THE BIG EASY

Another instance of the struggle against the criminalization of the poor is in the representation of defendants in the courts of New Orleans. Amid a deeply flawed law enforcement system, the Orleans Public Defenders, an entity that was completely reorganized after Hurricane Katrina in 2005, offers a remarkable exception. Public defenders are literally the first line of defense in protecting low-income people from high fines and fees. While even the ablest and most well-resourced defender will not always succeed in fending off a constitutional but fundamentally unfair prosecution, the presence of a defense attorney and the sand that a good defender can throw into the gears will often suffice to avert an injustice. In too many states, however, public defenders are virtually nonexistent. In others, they are hired on badly paid contracts with the courts and are more answerable to the judges than to their clients.

Though it operates on a hand-to-mouth budget—to the point where it announced in late 2015 that it would have to ration its representation and once asked people to participate in crowdfunding to help out—Orleans Public Defenders is widely respected for the professionalism of its work. Financing for the office, however, was already bad when Bobby Jindal was elected governor in 2007, and Jindal's slashes to the budget made everything vastly worse in a state that already had the highest incarceration rate in the country.[5] Grasping for straws (and public attention), in 2016 Orleans Public Defenders arranged for the American Civil Liberties Union to sue both Orleans Public Defenders themselves and the state Public Defender Board to make them do their job fully, which they hope will result in more funds. In 2017 the case was dismissed in federal court and superseded in state court with a new case brought by the Lawyers' Committee for Civil Rights, the Southern Poverty Law Center, and two private firms offering their services pro bono.

Danny Engelberg is chief of trials and part of the leadership of the deeply committed and tough team of defenders who dive into the muck every day to fight against racism, corruption, and avarice. Part of the issue, Danny says, is that the city continues to believe in the "broken windows" theory of law enforcement. Another problem is that the court system is financed by the large-scale use of extortionate fines and fees. Perhaps intended in part to make tourists feel safer, arrests for "obstruction of passage-ways," "drunk in public," loitering, and panhandling as well as traffic tickets and drug offenses bring in funds by the boatload. The city is more than half African American and arrestees are around 90 percent black.[6] Eighty-five percent of defendants are indigent for purposes of being eligible for a public defender.[7] In municipal court and traffic court every morning, people wait on a virtual assembly line, facing costly fines and fees for failing to pay overdue payments. Jon Wool, who works in New Orleans for the Vera Institute, says, "You go into a courtroom in New Orleans and the judge is likely to begin the day talking to the defendants and saying, 'Where's my money? I need money.' This is a quote."

In 2010, the Orleans Parish Criminal District Court judges were revealed to be financing personal medical and other insurance benefits for themselves through court fines and fees.[8] Further investigation showed that the judges spent more than $1.9 million on these items over a six-year period.[9] The district attorney and the Louisiana legislative auditor did their own investigations and confirmed the corruption.[10] Rafael Goyeneche III, the president of the Metropolitan Crime Commission, a local watchdog group, said, "The way Louisiana has funded the criminal system is to try and provide as many user fees as possible to finance it."[11]

Reform efforts outside the courts in New Orleans have made a little headway. The city jail is a major focus. A new structure, which cost $145 million, now replaces much larger structures that were uninhabitable and unspeakably dangerous for both inmates and staff. The MacArthur Justice Center, originally along with the Southern Poverty Law Center, and joined by the U.S. Department of Justice, sued the sheriff in 2012 to reduce the jail population and to improve conditions. They obtained a consent decree in 2013, and the jail population was reduced from 6,000 to 1,600 (not all of whom are being held in the new jail) as of June 2016.

The most far-reaching reform effort is a lawsuit that challenges the constitutionality of the whole system of imposing and collecting the torrent of fines and fees that holds thousands of New Orleans people in permanent thrall. As of May 2017, the case had survived multiple efforts to get it thrown out of court and the plaintiffs were about to argue a motion for a ruling that there is an unconstitutional conflict of interest in the whole system because the court, the district attorney, and the public defender all receive operating funds derived from fines, fees, and bail.[12]

In the midst of all of this, the public defenders make a difference every day. The funding crisis is both real and damaging, but Orleans Public Defenders is making a measurable difference in the lives of poor people living in Louisiana.

WHACK-A-MOLE: COUNTY BY COUNTY AND JUDGE BY JUDGE

Lawsuits have forced debtors' prisons out of business in increasing numbers, mostly in specific counties and municipalities, but there are more venues to be tackled. The state of Washington is one. That might be surprising, but lawyers and academics in the state have been pointing to the problem for years. Research in 2008 documented both at the state level and in particular counties not only the heavy-handed use of fines and fees but also their disproportionate impact on minorities and their negative effect on recidivism resulting from the incessant pressure to pay the debts.[13]

Following up, the ACLU of Washington and Columbia Legal Services studied four counties with the most egregious records.[14] On top of the state-imposed $500 victim penalty assessment (if applicable), the mandatory $100 DNA database fee, and the 12 percent interest rate on the original amount owed, each court has the discretion to impose a $100 annual collection fee and twenty other fees for such things as the cost of the public defender, having a jury trial, serving a warrant, and criminal filing fees.[15] Clark County, the report noted, imposed on virtually every indigent defendant a minimum of $800 for the cost of his or her public defender and a median criminal debt of $2,072 per case.[16]

Benton County was even worse. Twenty percent of its jail population consisted of people being sanctioned for nonpayment of criminal debt. Judge Robert Swisher of the Superior Court told Joseph Shapiro of National Public Radio that he knew someone could pay if he was wearing an expensive item such as a National

Football League team jacket or had a thousand-dollar display of tattoos on his arm.

With all of that information, Vanessa Hernandez and Prachi Dave of the ACLU of Washington, Nusrat Choudhury of the national ACLU, and the Terrell Marshall Law Group sued Benton County for multiple violations of the constitutions of both the United States and the state of Washington.[17] Plaintiff Jayne Fuentes's story epitomizes the attitude and behavior of the county. In 2010 and 2011, the court ordered her to pay $3,229 in criminal debt, including public defender fees, in relation to three misdemeanor theft convictions. The judge made no inquiry into her ability to pay, and the public defender made no argument, either. Fuentes had federal disability benefits until 2009 but lost them due to incarceration. An additional $2,486 was added in 2012 because of two more misdemeanor thefts, again with no judicial inquiry or any presentation from the public defender.

The saga went on. In 2013 the court ordered her onto a work crew doing manual labor to pay down her obligations, and once more there was no inquiry about her finances. In fact, she had just finished being incarcerated for nearly a year, and her income consisted of $200 monthly in food stamps and temporary housing assistance from the state Department of Corrections. She completed the work crew assignment in early 2014 but still owed money on the 2012 debts. Her part-time job and food stamps could not even pay for basic necessities, and she had to borrow from family members in order to squeak by and make some debt payments.

The legal issues were simple. The Benton County District Court was violating *Bearden* and *Gideon* as well as state law by systematically failing to ascertain the ability of defendants to pay fines, fees, and other levies and to provide effective counsel to the defendants. The case was settled in 2016 and the county stopped jailing people for their debts or ordering them to work crews for failure to pay, and also stopped issuing warrants over not making payments.

This is all good, but as Mike Brickner of the Ohio ACLU characterized the system, it's like whack-a-mole: you get one of the bad actors, but another one pops up.[18]

THE WORLD OF PRIVATE PROBATION

Kevin Thompson, an eighteen-year-old African American man in DeKalb County, Georgia, was arrested for driving without a license. Thompson was assessed $800 in fees and fines and made small payments, totaling $80, over thirty days. When he fell behind because his license suspension made it impossible for him to work, he was jailed for five days, even though he had appeared at every probation meeting. The judge held a perfunctory hearing, not asking meaningfully about Thompson's ability to pay and not asking at all why he did not have a lawyer. Thompson tried to explain that he was not able to work because of the license suspension. The judge was uninterested and sent him to jail.

For-profit probation is a special affliction.[19] Some public probation agencies overreach in the way Kevin Thompson experienced, but for-profit probation companies do it regularly. Georgia is the biggest player in the for-profit probation world, with about 250,000 cases in 2012, and its courts issued 124,788 arrest warrants for unpaid probation fees that year.[20] The private companies in the state collected nearly $100 million in fines, court costs, and restitution. Tennessee has somewhere between fifty thousand and eighty thousand cases, and the reach of for-profit goes as far as Michigan, Montana, Utah, and Washington.[21] Rutherford County in Tennessee was the prototype of overreaching by a for-profit probation company. PCC, Inc., collected $17 million in the county from 32,200 defendants in a recent year. "The county didn't pay for anyone to get that money," Judge Ben Hall McFarlin Jr. told a newspaper in defense of the privatization of probation in Rutherford County. "I don't see where the taxpayers would disagree with that."[22]

Actually, they might. Sheriff Robert Arnold told the local newspaper that 386 of his 837 inmates were there for probation violations, and he opined that the cost of running the jail could be cut significantly if there were not so many people jailed for misdemeanor violations of probation. The lead in the story focused on Amelia Lawrence, a student who had failed three times to call her probation officer and consequently was sentenced to eleven months and twenty-nine days in the county detention center. Taxpayers might wonder whether the cost of incarcerating Amelia Lawrence for nearly a year was worth it to them.[23]

A lawsuit filed in federal court by Alec Karakatsanis, now with Civil Rights Corps, along with the law firm of Baker, Donelson, Bearman, Caldwell & Berkowitz, called the county's policy an "extortion scheme" and "conspiracy" and said PCC charged $45 a month on top of all the other fines and fees for probation monitoring. It also charged $20 per drug test, which again was routine, and required such drug tests regularly, even if the debtor's offense had nothing at all to do with drugs. (It is also widely believed that the probation company often falsified the results.)[24] PCC charged for setup fees (whatever those are), community service participation fees, and fees for each rehab class it decided the debtor had to take.

No one ever asked debtors if they were able to pay, and the so-called probation officer placed a series of further financial hurdles before them if they wanted to ask the court for a ruling that they were truly indigent. The company charged $25 if a defendant requested a hearing before the judge and often required another $20 drug test as a prerequisite as well. The company routinely "lost" records of payments and thereby won any payment dispute with the debtor. And because PCC always paid itself first, debtors who paid enough to cover the original fine often still had a balance due; the money they paid had gone to the private company rather than the government. This in turn occasioned another year of probation and fees. And PCC often invented new rules or interpretations to add more debt and/or new grounds for accusing the debtor of having violated the terms of her probation.

Writing in Civil Rights Corps's case, federal judge Kevin Sharp said that private probation companies and PCC in particular "trap probationers in a pernicious cycle for years on end" and pointed to the experience of one plaintiff who he declared was "trapped" by the probation company for five years. At the end of 2015, the judge ordered PCC and the other defendants to change their policies pending trial. He also ordered that thirteen prisoners being held on probation violations be released immediately, and that almost ten thousand probationers facing bench warrants for probation violations not be subject to money bail. In light of the lawsuit and the judge's findings, the county ended its relationship with PCC and replaced it with a regimen it operated itself. The lawsuit continued, though, because the county's policies were still being contested. As of May 2017, negotiations are going on for a settlement which, if successful, will result in a big victory for the plaintiffs.

One of the first to sue private probation companies was the Southern Center for Human Rights. Founded by the legendary Stephen Bright and best known for its work on capital punishment cases, the Southern Center (and in particular staff attorney Sarah Geraghty) began to hear from people all over Georgia about how they had been mistreated in what should have been minor cases or not even cases at all.

Kevin Thompson's case, which Geraghty co-counseled with Nusrat Choudhury of the ACLU, and also the ACLU of Georgia, was one of the first cases.[25] Within two months the lawyers obtained a settlement from the county that created a detailed list of procedural protections for all defendants and included money damages for Mr. Thompson that allowed him to fulfill his dream of starting a towing business.[26] Geraghty went on to achieve another victory against two municipalities and the for-profit probation company in Grady County.[27]

In 2015 and 2016 the Georgia legislature responded partially to the overreaching. It created presumptions of financial hardship for defendants for disabilities, indigence, and recent incarceration, and placed limits on the probation companies, but Geraghty says it leaves plenty of room for the companies to continue to impose expensive and unnecessary tests. The work goes on, with the goal of getting rid of the for-profit companies altogether, reducing the fines and fees to reasonable levels, and repealing laws and ordinances that make no sense at all.

Alabama has made progress, too, getting rid of the for-profit probation company Judicial Correction Services throughout the state. The first step was a lawsuit in the town of Harpersville, which received national attention for the local court's jailing of indigent defendants and holding them in indefinite work release, with the probation company allegedly lying about the failure of debtors to respond to arrest warrants.[28]

Next came the case of Harriet Cleveland, of Montgomery, Alabama, which also became a national cause célèbre.[29] For Cleveland, a grandmother who had a daycare job until the recession interfered, the ordeal began when she was stopped at a police checkpoint in her African American neighborhood and ticketed for not having car insurance (which she did not have enough money to purchase) and for driving with a suspended license because she had not paid the full amount of an earlier ticket. She was put on "probation" with Judicial Correction Services, and after five years had paid more than $3,000 to Judicial and still owed $2,714, as probation fees and other debts mounted. She was jailed repeatedly, lost her car, went through bankruptcy, and ultimately lost her house. At one point she told the judge she had just found a job, but he sent her to jail anyway and she lost the job. No one ever asked if she could afford to pay the debts or told her that she had a right to counsel.[30] Finally she encountered a Southern Poverty Law Center lawyer at the courthouse when she was being sentenced yet again for falling behind in her payments.

This chance meeting ended her personal nightmare and ultimately changed the entire process in Montgomery.

Southern Poverty acquired new allies in 2014—Alec Karakatsanis (now at Civil Rights Corps) and Phil Telfeyan, the co-founders of Equal Justice Under Law, which now separately have litigation in numerous jurisdictions to challenge the constitutionality of debtors' prisons and money bail. Having been a federal public defender in Alabama after he graduated from Harvard Law School in 2008, Karakatsanis decided to start in that state. On the first day he returned to Montgomery City Court, he saw sixty-seven people, all black, and all with unpaid traffic tickets. The hearings lasted between ten seconds and a minute. Defendants pleaded their poverty and, having received a tongue-lashing, were sent to jail to work off their fines. Karakatsanis recalls a judge taunting a man with disabilities because he was unable to speak.

Karakatsanis was able to talk to some of the inmates, who had never had legal help before. One woman said she had been arrested at home in front of her children for a four-year-old traffic ticket. She became his first Equal Justice client. He filed a lawsuit on behalf of a group of plaintiffs and obtained a preliminary injunction, although the judges did not comply.[31] The city came to its senses and released everyone who was in jail for unpaid debt—about sixty people in all—and Southern Poverty and Karakatsanis jointly negotiated a settlement with the city, which ended Harriet Cleveland's ordeal, among other things.

Sam Brooke of Southern Poverty then wrote to about a hundred municipalities that had contracts with Judicial and urged them to end their relationships or risk being sued. They had a special asset on their side: the contracts had been illegal because they were not publicly bid, and also state law banned probation fees in municipal court. In October 2015, Judicial Correction Services pulled out of the state.

This was momentous for low-income people in Alabama, but it does not change the underlying situation. Public probation agencies can gouge poor people, too. Ferguson did not have such a contract with a private company, for example, and it behaved horribly all on its own.

DRIVER'S LICENSES: HOW CALIFORNIANS FOUGHT BACK

California uses traffic fines to raise money, but not as much as it used to. New statutes, the product of advocates and elected officials, are making some difference, as is a reduction in the number of tickets written by police.

Fredrick Jefferson's case offers a good example of the kind of problems that existed in California and the way the work of advocates has changed the system. Jefferson had been employed steadily as a heavy equipment mechanic in Los Angeles when he received a traffic ticket that cost him his driver's license and his job. He owed $5,000 for his exponentially expanded debt and became homeless, with a total cash income of $221 a month from state general assistance. Under the new law, he was given a payment plan of $1 a month and shortly thereafter received reinstatement of his driver's license.[32]

The full extent of the situation in California was brought to light in 2015 in an especially impressive advocacy report done jointly by five public interest law organizations. The report, "Not Just a Ferguson Problem: How Traffic Courts Drive Inequality in California," played a major role in increasing the momentum for reform. As the report documented, California had added a plethora of "penalty assessments" to its fines—among others, a state penalty assessment, a county penalty assessment, a contribution to the DNA identification fund, a state surcharge, a conviction assessment, contributions to court construction, court operations, emergency medical services, emergency medical air transportation, and night court.[33] In 2011, the actual cost of a $500 ticket, even when paid on time, was $1,829. A $100 ticket for failing to have proof of car insurance actually cost $490, plus another $325 if the driver did not pay on time or failed to appear in court.[34] California now has more than $10 billion in uncollected court-ordered debt.[35]

The state offers a community service option for those who cannot pay (although not all courts comply and others charge a fee to participate), but the fine for running a red light would take forty-nine hours to pay off—and that's assuming a person was in a position to miss more than a full week away from his regular job.[36]

The covered infractions were also vastly expanded to cover not only minor traffic things such as broken taillights, misplaced registration stickers, and failure to report a change of address, but also loitering, littering, carrying an open alcohol container in public, and failure to pay transit fare. All of these are subject to a further penalty and a license suspension if not paid on time. Then the private collections people with their rough tactics enter the picture in fifty-four of the fifty-eight counties, adding commissions of 13 to 17 percent. The underlying point is that the courts have become reliant on the fines and fees because their budgets were cut during the recession, which among other things is a clear conflict of interest.

People of color pay the highest price. In Oakland, where blacks make up less than a third of the city's population, 60 percent of those who lose their licenses are African American.[37] Likewise, African Americans account for 6 percent of San Francisco's population but comprised 70.4 percent of clients who came to an arrest and conviction clinic convened by the San Francisco Lawyers' Committee for Civil Rights in 2014. Statewide, African Americans are 60 percent more likely than non-Hispanic whites to lose their licenses, and Hispanics are 20 percent more likely.

An especially bizarre feature is that some courts require people to pay what they are alleged to owe even before they can get a hearing on their guilt or innocence and their ability to pay.[38] So even though state law requires an assessment of people's ability to pay, they cannot get that assessment unless they first pay what they allegedly owe. If they do not pay, they owe an added civil assessment fee of up to $300, which is routinely the full $300. The $300 goes entirely to help run the courts, so again there is a total conflict of interest.[39] Even if someone is ultimately found not guilty, there is no refund of the civil assessment.[40] The court is supposed to offer payment plans, reduced fines, and community service, but these are generally not mentioned in written materials, and they become irrelevant once a person pays the full amount and is found to be guilty.[41]

Elisa Della-Piana, then of the East Bay Community Law Center in Berkeley, told me about the partially successful fight in the legislature on the suspensions. In 2012, East Bay started to see a swell of clients with license suspension issues at the organization's weekly general clinic. Asking around, Elisa and her colleagues found that other providers were seeing the same thing. Suspensions had not been used much previously, but their role accelerated during the recession. Fines and fees went up, courts pushed harder on collections, and more people could not pay because they had lost their jobs.

The legal aid providers reached out to Mike Herald of the Western Center on Law and Poverty. Herald formed a coalition to press for action in Sacramento, and, along with colleagues in the legislature, Senator Robert Hertzberg led the way to partial success, first in 2015 and again in 2016.

While the first bill was pending, state chief justice Tani Cantil-Sakauye called for emergency steps to ameliorate the harsh impact of the existing law wherever possible. With her leadership, the state Judicial Council promulgated a new rule that banned the practice of refusing an initial hearing unless the defendant paid the ticket and costs first. The rule change did not cover requests for a hearing after a person misses a court date or a payment deadline—under those circumstances, defendants still have to pay in full before being allowed a court hearing.

The first new law went into effect on October 1, 2015. For payments due before January 2, 2013, it created an amnesty that cut in half the amount owed on every debt, reduced the debt of low-income debtors by 80 percent, and cut out the $300 civil assessment fee for low-income debtors, although courts were authorized to impose a new $50 fee to process amnesty applications, which most courts imposed. It also exempted from payments people with no income other than public benefits. People who establish a new plan and are in "good standing" on their payments can get their licenses back. However, measures such as garnishing wages, seizing bank accounts, and tax refunds remain available.

The 2015 law was an important step, but it falls short of doing all it should. It offers no relief to those who are barred from the courts because they are delinquent on a payment or fail to appear for a court date unless they first pay what the court says they owe. "Pay to play," people called it. Senator Hertzberg, the Western Center, and others offered a bill in 2016 that banned officials from suspending licenses for the failure to appear in court or pay traffic tickets. Their bill did not succeed, but they did get the previous amnesty extended to cover debts incurred up until the beginning of 2017. Past parking tickets and car tow fees are still not covered in the amnesty, and there are still many criminal charges, such as passing bad checks, that have nothing to do with driving but can result in driver's license suspensions and in some cases should not be offenses at all.

In January 2017 Governor Jerry Brown proposed in his budget to repeal license suspension for failure to pay tickets, and Mike Herald predicted in April that the legislature would accept it. At the same time Senator Hertzberg proposed permanently reducing fines on low-income people and requiring payments based on a person's ability to pay. This, too, was still pending in April 2017.

The story of license suspensions in California reveals both the extent of the injury governments are willing to inflict on low-income people in order to balance their books and the results that advocacy can achieve to reduce the damage.

THE PHILADELPHIA STORY

In 2009 the *Philadelphia Inquirer* ran a story headlined "Violent Criminals Flout Broken Bail System" as part of a high-profile series called "Justice: Delayed, Dismissed, Denied." The piece documented the long-standing incompetence of the three-hundred-year-old office of the elected court clerk—*elected* is the key word here—which had failed for decades to maintain proper court records and collect bail money and fines in criminal cases. When the recession caused an immediate need for funds to run the courts, court officials and politicians embarrassed by the news story panicked.[42] The city abolished the elected office of clerk and handed responsibility for the collection of fees and fines to the courts. Pamela P. Dembe, the chief common pleas judge, took the lead to fix things.[43] What followed was a campaign of harassment, primarily of poor people, of momentous proportion.

Judge Dembe determined that, going back to the 1970s, the city was owed $1.5 billion in unpaid criminal debt that no one had ever tried to collect—about $1 billion in forfeited bail for missed court appearances and $500 million more in supervision fees, restitution, fines, and costs. Without any investigation of the accuracy of the debts, the court relied on a flawed computer database to send payment notices (some for bills dating back decades) to more than 320,000 people—one in five people in the city, and overwhelmingly those with low incomes.[44]

Most people had no idea what was going on. They faced demands as large as $100,000 and even more. Phone calls and threatening letters followed the initial notices. Community Legal

Services, one of the most respected legal aid organizations in the country, and others helped as many clients as their capacity allowed—records were often missing and many debts were clearly not correct—but they could serve only a small fraction of those who had been buried in the avalanche. Local media headlined the story of a woman who was told in 2009 that she owed $900 for a hearing she had missed in 1990. She had been in jail at the time of the hearing but could not prove it because the prison's records had been destroyed by a flood in 1991.[45] She was far from the only one caught up in the mess.

Community Legal Services, particularly in the person of Sharon Dietrich, put together a coalition that included the ACLU of Pennsylvania, the Philadelphia Defender Association, and social service and community organizations. The coalition met with people from the courts, the mayor, and other key individuals and argued not only the injustice of balancing the courts' books by punishing the poor but also that the cost of the enforcement would inevitably be greater than what the effort would return. In addition, Community Legal Services ran a media campaign that garnered attention even around the world. Meanwhile, people were picking up cans and scrap metal and selling plasma so they could make the payments. They were terrified of going to jail.

In September 2014, the city and the courts backed down, at least in part. They announced that bail debts dating back before March 4, 2010 (though not other court debts), would no longer be collected. Besides being relieved of the obligation and the stress, thousands of Philadelphians would become eligible for expungement and pardon of their criminal records and for public benefits that had not been available to people with bail debts.

Judge Dembe's harsh response was revealing. "Deep in our little hearts, we knew we could never collect that much," she said. "But it was a goal to shoot for. And shoot for it we did."[46]

In 2016, the court wrote off the last $1 billion in bail judgments, but the debt from the old fines and fees themselves is still on the books. This debt still creates barriers to expungement and public benefits, but at least there is no harassment occurring and no incarceration for the debt.

Nonetheless, the liability is still unacceptably large and leaves people with lifelong burdens.

3

Money Bail

Sixteen-year-old Kalief Browder was locked up for three years at Rikers Island in New York City, waiting for a trial on a crime he did not commit, simply because he could not make bail. Browder's ordeal epitomizes the inequity of our bail system and the way it contributes to the criminalization of poverty. As Jennifer Gonnerman recounts in a series of heartbreaking articles in the *New Yorker*, Browder was arrested in 2010 and accused of stealing a backpack, which probably never happened, and then sent, horribly for a sixteen-year-old, to Rikers Island. Because the alleged crime occurred in the Bronx, Browder's case was handled in an unbelievably overcrowded, understaffed court, with a docket that is years behind. And to make matters worse, he was not represented by a full-time public defender but by a private lawyer on contract with the court system (which too often means that the client receives substandard representation).

Without inquiring into his family's financial circumstances, a routine omission, the judge set bail at $3,000 because Browder was already on probation from a previous guilty plea to a joyride in a stolen delivery truck. His family could not raise the $3,000. He was offered plea deals in the backpack theft but was unwilling to plead guilty to a crime he did not commit, preferring to exercise his right to a trial, which, despite a so-called speedy-trial statute, was anything but speedy in the Bronx. While in jail, Browder's abuse by both guards and inmates was captured on videotape. He spent two of his three years, eight hundred days, at Rikers in solitary confinement and tried to commit suicide several times. By the time he got a better lawyer and got out, he had become deeply paranoid. He tried to put his life back together: he went to school and, because of the news coverage of his story, met various celebrities who tried to help. He did not recover from his ordeal and committed suicide in June 2015.[1]

Untreated mental illness that began in jail, solitary confinement, abuse by correctional officers and other inmates, a lousy lawyer, and a dysfunctional court all played a role in Kalief Browder's tragedy. But Browder should not have been at Rikers in the first place; the only reason he was there was that his family was too poor to make his bail.

Americans are generally aware that at any given moment, 2.2 million people are locked up in our prisons and jails, 700,000 of them in our county and city jails. What most don't know is that, over the course of a given year, a total of 11.7 million people spend some amount of time in America's county and city jails, double the number in 1983.[2] Three-fifths of them have not been found guilty of anything, and three-fourths, both convicted and pretrial detainees, are there for nonviolent traffic and other low-level offenses. African Americans are detained at rates nearly five times greater than whites and three times higher than Latinos.[3] The total cost is $9 billion a year.

Why? Two simple words: money bail.

Money bail—meaning a sum of money that a defendant is ordered to place with the court ostensibly as a guarantee that he or she will appear for trial—is utilized for offenses ranging from the most heinous (if the judge believes the defendant should be allowed bail at all) down to the lowest-level crimes. Even people accused of trivial violations are often held pending trial unless they can post bail, which is usually not possible for those who are indigent. (In a minority of states, substantial numbers of defendants are released on their own recognizance, meaning they are trusted to appear for trial.) Minor offenses can result in bail as high as $10,000. A few defendants will be able to pay in cash, but most defendants must retain the services of a bail bondsman, who charges 10 percent or more of the total for a secured bond issued by an insurance company (an amount that is not refunded even if the defendant is not found guilty). Routinely, low-income defendants cannot afford to pay the bail bondsman and therefore plead guilty even though they are innocent, in order to get out of jail.

The picture has changed for the worse over recent years. Enormous numbers of people are now arrested for low-level offenses and large percentages of those are held in jail pending payment for bail instead of simply being released to await trial. The vast majority of those in jail are poor or near poor and do not have the money to pay the bail bondsman the fee for the surety bond.

In the 1960s as a young Department of Justice lawyer and then a staffer to Robert Kennedy in the Senate, I knew that Kennedy, as attorney general, and the then brand-new Vera Institute in New York City had taken initial steps to reform the country's bail system. The idea, as valid now as then, was that most accused people let out without a cash payment would neither endanger the community nor fail to show up for trial. Demonstrations of the concept proved it worked. New York passed a law—still in effect—that outlined nine criteria to determine whether to hold a person pending trial, to release him but only if bail is posted, or to release him on recognizance with no money paid. Judges are instructed to take into account such matters as character, employment, financial resources, ties to the community, criminal record, and previous flight. It seemed as though the idea of release on recognizance would spread.

Instead, rising crime rates starting in the 1970s caused politicians to fan fears that had little basis in fact and a larger genesis in racism. Judges, especially judges who would have to stand for reelection, got scared of releasing people on recognizance when there was even a modicum of perceived possibility that they might offend again while awaiting trial. The era of mass incarceration was under way. In 1975, I became the director of the New York Division for Youth, the state's youth correction agency, and found myself under attack for pursuing reform at a time that turned out to be the beginning of the rush to lock up large numbers of people, especially African American men and boys.

Bail reform in the states stalled, aided and abetted by the bail bondsmen lobby. We hear a lot about the political power of the correctional officers unions, but bail bondsmen wield similar clout. The unions pushed with great success for the building of more and more prisons and jails, and bail bondsmen helped with equal success to make sure the ever-bigger jails would always be full to overflowing. About fifteen thousand bail bond agents nationally write some $14 billion in bonds each year; these in turn are backed by powerful insurance companies that also have significant political power.[4] Bail bonds are a big and lucrative business.

The resulting structure is a travesty. In New York, Brooklyn Defender Services special litigation counsel Susannah Karlsson says, "It's a broken record. You get only two choices, put up cash or deal with a bail bondsman." The practice leaves out use of the criteria that would lead to release on recognizance. Karlsson continues, "Until very recently, I could count on one hand how many times I heard of those other criteria for release being used in Brooklyn."

Money bail is ruining the lives of literally millions of poor people and costing the country unnecessary billions of dollars in incarceration costs every year. Local jail populations grew by 19.8 percent just between 2000 and 2014, with pretrial detention accounting for 95 percent of that growth. Just as one example, but typical of big cities around the country, is Philadelphia, where the cost of running the jails is $110 to $120 per inmate per day.[5] The single feature shared by almost every defendant in pretrial detention is that they are poor. Rich people make bail; poor people don't. Regardless of actual guilt or innocence, poor people are criminalized for their inability to buy their way out of jail.

The major shortage of judges, prosecutors, and public defenders, coupled with the number of people being held in jail awaiting trial, has led to a crisis in which it is not possible for every defendant who wants a day in court to get one. So the courts need a way to keep the trials from taking place. By imprisoning poor people who cannot put up money for bail, the system uses the threat or reality of extended imprisonment to extract guilty pleas, even from people who are innocent or have other valid defenses. Not able to get a timely trial, they have only one option—plead guilty. It is a Hobson's choice, more so even than many of the defendants realize, because the guilty pleas have serious collateral consequences they may not even be aware of and which stay with them for the rest of their lives. But pleading guilty is what they do by the thousands, every day, all over America.

And, ironically, when they plead guilty, they receive a sentence of credit for time served and they go home. While they were presumed innocent, they were too dangerous or unreliable to be released, but once convicted they are sent home.

Karlsson says it has gotten worse over the years. "Senior practitioners remember a time when only clients charged with serious felonies had to make bail unless they were held without bail, but now it's pretrial incarceration en masse," she says. "Even clients charged with petty, non-jailable offenses can have bail set on them nowadays. The predictable result is that many of our clients take a plea in order to get out rather than fight the case while sitting in jail, even if they have a great defense or are totally innocent."

Getting rid of money bail is far from all that is needed to fix Rikers Island in New York, but it would certainly help. In the course of a year, about 45,000 people are jailed there solely because they cannot afford bail.[6] On any given day, 1,500 people have been there for over a year without a trial and 400 for more than two years without being tried.[7] Rikers has a capacity of 9,600 inmates, averages about 11,000 on a daily basis, and balloons to 15,000 from time to time. Of the 77,000 people who come through there during the year, 85 percent have not yet been convicted of a crime.[8] In 2010, Human Rights Watch calculated that New York City was paying $42 million annually to lock up non-felony defendants.[9]

It is patently obvious that this situation is destroying lives, and there are concrete numbers. The New York City Criminal Justice Agency reported in 2012 that 50 percent of defendants not detained before trial over a ten-year period were convicted versus 92 percent of those who had been detained. Examination of the data showed that the detention itself was the greatest predictor because of the pressure on defendants to plead guilty.[10] A study supported by the Houston-based John and Laura Arnold Foundation, looking at 153,000 arrests and bookings into jails in Kentucky, found that even a low-risk defendant serving a two- to three-day jail stint was 40 percent more likely to commit new crimes than similar defendants held less than twenty-four hours, with longer stints resulting in higher likelihoods of committing new crimes.[11]

New York State's former chief judge Jonathan Lippman told the *New York Times*, "You have to eliminate cash bail."[12] Speaking to the *New York Observer*, he went on to say that the bail system is "totally ass-backwards in every respect. You have people who can't make $500 bail who end up rotting in jails or prison, losing their jobs, being separated from their families, while they are absolutely no threat to anyone."[13] In 2013, when he was still chief judge, Lippman made a serious effort to reduce the use of money bail by sending a set of reform bills to the legislature. He batted zero. The bail-bond industry and the insurance interests carried the day.

THE WINDS OF REFORM

Tim Murray and the Pretrial Justice Institute have been working for change for a long time, and they are beginning to see improvement in the system. "We're at an unprecedented point in our examination of policies and practices at the front end of the justice system," he told me. "There's an awakening that decisions that were deemed inconsequential have a profound and lasting impact."

Murray points to a number of converging developments regarding bail that could be a happy perfect storm: "Demonstrations of the failures of the current bail system have been dramatized much more and the introduction of statistical science has moved the conversation as well." As a consequence, Murray says, "I've never seen so much discussion nationally. The conversation has veered toward asking why we are locking up so many people and spending so much money." He thinks that "if it is orchestrated and nurtured correctly, there could be a national movement to fix much of what is broken."

Among the specific convergences, Murray mentioned the Conference of Chief Justices of the state courts, which came out with a unanimous call for bail reform. The National Association of Chiefs of Police has called for a variety of reforms, as have the National Association of Counties, the Conference of State Court Administrators, and the defense community. Public opinion studies show that the public, too, thinks current practices do not make sense. The MacArthur Foundation and the Arnold Foundation are investing substantially in reform efforts, following the long-standing leadership of the Public Welfare Foundation.

MacArthur has chosen twenty sites around the country and is asking each jurisdiction to look at who is in its jails and why they are there, planning for a total investment of $75 million over the coming years and discussing significant increases beyond that.

A key development in moving away from money bail is the work of the Arnold Foundation. Reformers agree that a restructuring of bail must include a risk-based assessment of defendants to identify those who pose unmanageable levels of risk. Having a formal risk assessment mechanism is crucial to the regimes of the pathbreaking jurisdictions of Kentucky and the District of Columbia, which are generally considered as working well. Nonetheless, people on both ends of the ideological continuum worry. Some on the left worry that risk assessment would be used as a pretext to keep minorities incarcerated, and conservatives worry that it will result in releasing people who would be dangers to the community.

Hence the important work of the Arnold Foundation, which invested $1.2 million to create the Public Safety Assessment, an evidence-based algorithm that works in real time to assess the level of risk posed by defendants. After analyzing data on 1.5 million criminal cases drawn from more than three hundred U.S. jurisdictions, the Arnold Foundation researchers found that age, criminal record with greater weight for more recent offenses, and previous failures to appear in court are the most salient factors for assessing risk, while matters such as employment status, community ties, and histories of drug and alcohol use are of less value. As of early 2017, twenty-nine jurisdictions were using the assessment tools or working toward implementing them, and a hundred or more are interested.[14]

The District of Columbia has long been the leader in bail reform. Tim Murray calls it "the gold standard." The law in the District does allow judges to require defendants to put up a surety bond in order to be released, but the courts have not used the authority in many decades. The District's position in the vanguard of reform was a happy accident stemming from a conservative initiative—preventive detention, the idea of holding defendants pending trial to keep them from committing further crimes (or, among its most extreme adherents, holding people deemed dangerous even if they have committed no current crime). In 1984 Congress enacted a relatively moderate version of preventive detention for the federal system and the District, which the District implemented in an especially thoughtful way.

The heart of the District's law is a presumption of pretrial release, and it works—88 percent of all people who come into the system are released on their own recognizance. D.C.'s law bans anyone from being held pretrial simply due to inability to pay the bond, which adds to the push for release. Tim Murray says the lessons learned from those policies are finally seeping into other jurisdictions.

Community-based, nonprofit bail funds that started up in 2007 in the Bronx and later in Brooklyn and elsewhere have had near-perfect records in getting people to show up in court. They bypass the bail bondsmen, whose fees defendants never recoup even if they are acquitted or charges are dropped. Taken to scale, these bail funds would both reduce the cost to taxpayers and alleviate significant destruction in human lives. Releasing defendants on recognizance would be an even better and less expensive policy, but the bond funds are a distinct improvement on the current profit-making system.

Kentucky adopted a risk assessment system many years ago and has done well on court appearance rates, with low recidivism.[15] The state installed the Arnold assessment algorithm in 2013, stimulating a new statewide campaign among public defenders for use of the tool. Murray says that many fewer people are now detained for not having money than at any other time in the state's history.

One particularly interesting recent development was the decision of New Jersey to completely retool its pretrial justice legislation. To make its reform possible, it adopted a state constitutional amendment that empowers its justice system to assess pretrial danger and then passed legislation to use the Arnold algorithm. The special importance of New Jersey's decision is that the state is not exceptionally liberal, and it is a bastion of the bail bond industry and for-profit influence. Yet Governor Chris Christie championed the effort in tandem with civil rights organizations and the state supreme court.[16]

Charlotte, North Carolina, found that using the Arnold tool for one year reduced its jail population by 20 percent with no increase in reported crime.[17] States including Colorado and Arizona and local leaders such as Sheriff Tom Dart in Cook County, Illinois, are particular bright lights in the process, too. So is Arthur Pepin, the director of New Mexico's Administrative Office of the Courts, whose leadership in Albuquerque led to a 38 percent drop in the county jail's population in two years, saving more than $5 million and keeping hundreds of lives intact.[18]

Joining the growing reform group in early 2017, Maryland's highest court with the strong support of state attorney general Brian Frosh changed court rules on bail to impose the "least onerous" conditions when setting bail for a defendant who is not seen as a danger or a flight risk.[19] The Maryland story illustrates the politics of all of this. After the court acted, the bail bond lobby went to the legislature seeking to nullify the new rules. They failed, but not as easily as the reformers would have preferred.

In the wake of the Kalief Browder tragedy, New York City mayor Bill de Blasio proposed in 2015 to spend $18 million annually to triple the number of defendants under pretrial supervision in the community instead of being in jail, saving substantially on jail costs. The city estimated that this initiative would serve 3,400 people who would otherwise be in jail, about 30 percent of the average census at Rikers now. The mayor's proposal was not universally applauded, however. Robin Steinberg, the executive director of the Bronx Defenders, and her board chair, David Feige, were blunt in an op-ed for the Marshall Project about the effects on their clients of what they felt were unnecessary supervision programs: "Guilty or innocent, the urge to intervene in the lives of those we shovel into the criminal justice system has proven almost irresistible to politicians over the years. So despite the fact that the most effective method of ensuring that people return to court is to just release them with nothing more than a friendly reminder of their court dates via calls or text messages, the city has already made clear that it will aim to create a 'pretrial-services system' at an estimated annual cost of $18 million."

In fact, Steinberg and Feige say, the proposal is a combination of expensive and unnecessary hurdles for the accused to jump over, with failure resulting in incarceration. So there may be drug education programs, reporting weekly to a pretrial-services officer, drug testing, and more—all for a person who is perhaps accused of shoplifting and claims to be innocent. Besides, they conclude, judges have the option right now of setting a personal-recognizance bond or an arrangement involving the signing of a promissory note rather than paying cash up front. Of course Steinberg and Feige are all too aware that judges do not use that option.[20]

Susannah Karlsson says, "What makes people come back to court is a reminder and a metro card, not money, not an ankle bracelet, not a social worker—a phone call and a metro card."

So what is going on? Politics, of course, which is quite divergent from what the best policy would be. "While 'supervision' may sound good on the evening news," Steinberg and Feige say, "it is a terrible thing for those caught up in it—many of them struggling to get by, working two jobs with inflexible hours while juggling childcare and other responsibilities. For them, the bureaucratic necessities of compliance can become terribly destabilizing."

Tim Murray of the Pretrial Justice Institute says the New York pushback against pretrial supervision is a unique position. He says supervised release has been used effectively in numerous jurisdictions, including the District of Columbia, for decades. He thinks that if supervised release is the price of keeping people from rotting in jail because they cannot afford money bail, it is worth it.

Susannah Karlsson is working on reform from the bottom up, enlisting her colleagues at Brooklyn Defender Services to press judges to make full use of release on recognizance as set out in the pathbreaking law of the 1960s. Because such arguments were made only here and there over the years, they were unsuccessful and no case law limiting the use of money bail developed.

The renewed public concern about excessive use of money bail has opened the door for a new wave of advocacy. Karlsson says that "there is finally a legal climate where New York's non-monetary bail options may finally be taken off the shelf" and can lead to judicial innovations such as the creation of a special judge in criminal court to take a second look at bail decisions and regular challenges by defense lawyers of the constitutionality of bail decisions.

"Changing a culture in a way that thinks about bail systematically is difficult," Brooklyn Defender Services executive director Lisa Schreibersdorf added, "so we are using previously underutilized techniques to test the ingrained notions about bail. We think we can get rulings that spell out what judges should be thinking about—including the financial circumstances of our clients, the fact that people should not be in jails simply because they cannot afford to post bail, and a policy that money bail is inappropriate in almost all low-level cases." Speaking in the summer of 2015, not long after the death of Kalief Browder, Karlsson said this was a time of particular opportunity. "We have been trying to change the conversation, and we are finally in a moment where the public is ready to concede that pretrial detention has dire consequences and is almost always unnecessary."

Symbiotic with the work on bail, in New York and no doubt elsewhere, is the need for reexamination of the effectiveness of speedy-trial statutes. The long pretrial stays in Rikers and other big-city and big-county jails are obvious antipathies to the very idea of having speedy trials. How these statutes work—what counts toward mandated time limits within which a trial must take place, and what does not—is complicated, but the basic point is that delays related to backlogs in the courts are not counted against the clock. Kalief Browder had a lawyer and was prepared to go to trial, but under the current system, the clock stopped every time there was a delay due to unrelated backlogs at the court.

Another front in the fight against money bail has been opened by Alec Karakatsanis of Civil Rights Corps and Phil Telfeyan of Equal Justice Under Law, and ArchCity Defenders and Thomas Harvey, in partnership with a growing number of private law firms contributing their services pro bono. As Karakatsanis says, judges and others "claim to be outraged by debtors' prisons, but every state is doing the same thing—holding innocent people prior to trial—and we call it the bail system. Five hundred thousand people are in jail every day because they can't afford bond."

Karakatsanis worries that some jurisdictions that adopt the risk assessment approach will do so in a bastardized way, where it is grafted onto a money bail system and consequently does little to improve things except to provide a stronger basis for holding people who can pay but nonetheless should not be released. And he and others also worry that even without being tacked on to the money bail system, risk assessment will be used in a racially disproportionate way—for example, using previous arrest records, which may penalize defendants of color.

Karakatsanis and others have decided to attack money bail on the same theory that is involved in *Bearden v. Georgia*—that money bail for indigent people is unconstitutional without an inquiry into defendants' ability to pay, and extrapolating from that, the whole system should be based on release on recognizance plus a risk assessment analysis. He understands that people of any income level may need to be held because they present a risk to the community, but believes applying a *Bearden* approach will highlight the need for a careful inquiry into risk before someone who is indigent can be held.

Having litigated in the federal courts in Alabama and knowing the judges, Karakatsanis decided to test bail practices there. In 2015 he filed his first bail challenge, against the town of Clanton, Alabama. He sent the papers to the Department of Justice, which filed a statement of interest in the case. The Equal Justice website says, "In an historic moment for the American criminal legal system, the United States announced its official position that detaining people solely because of their poverty is unconstitutional." Shortly after, the website continues, "the City of Clanton announced that it would reform its bail system to stop using secure money bond for new arrestees. Arrestees will no longer be held in jail until they can pay money for their freedom."[21] This means they will be released on unsecured bonds, which will be canceled when the person shows up for trial. It is not the same as release on recognizance, because defendants released on unsecured bonds will have to pay if they do not appear in court, but it is a big step nonetheless.

Beyond the legal theory, Karakatsanis's strategy was to begin in small jurisdictions that would not have much of a revenue concern about not using money bail and also would not want to spend the money to fight the case. By the fall of 2015, he had filed ten such class action challenges in eight states, resulting in reformed bail practices for arrestees in cities and counties in Alabama, Missouri, Mississippi, and Louisiana; twenty counties in Alabama stopped using secured bonds. Working with Arch-City Defenders, the lawyers obtained a decision in federal court against Velda City, Missouri, affirming that the use of secured money bail to detain impoverished people after arrest violates the Constitution. Similar suits are at various stages in Alabama, Mississippi, Tennessee, and Georgia.

By 2017 the lawyers had moved on to larger cases challenging money bail in the city and county of San Francisco; the state of California; Harris County, Texas, which includes the city of Houston; Cook County, Illinois, which includes Chicago; and the Commonwealth of Massachusetts. In San Francisco, City Attorney Dennis Herrera and Sheriff Vicki Hennessy support the lawsuit, and Senator Robert Hertzberg is pushing statewide legislation.[22]

The Houston case is the most important, by far. The county sheriff, the district attorney, and a criminal judge—all newly elected in 2016—support the plaintiffs.[23] And in April 2017, federal Judge Lee Rosenthal ruled preliminarily in a 192-page opinion after a lengthy hearing that the bail system in Harris County is unconstitutional.[24] Given the extensive evidence of the arbitrary way in which bail is administered in Harris County, including a disturbing film of judges treating defendants horribly, the judge implied strongly that her final decision would be the same as her preliminary ruling.

For the first time in half a century, dents are occurring in the money bail system that has ruined the lives of so many poor people. A letter sent by the Department of Justice in August 2016 to state chief justices and court administrators summed up, "Bail that is set without regard to defendants' financial capacity can result in the incarceration of individuals not because they pose a threat to public safety or a flight risk, but rather because they cannot afford the assigned bail amount." Robert Kennedy would be pleased.

4

The Criminalization of Mental Illness

Darren Rainey might not be dead now if, when we closed mental hospitals in the 1960s, we had made major investments in community-based mental health services. He might not be dead now if we hadn't started incarcerating people at astronomically high rates in the 1970s. He might not be dead now if we hadn't slashed addiction treatment funds in the 1980s. He might not be dead now if, in the 1990s, we hadn't hired private companies to run our jails and prisons or portions of them and paid them so little that they could recruit only correctional staff who were untrained, incompetent, and too often sadistic, and mental health professionals who were stretched too far, were too frequently underqualified, and often operate under horrifying conditions. But he is dead, because what we did do in the wake of the deinstitutionalization of mental hospitals over the past half century was the worst possible combination of choices we could have made.

Schizophrenic, African American, poor, fifty years old, and doing time for a drug conviction, Rainey was an inmate at the Dade Correctional Institution of the Florida Department of

Corrections, and specifically at the Transitional Care Unit or mental health ward when he died on June 23, 2012. Correctional officers there had rigged a shower with water at the scalding temperature of 180 degrees to torture prisoners whom they deemed uncooperative. Darren Rainey had defecated on the floor of his cell and would not clean it up. As punishment, the officers put him in the shower for almost two hours, taunting him as he screamed in panic and pain. Ultimately, Rainey was scalded to death. Inmate Mark Joiner remembered. "I heard them lock the shower door, and they were mocking him," Joiner said. "He was crying, please stop, please stop. And they just said, 'Enjoy your shower,' and left."[1]

Florida has the third-largest prison population in the country. Between 1996 and 2014, the number of Florida's prisoners with mental disabilities grew by 153 percent.[2] Yet Florida spends less money per capita on mental health than any state except Idaho.

A number of sources said the shower torture was only one of the methods the guards at Dade Correctional used to keep mentally ill prisoners in line. Richard Mair, also in the mental health unit, hanged himself from an air-conditioning vent three months after Rainey's death. He left a note saying that he and other prisoners were routinely abused physically and sexually by guards. The note went on to say that "if they didn't like you, they put you on a starvation diet," and that guards forced white and black inmates to fight each other while the guards placed bets on who would win.[3] The mental health professionals employed by for-profit companies to work in the prison stayed silent.

Mental illness and addiction are pathways to poverty, and poverty is a pathway to mental illness and addiction. The toxic stress that is emblematic of people coping with poverty culminates all too regularly in mental illness and addiction. Research shows that 8.7 percent of adults with incomes below the poverty line suffer from serious psychological distress, compared with 1.2 percent of adults with incomes above 400 percent of the poverty line.[4] People in poverty are twice as likely to suffer from serious mental illness as the average person.[5] Unemployment and depression are linked so closely that the Centers for Disease Control and Prevention have pronounced unemployment to be a public health concern.[6] The lack of mental health and addiction services in low-income communities and the high incidence of mental health and addiction issues in the inmate population are linked. For too many of the poor, our jails and prisons are the mental health system of today. By substituting prisons and jails for mental hospitals, we have effectively criminalized mental illness along with the poverty that is often its source.

Once begun, the cycle continues. Previously incarcerated people with major psychiatric disorders are 2.4 times more likely to be reincarcerated than people without such disorders. The incidence rises to 3.3 times more likely for those with bipolar disorders.[7]

FROM HOSPITAL ROOMS TO PRISON CELLS

In the same decades that saw the rise of mass incarceration, the number of beds available in state mental hospitals across the country dropped from 339 beds per 100,000 people in 1955 to under 20 beds per 100,000 people by 2015.[8] There are now ten times as many mentally ill people in our prisons and jails as there are in state mental institutions.[9] Dr. E. Fuller Torrey of the Treatment

Advocacy Center says, "We've basically gone back to where we were 170 years ago."[10] Obviously not every person deinstitutionalized was "transinstitutionalized," to use Dean Aufderheide's evocative term for shifts from mental health hospitals to prisons, but the percentage of inmates with mental health problems now is catastrophic.[11]

Various studies place the number of inmates in jails and prisons with serious mental illness at 300,000 to 360,000 individuals.[12] Serious mental illness characterizes one in seven men and almost a third of women in jails, four to six times higher than in the population as a whole.[13] Specific institutions and systems have higher numbers. For example, Rikers reports that nearly 40 percent of its population has been diagnosed with mental illness.[14] Overall, out of the increase from 500,000 people in prison and jail populations in the late 1970s to the more than two million now, a rough estimate would be that up to a quarter of the increase is due specifically to the incarceration of people with mental illness.[15] Recent data say that 83 percent of jail inmates with mental illness do not get treatment upon coming into the jail.[16] The National Alliance on Mental Illness estimates that 25 to 40 percent of people with mental illness are incarcerated at some point in their lives.[17]

The case of Darren Rainey and the situation in Florida unfortunately mirror too many situations all over the country. Too often, prison systems are riddled with insufficiently trained and even brutal guards, and mentally ill inmates face the worst abuse. Even in better systems, cellblocks for the mentally ill are woefully understaffed and the staff that exists is grossly undertrained for the job. The overutilization of solitary confinement with its deeply damaging effects is just one of the consequences.

In its powerful report "Callous and Cruel," Human Rights Watch reserves the ultimate negative rating of "a culture of abuse" for Rikers and the Orleans Parish Jail in New Orleans. The Rikers story emerges clearly from the litany of settlements of lawsuits brought by individual plaintiffs—one after another, many of them mentally ill. Two who were mentally ill were Jerome Murdaugh and Jason Echevarria. Murdaugh, fifty-six, mentally ill, an ex-Marine, homeless, was arrested for trespassing, could not make $2,500 bail, was left in a cell for four hours where the temperature was 101 degrees, and died. The city settled for $2.25 million.[18] Echevarria, twenty-five, was mentally ill and swallowed toxic soap. Staff did nothing and he died. The city settled for $3.8 million and a captain at Rikers was convicted and sentenced to five years.[19] At the end of the day, it would have been cheaper to treat Murdaugh and Echevarria properly.

Perhaps Corizon, the largest for-profit medical and mental health provider in the country for prisons, jails, and detention centers, represents best the consequences of the transformation from mental hospital rooms to prison cells. Corizon is the result of a 2011 merger between Prison Health Services and Correctional Medical Services, and the company's website boasts of serving 531 correctional facilities and 335,000 prisoners in twenty-seven states. Corizon's revenue is somewhere around $1.5 billion.[20]

One does not have to dig very deeply to see the sordid trail Corizon and its two predecessors have left. The *New York Times* did a yearlong investigation into prison health in 2005 and found story after story of horrible health and mental health care by Prison Health Services that led to death.[21] Just since 2012, Corizon has lost statewide contracts in Maine, Maryland, Minnesota, and Pennsylvania. In 2013, the debt-rating company Moody's twice downgraded Corizon's $360 million debt, citing its recent contract losses, and in mid-2015, Corizon's contract at Rikers was not renewed.[22]

In late 2015, Corizon left Florida one step ahead of the sheriff, so to speak, after the *Palm Beach Post* ran an award-winning series about the surge in inmate deaths and patient neglect following the state's decision in 2011 to contract out the delivery of medical and mental health care to Corizon and Wexford Health Sources (the company charged with providing care to Darren Rainey).[23] It is a devil's bargain: the state wants bare-bones services, and Corizon and others are willing to provide services that they have to know are inadequate in both quantity and quality.

THE CHANGE AGENTS

Sheriff Thomas Dart of Cook County in Illinois—with the second-largest jail in the country after Los Angeles County—represents the kind of reform leadership we need. With as many as a third of the county jail's eight thousand inmates suffering from mental illness, he refers to the jail as the largest mental institution in the country and appointed a PhD clinical psychologist, Dr. N'neka Jones Tapia, to be the warden.[24] "The person isn't choosing to be schizophrenic," Dart says. "The vast majority of mentally ill people are here for nonviolent crimes, like stealing food to survive or breaking into places, usually looking for somewhere to sleep, or getting caught with drugs because they are self-medicating. How is it different from locking up diabetics? Jails were never meant to be mental hospitals."[25]

Tapia was in charge of mental health care at the jail before she became the warden, so change had already begun. Now all inmates see a clinician when they arrive, during which a mental health history is taken, a proper diagnosis is made, and medication is prescribed. The jail sends a report to the arraigning judges in the hope that they will refer arrestees to mental health care instead of jail. They enroll arrestees in a health insurance plan if they can, to facilitate case management when they are released.

Dr. Tapia is most proud of the mental health transition center that she started in 2014. It serves about fifteen inmates at a time, people who suffer from mental health issues including depression, bipolar disorders, and schizophrenia, and provides cognitive behavioral therapy, job readiness skills, and extra recreation. A year later, none of the forty-three former inmates who participated had been rearrested.[26] In 2016 the county opened a Community Triage Center on the South Side of the city, aimed at keeping people out of jails and hospitals. It is open 24/7 and offers assessment, support, and referrals. People can walk in, and police can bring people in.[27]

The jail—infamous for its overcrowding, gangs, and decrepit physical condition—is under federal oversight and has really only begun to improve. Over the three years beginning in 2014, the jail reduced its population by 25 percent—by about seven hundred people—to the lowest level since 1991.[28]

On the other hand, Cook County Board of Commissioners president Toni Preckwinkle acknowledges that 70 percent of the population consists of people charged with nonviolent crimes, many of whom have behavioral and mental health issues, and are there only because they cannot afford bail.[29] In October 2016

Alec Karakatsanis of Civil Rights Corps, the MacArthur Justice Center, and a private law firm filed a lawsuit challenging the county's bail system as unconstitutional.[30] So there is still overcrowding, although less, and there are still long waits for trial and even arraignment. There are still gang rivalries. The jail itself is falling apart physically and there is little for inmates to do other than watch television and sleep. The state of Illinois made huge cuts in the mental health budget four years in a row and two state facilities had to be closed altogether.[31] Nonetheless, the Cook County Jail is going in the right direction.

Los Angeles is the home of the largest county jail system in the country, including some four thousand mentally ill inmates—the largest mentally ill population in any jail and the largest mental health facility of any kind (vying with Cook County). Lee Baca, the previous sheriff, who steadfastly denied there were any major problems in the county jails, is finally gone. The new sheriff, Jim McDonnell, says he wants "to write a new chapter in the care of those suffering from mental illness who end up in our jails, and will eventually return to our communities." Margaret Winter, until 2016 the associate director of the ACLU National Prison Project, said, "This is one of the few times in my career that I've seen reform on such a big scale. Not that there aren't still significant problems, but this is a major, real thing."[32]

Advocacy, journalism, and politics focused on the Los Angeles jails have been going on for decades. In addition to the U.S. Department of Justice, which began investigating the jail in 1996, litigation has repeatedly been undertaken by groups of inmates represented by public-interest lawyers and private law firms working pro bono. And there has been a steady drumbeat of coverage by the *Los Angeles Times* and others. Winter, who has been working on cases in the jails since 2007, says, "I'd never seen anything comparable to the horror, the abuse of the mentally ill, the overcrowding, the dungeonlike conditions."[33]

The momentum for change accelerated in August 2015, when, after a series of agreements and settlements failed to produce lasting change, the Department of Justice, the county of Los Angeles, and Sheriff McDonnell reached a comprehensive settlement that addressed the grossly inadequate mental health care and routine excessive force; court oversight and an independent monitor would ensure the jail implemented the reforms.[34] The fifty-eight-page agreement includes measures to reduce suicides, ensure better assessment of prisoners' mental health, improve crisis intervention and other staff training, reduce excessive force generally, allow inmates to spend more time out of their cells, and hire five hundred more staff, including more mental health professionals.[35]

In 2013 McDonnell brought in Terri McDonald as assistant sheriff to run the jails, and by most accounts the level of violence decreased in the three years she served, ending at the close of 2015. Assaults on deputies and beatings of inmates decreased markedly. Miriam Krinsky, who had been the executive director of the Citizens' Commission on Jail Violence and later a top aide to McDonnell after a stellar career as a prosecutor and a child advocate, says she felt a powerful "tenseness" in the jails when she visited in the Baca era, but that is "not the way they feel today." Peter Eliasberg, the legal director of the Southern California ACLU, points to a "dramatic decrease in the brutal beatings."

Implementation of the 2015 agreements is still a major challenge, and the aged, dilapidated, and pest-infested Men's Central Jail has yet to be replaced, although the county Board of Supervisors has approved a $2 billion replacement plan.[36] Not surprisingly and not incorrectly, advocates for the homeless and mentally ill former inmates say the settlement does not break the cycle between Skid Row and jail cells.[37] Mark-Anthony Johnson, with Dignity and Power Now, said, "The Sheriff's Department needs to separate itself from being a mental health provider. Those folks who are mentally ill, our loved ones, need to be in the community, in community-based treatment."[38]

The year 2017 began with further positive developments. The sheriff's department announced it would add twenty-five staff members to increase the size of its Mental Evaluation Teams from ten to twenty-three, and that it would create a triage help desk for residents to call during a psychological crisis. Maya Lau of the *Los Angeles Times* reported that the county's Mental Evaluation Teams had "diverted 99 percent of the 1,200 people they encountered away from the criminal justice system" over the previous year.[39] In addition, the county opened a sobering center aimed at keeping intoxicated people out of jail.[40] And the county created a Sheriff Civilian Oversight Commission, constituting the first all-civilian review board the county had ever assigned to monitor the agency.[41]

The forces necessary for change seem better aligned than they have been at any time in the mass incarceration era, at least insofar as improving the jails overall is concerned. Mental health is another matter. With budgets perennially tight, breaking the unending cycle of homelessness and jail and improving community-based mental health services as a whole remains a challenge. The decriminalization of mental health is a long-term project.

In response to Darren Rainey's death in Florida, the state did nothing despite credible witnesses among inmates and a few professionals at the prison until Julie Brown of the *Miami Herald* bit onto the issue and would not let go. People then noticed, actively among the general public and some legislators, and reluctantly in the executive branch of the state, but no one was prosecuted for Rainey's death. A negative autopsy was finally finished in January 2016, finding that Rainey had died from "complications of schizophrenia, heart disease, and 'confinement' from the shower," although Brown found a never-released preliminary report written the day of the autopsy that refers to "visible trauma throughout the decedent's body." Then, in March 2017, almost five years after Rainey's death, the prosecutors finally issued a 101-page investigation report concluding that the corrections officers had committed no crime. Brown and others interested in the case found inconsistencies in the report itself and reported intimidation of some staff who knew what had really happened, as well as pointing out that the testimony of inmates was not believed.[42]

Dade is still the deadliest prison in Florida, but at least a few constructive things did happen regarding the system and the Dade Transitional Care Unit.

Julie Brown's reporting did result in a shakeup of the leadership of the state Department of Corrections and some reforms. The most important concrete step at the Transitional Care Unit, probably helped along by Brown's reporting, was the settlement in May 2015 of a lawsuit regarding the conditions there. The lawsuit was brought by Disability Rights of Florida along with Peter Sleasman, now at Disability Rights, and the law firm of Holland & Knight (which is perhaps the most powerful law firm in the state). It alleged systematic abuse and discrimination against prisoners in the mental health unit, including brutality, deprivation of food, and physical and verbal harassment.[43]

The settlement agreement is comprehensive. It has substantive reforms, implementation steps, and the consequences of breach of the agreement—all in considerable detail.[44] Sleasman says the settlement caused significant change. The security staff was cleaned out. A new video and audio recording system was installed. Sleasman made several visits toward developing a plan of compliance on the content of mental health treatment. As of May 2017 the settlement was about to expire, but a few weeks earlier the state had fired its health and mental health contractor for poor performance at Dade and two other facilities. Sleasman told me that he intended to ask the court to extend the life of the settlement in order to monitor the uncertainty associated with the removal of the contractor.

In November 2014, Sleasman also brought a wrongful death suit on behalf of Darren Rainey's family. He referred it to private counsel and it is still pending as of May 2017. It was suspended for a period of time and as of May 2017 had resumed discovery. Sleasman told me that the prospect for the lawsuit is uncertain due to the dispute stirred up by the claim in the autopsy that Rainey was not scalded.

And finally, in June 2014, the Florida ACLU and a number of other organizations asked the U.S. Department of Justice to investigate the death of Darren Rainey and the treatment of mentally ill inmates in the entire Florida correctional system.[45] In May 2015, Justice began a criminal investigation of Darren Rainey's death, announcing that it was considering a "pattern or practice" probe into allegations of mistreatment of mentally ill inmates across all of Florida's prisons.[46] As of May 2017, no public outcome had emerged from the investigation, and with the change in administration it seems unlikely that the investigation will produce anything positive.

In New York, five successful class action suits have been brought against Rikers over the past twenty-five-plus years. Each addressed the excessive force and the other abuses. Some of them did make a significant difference about specific problems. Others made a difference for a while but fell apart when the court orders expired. Although not focused only on inmates with mental health issues, they are relevant because, while 40 percent of the inmates have mental illness, 75 percent of the injuries inflicted on inmates are directed at those with mental illness.[47]

An unsung hero, a lawyer named Jonathan Chasan, has become visible as the Rikers tragedy finally became a public issue. He works at the Prisoners' Rights Project of the Legal Aid Society, and he has been working since 1980 to protect inmates at Rikers from being subjected to excessive force. His most important success was a class action in 1993 taking on the main solitary imprisonment unit at the prison, in the course of which he brought out that guards had seriously injured—broken bones and perforated eardrums and more—three hundred or more prisoners over the five years prior to the litigation. The class action forced many changes in the unit, including the installation of three hundred video cameras. It made a difference until the settlement agreement expired and things regressed.[48]

In 2012, Chasan and the Legal Aid Society sued along with two private law firms, Ropes & Gray and Emery, Celli, Brinckerhoff & Abady (in particular, Jonathan Abady), to stop the violence against adolescent inmates. Because of the peculiarity of New York state law, people as young as sixteen can be locked up at Rikers, and they are particularly vulnerable to abuse from both guards and other inmates. (The law was finally changed in 2017.) The case is *Nunez v. New York*, and the ninety-six-page complaint the lawyers filed was a blockbuster. In addition to the named plaintiffs, each of whom had been attacked savagely by staff, it recounted a long list of settlements, each of which had cost the city hundreds of thousands of dollars or more.[49]

As the lawyers were preparing and filing *Nunez*, the federal government was doing its own investigation. In the same time frame, Michael Winerip and Michael Schwirtz of the *New York Times* published a powerful account of the mental illness and brutality in Rikers. Drawing on a secret city study that was leaked to them, the reporters did further investigative work on the 129 cases discussed in the study, which had not named names, and were able to identify inmate victims and write about the specifics of their ordeals.[50] This was of great value to the lawyers.

Mayor Bill de Blasio, then new to the job, undertook efforts at change, too. Mayor de Blasio had begun from the outset of his administration to invest in improving Rikers, including launching specialized therapeutic initiatives that reward improved behavior and the scaling down of solitary confinement.

The Department of Justice reported in 2014 that it had found "a deep-seated culture of violence." The federal report paid particular attention to inmates with mental illness, who sustained three-fourths of injuries, and younger inmates, finding that 44 percent of them had been subject to the use of force, resulting in serious injury in numerous cases. The United States filed its own lawsuit and then joined the *Nunez* case in late 2014. As Jennifer Gonnerman wrote in the *New Yorker*, Jonathan Chasan had "acquired the ultimate ally."[51]

Settlement negotiations in *Nunez* culminated in a sixty-three-page agreement in June 2015, which was accepted by federal judge Laura Taylor Swain that fall. Some of the reforms had already been put into place by the de Blasio administration, but the lawyers on the plaintiffs' side quite correctly wanted them in the agreement, to make them subject to court sanctions if backsliding occurs down the road. U.S. attorney Preet Bharara called it a "groundbreaking framework" that would "fix a broken system and dismantle a decades long culture of violence." Mayor de Blasio said there had already been "extraordinary steps to reform Rikers" and the "agreement represents another strong step toward our goal of reversing the decades of abuse." Not surprisingly, Norman Seabrook, the head of the correctional officers' union, was decidedly less enthusiastic.[52]

The agreement covered the entire institution, with specific attention to young inmates. There are new requirements and standards for reporting and investigations of force, greater accountability for staff who engage in force, an early warning system for identifying incipient force by staff, 7,800 new cameras, a pilot program for body cameras, video cameras to record the removals of prisoners from their cells, computerized data on force, more care in staff hiring, improved screening for promotions, additional staff training, anonymous reporting, and notification to the U.S. attorney of possible criminality in the use of force.[53] The new force policy includes an explicit ban on blows to the head, face, groin, neck, kidneys, and spinal column, as well as kicks and choke holds, with an exception for guards who believe they are in imminent danger of death or serious injury.[54]

The requirements regarding youth are detailed as well. The headline is the ending of solitary confinement for sixteen- and seventeen-year-olds, which had already been ordered administratively, along with prohibiting the use of isolation for eighteen-year-olds with serious mental illness. In addition, there are particulars on staff ratios, daily inspection of housing areas, classification, programming, transfers for youth at risk, supervision procedures, staff training, and a review of the inmate disciplinary process. The city promised to make "best efforts" to find an alternative site not on Rikers for youth under eighteen, and in July 2016 it made a concrete proposal to move two hundred sixteen- and seventeen-year-olds to a site in the Bronx.[55] An independent monitor is overseeing compliance.[56] Best of all regarding youth, the state legislature finally acted in 2017 to treat most youth under eighteen as juveniles, which means they will not be held in Rikers at all.

Throwing Corizon out of Rikers was another important event. The unfortunate thing is how many people already knew how bad Corizon and Prison Health Services were and did nothing about it. The first sentence of Michael Winerip and Michael Schwirtz's *New York Times* story on the demise of Corizon was, "New York

City officials have known for years about serious problems with Corizon." Corizon and PHS had been there for fifteen "troubled" years, the reporters wrote, and cited a new report by the city's Department of Investigation that Corizon "had hired doctors and mental health workers with disciplinary problems and criminal convictions, including for murder and kidnapping" and its employees "may have contributed to at least two recent inmate deaths."[57]

A definite feel-good moment occurred in early December 2015 when the city swore in 592 new corrections officers. They were the first of almost 1,800 new officers to be hired over three years and the largest class in the city's history. Speaking to the group, Mayor de Blasio stressed their qualifications—fifty-seven had served in the military and more than a hundred had civil service experience. Michael Schwirtz of the *Times* quoted a number who expressed idealistic reasons for taking the jobs.[58]

Of course, the bottom line is to take on the dysfunctional culture at Rikers, and specifically the lack of transparency, outmoded infrastructure, and hostility to civilian oversight, all of which must be tackled to solve the problem of excessive force.[59] Highly respected leaders said for years that no strategy could succeed in reforming Rikers and that the only appropriate action is to close it. In March 2017, in the light of a devastating ninety-seven-page report written by a distinguished independent commission, Mayor de Blasio finally stated an intention to close the facility. This was certainly important, although the small print in the plan said that it would be done over a ten-year period and will be conditioned on getting the population down to five thousand inmates. Still, what the mayor and his staff are doing now, along with the pressure of the federal government and other advocates, is vital. Closing the place is far off, and the people now locked up there deserve a far less destructive environment. What has been accomplished by the city administration and the ramped-up outside advocacy efforts—important and worthwhile as it all is—is only the beginning.

The worst part of all of this is the horrific abuse of the inmates. But ending that abuse is just the tip of a huge iceberg of mass incarceration and the acute shortage of mental health and addiction services in communities. Improving mental health and addiction services in jails and prisons is just the first step. Ending mass incarceration is essential if we are to reduce the number of people with mental illness who are locked up. And creating accessible behavioral health services for low-income people in the community is crucial to keep them from having to do time in jail or prison in order to get treatment.

There is no magic way to accomplish either prison reform or improvement in services for the mentally ill or treatment for those with addictions (often the same people). What gets fixed all too often gets unfixed after a while. In some states, a governor or legislative leadership or even a progressive corrections commissioner will lead the way to change, but governors and legislators and commissioners come and go. Outsiders—lawyers, other advocates, and journalists—are more often the catalyst for change and must be the force for keeping it, once achieved. But it must be noted that, all along, there are caring and courageous mental health professionals who stay at it day after day and press for change whenever they can get a hearing.

The fundamental issue, though, is that the culture of the

system has to change, and that, of course, is the hardest thing of all. The even bigger question is how we improve mental health and addiction services generally so we do not send people to prison only because we do not know what else to do with them. Difficult as it is to reform debtors' prisons and money bail, the mess we have made by using jails and prisons in lieu of appropriate mental health services is even harder to repair. Certainly, services in jails and prisons should be improved, but the real answer is community-based behavioral health services that help prevent people from committing crimes and divert at least minor offenders from being placed in correctional settings. Darren Rainey should not have died in vain.

5

Child Support: Criminalizing Poor Fathers

Walter Scott of North Charleston, South Carolina, died because he could not pay his child support. An African American man, he ran away from a police officer who had stopped him for driving while black. He ran because he was terrified he would be jailed for being delinquent in paying child support. He was unarmed, and the police officer shot him in the back.

Imprisoning people delinquent on child support payments is a more complicated form of debtors' prisons. The state's interest in squeezing fines and fees from low-income people when they have committed a minor infraction is hardly compelling, although fines and fees set at reasonable levels for real offenses from people who can pay are not problematic. But in general the loss to the state in not collecting a fee to finance its court system is only a loss of revenue for the state.

By contrast, the nonpayment of child support is typically a loss of revenue to a child. (There are still instances when child support money goes to the state and not the child).[1] A parent who can afford to pay child support and fails to do so is reneging on a fundamental responsibility. To put a "deadbeat dad" in jail—it is usually the father—for not paying when he could pay is a proposition hardly anyone would oppose.[2] But it is useless and almost inevitably destructive to imprison a man who cannot meet his obligation.

Child support is vital. It lifts about one million people out of poverty. In 2014, the federal Child Support Enforcement program alone collected $28.2 billion in child support payments for families.[3] In 2011, child support constituted 17 percent of the income of those mothers receiving it. Child support received by custodial parents with incomes below the poverty line accounted for a whopping 52 percent of their income.[4] Child support is a powerful anti-poverty strategy.

Constitutional law and federal policy mandate that a noncustodial parent who does not have the ability to pay child support may not be incarcerated. As Vicki Turetsky, President Obama's commissioner of the federal Office of Child Support Enforcement, says, "Every parent has a responsibility to support their kids to the best of their ability," but quickly adds, "Jail is appropriate for someone who is actively hiding assets, and not appropriate for someone who couldn't pay the order in the first place."[5] Yet a number of states and individual judges still send indigent parents owing child support to jail, either by ignoring the law or by finding ability to pay where it does not exist. In addition, in many states, arrears in child support payments mount up while a parent is in prison for a crime other than owing child support.

A proper approach begins with figuring out how much a

low-income parent can pay, if anything at all. His obligation should be fairly calculated and not impossible to meet from the outset; many fathers are doomed to be jailed because the calculation was unreasonable from the start.[6] A separate challenge is how to get more states to stop allowing the mounting up of charges during incarceration. Fathers should also be provided a lawyer for court hearings on payment of child support; those who do are much more likely to be able to prove their indigence. Since a considerable number of states criminalize nonpayment with incarceration, the liberty of a father in a child support hearing is often at risk—typically the standard for requiring a lawyer.

The incidence of indigence among fathers is very large. The Urban Institute studied nine states in 2007 and found that 70 percent of child support debt was owed by people with incomes of less than $10,000. Yet in many states the obligation to pay is based on an assumption that the father has a full-time minimum-wage or even median-wage job. As a result, low-income fathers were being expected to pay an average of 83 percent of their income for child support.[7]

And, because child support payments in fourteen states do not pause for incarceration, fathers with child support orders go into prison owing an average of $10,000 and come out owing an average of $20,000, plus interest and penalties.[8] What we hope to achieve by criminalizing the poverty of fathers in this way is not clear. But it is clear that this approach makes a bad situation worse and does little to help the children who are not receiving the support due them.

Vicki Turetsky, the federal commissioner, says that in general, state child support guidelines for parent payments are moving in a constructive direction. Most states now take into account the income of both parents in setting court orders, which is more realistic. But the problems continue for low-income parents, because some states still base child support obligations on "imputed" incomes—assumed or fictitious income—rather than evidence of an actual ability to pay, even though ability to pay is the federal law. This results in unsustainable payments, uncollectible debt, illegal income generation, reduced parental contact, and jail.

"Parents who are truly destitute go to jail over and over again for child support simply because they're poor," Sarah Geraghty of the Southern Center for Human Rights says.[9] "You see a room full of indigent parents—most of them African American—and you have a judge and attorney general, both of whom are white. The hearings often take only 15 seconds. The judge asks, 'Do you have any money to pay?' The person pleads and the judge says, 'OK you're going to jail.'"[10]

In 2002, Elaine Sorensen of the Urban Institute analyzed data from the U.S. Bureau of Justice Statistics and concluded that nationally about ten thousand men are in jail for falling behind in their child support obligations. A 2009 survey in South Carolina showed that one out of every eight inmates in the state was there because he could not pay child support. In 2010 in Georgia, 3,500 parents were jailed for nonpayment of child support. Not surprisingly, those two states are among the fourteen that do not allow a pause in the growing obligation while fathers are incarcerated for committing an unrelated crime. And the two states are among the five nationally that do not provide a lawyer—Florida, Maine, and Ohio being the others. But they are not alone in locking up men who cannot pay. The newspaper in Hackensack, New

Jersey, recorded 1,800 parents jailed or put on ankle monitors in two New Jersey counties in 2013 for being delinquent on child support payments.[11]

Having a lawyer would make a big difference. The Supreme Court had a chance to help in 2011 in *Turner v. Rogers* but failed to rise to the occasion.[12] Physical liberty is the most important liberty right we have. When a person is about to lose his liberty, he should be provided a lawyer if he cannot afford one. The Supreme Court did not see it that way. Technically, nonpayment of child support is not a criminal procedure; it is a civil contempt procedure. In principle, a father is being coerced to pay, not punished. In the eyes of the court, such a man has the keys to the jail in his pocket: if he pays, he gets out, so there is no need for a lawyer. But in the case of an indigent parent this is a catch-22, because he has no money. Thus he has no key to the jail in his pocket and risks being punished for his poverty by being deprived of his liberty. In reality, the situation is no different as a practical matter from the reason *Gideon* requires a lawyer in a criminal matter. The Court is wrong; he should have a lawyer.

The Court in *Turner v. Rogers* said instead that a father *might* be entitled to a lawyer if the other side, such as the state, has a lawyer. But if the other side—say, the mother of the children—has no lawyer, the Court says, it would be unfair to give the father one. One wonders whether it occurred to the Court that it could require lawyers for both sides.

Although it did not require the appointment of a lawyer, the Supreme Court did rule, à la *Bearden*, that the trial court has to allow the defendant to explain his economic situation and then determine whether the defendant has the ability to pay. (In fact, the court in this case did not do those things, so Turner won.) But no lawyer was required. I think some members of the Supreme Court, including one or more in the majority, have no idea what happens widely and routinely in courtrooms in our country. Whether the case is child support or any other of the myriad examples of debtors' prisons, *Bearden*'s requirement that a defendant's ability to pay be taken into account is a fiction in many jurisdictions. The way to put teeth into *Bearden* is to provide a lawyer.

Turetsky goes further, arguing that providing legal representation does not dig deeply enough. She contends that public policy and children will be better served by greatly reducing the use of civil contempt to collect child support and finding other means of getting obligations paid, such as garnishment of salary. She believes that the adversarial nature of the current process is destructive and not cost-effective. Custodial parents often shun the use of the court because of its deeply negative consequences for the noncustodial parent. In addition, court-ordered payments often bring forth payment from family members who really cannot afford it or result in new offenses to get the money. Illinois reduced its use of contempt by two-thirds and consequently increased its non-payroll-withholding collections such as tax refunds by $14.5 million between 2010 and 2013. Florida decided that civil contempt is the least cost-effective strategy, and other states are implementing or considering changes in their policies.

For very good reasons we have toughened and toughened again our policies on child support.[13] The "won't pay" fathers had a free ride for years before that. It is much harder for them to go scot-free now, with garnishment, bank account seizures, and suspension of driver's licenses and even professional licenses to reach their assets and put pressure on them to pay. But to the extent we continue to use the courts to collect child support, it would be helpful to have lawyers to make sure the "can't pays" have a fair chance to make their case to the court.

The Obama administration proposed and finally adopted regulations that improve the system in important ways, but only after Republican opposition delayed the final rule until a month before President Obama left office.[14] Three provisions in particular are of major significance. Perhaps the most important requires that states take into account noncustodial parents' actual ability to pay when setting child support obligations. This step takes on frontally the longtime practice in many states of using unrealistic non-individualized methods to set support levels, with devastating consequences for low-income noncustodial parents. A second requires states not to treat incarceration as "voluntary unemployment," a euphemism if ever there was one. This will prevent the piling up of arrears while the father is in prison. There has been improvement on this—thirty-six states now allow inmates to ask for modification in their support orders and provide help to the inmate to understand how to do that.[15] The new regulations make the policy mandatory. Finally, the regulations place into federal law the holding in *Turner v. Rogers* that judges presiding over noncustodial parents brought into court for nonpayment of support must determine the defendant's ability to pay before sending him or her to jail.

The problems with the child support system itself are bad enough, but mass incarceration along with its effects on children is even more staggering. One in twenty-eight children has a parent in jail or prison, and one in nine African American children does.[16] The damage that mass incarceration does to children and families goes far beyond the fact that Dad is unable to pay child support while he is in prison. And along with mass incarceration, there are enormous issues of unemployment, low-wage jobs, and racism. The deeper challenges are to attend to those problems. Some good people promote fatherhood as a behavioral goal, and there is value to that, but rather than criminalize indigent fathers' poverty, we must dig all the way to the roots if we want to help families achieve what they want and deserve for their children.

6

Criminalizing Public Benefits

Rebecca Vallas remembers vividly her first case, which was when she was still in law school. Her client was a food stamps recipient accused of an "intentional program violation," which could have ended in a criminal prosecution as well as loss of the food stamps. I'll call her Mom because she is representative of mothers everywhere with similar stories. Mom was a forty-year-old woman with a twelve-year-old daughter. Mom had worked hard for years in a series of low-wage jobs, but her daughter had a disability and as the daughter got older Mom could not hold a steady job. As a result, Mom was receiving food stamps for the family and disability benefits for her daughter. But even though their income was well below the poverty line, it was too high to be eligible for welfare (which is the case in most states). They had lost their home and were living in a long-stay motel, and they were so poor they had to choose which utility bill to pay each month. Out of desperation Mom was selling her plasma, which constituted the alleged "intentional program violation."

The authorities went after Mom to cut off her food stamps for not reporting the added income. She found her way to the Legal Aid Justice Center in Virginia, which sent her to the University of Virginia Law School public benefits clinic and Vallas. Vallas represented her at a hearing that lasted seven hours. Three people were arrayed against her—a caseworker, a law enforcement officer, and an inspector general. With Vallas's help, Mom won. But the vast majority of people in such situations have no lawyer and therefore lose their benefits and sometimes even end up imprisoned. Such penalties occur all too regularly.

Criminalization of public benefits takes two forms: situations like that of Mom, where the beneficiary of a public benefit is accused of cheating; and being barred from access to the public safety net altogether as a collateral consequence of a prior criminal conviction or even just an arrest.

Mom's experience was not unusual. "Criminalization" is a key strategy in today's cruel world of diminished public benefits for people with very low incomes. In too many parts of the country, the reigning bureaucratic culture assumes that applicants and recipients are dishonest and fraudulent in one way or another. Lacing public benefits with harsh rules and making violation of those rules into crimes are the products of decades of policies meant to punish struggling mothers and children. Punishing the poor is hardly a new idea, but it had become less pervasive with the Great Depression and the New Deal and through the period of the Great Society and the civil rights movement. Since then our attitudes have gradually coarsened again and the nasty side has returned.

Punishing people for missteps with public benefits cuts a wide swath, and while violations of the rules for Temporary Assistance for Needy Families (TANF, formerly known as welfare) and unemployment insurance are the primary reasons people are penalized, along with food stamps, these violations are not unique. Violations of the rules of Supplemental Security Income, or SSI, which provides income to people with disabilities and elderly people who have very low incomes, are also used to criminalize poverty. The most a person can receive under SSI is $735 a month, but a recipient can be docked or terminated if, for example, she pays less for room and board than what the government deems a fair amount; according to the rules, this "discount" counts as extra income. The government also calls it extra income if a friend or relative gives the person some money to help get by. And a stint in a hospital for more than thirty days that is paid for by Medicaid can be counted as an SSI overpayment and place the beneficiary in jeopardy of being penalized.

WELFARE

The negative politics around public benefits went into high gear with President Reagan and climaxed with President Clinton's decision to sign the Personal Responsibility and Work Opportunity Act in 1996 (although the Trump administration may take us to a further low). "Welfare reform" joined mass incarceration as a way to do racial politics without using the *n*-word: jail for the men, ending welfare for the women and children, with race playing a role in all of it.

The most important feature in the 1996 law was to end the legal right to federally funded welfare benefits (although benefit levels were already very low in some states) and replace it with block grants to the states; many states accepted the consequent invitation to invent new punitive measures to apply to their recipients and applicants. The new form of welfare, TANF, allows the states to deny help to anyone they choose, so long as they do not violate the Constitution or other federal laws including civil rights laws. The 1996 act also imposed a lifetime limit of five years for families to receive TANF funds and gave authority for states to impose even shorter time limits, even though the money is entirely federal. The underlying goal was to reduce the number of people on TANF to levels as close to zero as possible in as many states as possible.

Criminalization is a key component of that strategy. Welfare fraud warnings are publicized. The authorities check for arrest warrants pending for the applicant and whether she has been convicted of a drug-related crime, either of which would disqualify her completely from aid, an approach that severely diminishes employment prospects. Twelve states have drug testing for TANF, and every year legislators in other states introduce bills to require it, even though a number of courts have already ruled it to be unconstitutional. In some states, home visits are used to look for evidence that the recipient has income or assets she did not report or a boyfriend who "should not be there." In many states, TANF payments have to be repaid to the state by the father of a child as part of his child support obligation, so child support may never reach the child for which it is intended. If he figures it is a waste of his meager income to pay back the state, he can be sent to jail. People get the message and do not even apply.[1]

Frequently, states punish recipients who are late or absent for work assignments or office appointments by kicking them off the rolls—no excuses and no due process—for two or three months the first time, longer the second time, and, in some states, for life the third time.

Shutting the front door has an even bigger punch in reducing the rolls than kicking people off. States have reduced eligibility by lowering the income levels above which people do not qualify (think of Mom above), and they discourage applications by making sure the lines are so long that people can wait all day and still not be served by closing time. They operate work programs so unpleasant that large numbers of eligible recipients, hearing about them, will not bother to apply, and they ask privacy-violating and obnoxious personal questions of those who do get to the desk.

Criminalization is not so much a strategy to actually put people in jail for welfare fraud and other infractions as it is a method to scare them away from even applying for benefits. The broader strategy is for the states to keep the rolls down to a size that can be "drown[ed] in a bathtub," to adapt the infamous phrase Grover Norquist used of the size of the federal government. Most of the states followed the strategy.

Attorney Rebecca Vallas elaborates on the way help for the lowest-income people, originally designed to help the poor, has since morphed into ways designed to punish them: "The welfare system has become a tool for catching criminals—police actually rely on social service offices to run checks and even fingerprints. The process almost looks like getting booked. [Applicants] have to give personal information, sign a slew of documents, let them into your house and do spot checks, give over your biometrics and social security number, and let them look into your past. And of course the felony drug ban. It's policing the poor."

Kansas offers a case study of one state's punitive approach. In 2015, Kansas enacted a law putting a daily maximum of $25 on the amount that TANF recipients could withdraw from ATM machines using their electronic benefit cards. With all the senseless limitations that have been placed on TANF, this was a first. Most ATMs do not give out $25 bills, so the limit was effectively $20, and there was also a $1 administrative charge from the state for every withdrawal. As State Senator Oletha Faust-Goudeau declared, any daily limit could create significant problems for TANF beneficiaries, making it almost impossible, for example, for her constituents to withdraw what they would need to pay their rent on time each month.[2]

Ultimately the state backed down, but it did not happen by the goodness of Kansas's heart. Before the law was implemented, the federal Department of Health and Human Services under the Obama administration carried on a lengthy correspondence with Governor Sam Brownback about whether the state law was barred by the federal law. The federal government stopped short of saying the state law was invalid, but it sowed enough doubt into the state's thinking that Kansas dropped the idea. (It remains to be seen what role the Trump administration will play in curtailing egregious state policies.)

Press coverage was important, too. The *Wichita Eagle*, part of the McClatchy chain of newspapers, opined against the policy and did an excellent job of explaining the intricacies of the federal law and the federal-state relationship, and it and many other newspapers and television and radio stations stayed with the story. The attention that television's faux news moderator Jon Stewart paid to the issue didn't hurt, either. Poking hard at

Kansas, Stewart said the restrictions treat a TANF recipient "like a bad child. You haven't recovered from the national economic collapse? [Bleep] you. No movies."[3] Maybe the federal government would have gotten Kansas to back down anyway, but the press coverage definitely helped.

That is the good part of the story. Sad to say, the demise of the $25-a-day limit was actually an exception to Kansas's retrogression. After Governor Brownback was elected in 2010 and there was a further turn to the right in the legislature, the state went to work on TANF. Beginning in 2011, Kansas put tougher sanctions into place for such things as failing to show up for an appointment with the TANF office, and instituted stricter eligibility requirements, such as including the income of a cohabitating partner or spouse who is not the parent of resident children and has no legal obligation to support them. The state's next move was to require TANF applicants to make a minimum of twenty job contacts before the authorities would even consider an application for cash assistance (with no help provided for childcare or transportation while looking for a job). Not surprisingly, the state's caseload fell by 60 percent between 2006 and 2014.[4]

Kansas kept on. A 2015 law shortened lifetime eligibility from forty-eight months (already shorter than the federal sixty-month limit) to thirty-six months. It prohibits TANF recipients from spending benefits on taking children to swimming pools and on movie tickets, among other things. TANF recipients who commit welfare fraud are banned for life, and adults convicted of two drug felonies are permanently barred from food stamps. All of these measures are completely permissible under the federal law.

Barely 3 million people receive TANF now, less than 1 percent of the population. Almost half of those are in California and New York, so the remaining 1.7 million are divided among forty-eight states and the District of Columbia. And the numbers are still going down, 600,000 fewer in 2013 and 2014 alone.

Having fewer people on TANF would be good if it was because fewer people were poor, but that is not the case. Welfare is dead in most of the country. No wonder we have 15 million people with incomes below half the poverty line and 7.5 million people whose only income is from food stamps—which is just over $6,000 a year for a family of three, less than a third of the poverty line. We still have 43 million people in poverty as well as 15 million in deep poverty, mainly because the recovery from the Great Recession has not reached them.

Our safety net for the lowest-income people is in tatters—consisting only of food stamps and, for some, Medicaid. We urgently need to invent a new, decent system, one that is connected to the realities of the job market and how much it costs to live at even the most rudimentary level. However, the results of the 2016 election do not bode well for a more humane approach.

With Congressman Paul Ryan calling the shots on domestic policy, the "success" of welfare "reform" is poised to migrate the block grant idea in multiple directions. Medicaid, SNAP (food stamps), housing vouchers, and perhaps a dozen other programs, totaling in all well over half a trillion dollars annually, are in jeopardy, and may have been transformed by the time this book appears. This constitutes the dream for decades of enemies of the New Deal and the Great Society. Now they have their chance—an upheaval of immense size, a truly profound and radical revolution. These are successful and proven programs that have made a positive difference for millions and millions of people. It does not matter. This is about ideology, not real people.

Block grant, someone says. What's so bad about that? Sending funds to the states to decide how to spend it—aren't states closer to the people? Here is what happens in reality. First, the funding stagnates. Many of the programs are funded based on the number of beneficiaries, but the block grant for each recipient has a capped amount. The funding quickly falls behind. Does the incidence of illness go down because the funds wither? The opposite is more likely. Second, perhaps the blue states spend wisely the funds they do have, but the red states, probably not. With the block grant, SNAP eligibility and benefit levels would be up to the state. Are people less hungry in Mississippi than they are in Minnesota? With block grants, need will be irrelevant in many states. Third, as in TANF, punitive policies, especially for the lowest-income people, are offered an open invitation. When the money has diminished in amount, one way to ration it is to scare people away from asking for it.

UNEMPLOYMENT INSURANCE

Unemployment insurance has been a mainstay of our economic safety net since 1935, along with Social Security (and, less successfully, welfare, now called TANF), all parts of the historic Social Security Act of 1935. Unlike the near demise of TANF, we still think of unemployment insurance as a pillar of our support for people having a hard time—unless we look more closely. It still works reasonably well in recessions—keeping five million people out of poverty in the recent Great Recession—but otherwise is in a gradual deterioration that has been going on for many years.

Two phenomena tell the story. One is the major changes in our economy over the last forty years. The other, more recent, is the specific state-by-state cuts in benefit structures, including here and there some of the punitive measures like those imposed on TANF.

Unemployment insurance was designed for male industrial workers who tended to stay in the same company for their entire lives, punctuated by layoffs in recessions. A significant number of the unemployed were never qualified because they had quit, not because they were laid off. We have had massive changes since that was the state of things. Women (and many men) now go in and out of the labor force and have part-time, temporary, seasonal, or leased work, or low-wage jobs that do not qualify for benefits. Independent contractors (many so-called) and the holders of the now ubiquitous on-demand jobs are not covered. Currently, only one in four unemployed workers receives benefits after losing a job,[5] versus three out of four in 1975.[6]

Unemployment insurance has always firmly been seen as assistance for the "deserving poor." In today's world, though, slashing the length and the amount of benefits is prevalent, along with other steps to keep the rolls down.

Along with other consequences of North Carolina's hard turn to the right, the state cut unemployment insurance down to one in ten unemployed workers there, the lowest level in the nation.[7] George Wentworth of the National Employment Law Project said, "No state has ever inflicted such extensive damage to its unemployment insurance program in such a short time as North Carolina did with House Bill 4."[8] Florida reduced its coverage to 11 percent of its jobless workers after a series of cuts in eligibility.[9] Missouri, with a newly minted Republican governor and a Republican legislature in 2017, made reducing eligibility from twenty to thirteen weeks one of its highest priorities with its newly obtained power.[10] Kentucky is more than halving the number of offices that can handle unemployment insurance claims.[11] Employers have begun to hire companies to fight claims, resulting in applicants going into deep debt trying to assert their rights.[12]

Governor Scott Walker of Wisconsin required some recipients of unemployment insurance to take a drug test, with benefits denied if the person fails the test or refuses to take it.[13] Several dozen states have considered drug tests for unemployment insurance, as well as for SNAP, Medicaid, and various local benefits, to go along with the dozen states that already have laws mandating drug testing of TANF recipients despite the court decisions declaring such statutes unconstitutional.[14]

The worst of the worst is Michigan. You remember Hal, the rogue computer in the film *2001*? It is back, this time installed in Michigan's Unemployment Insurance Agency, merged by Michigan governor Rick Snyder into something called the Michigan Talent Investment Agency. When Snyder took office in 2011, he decided to computerize the state's unemployment insurance program and spent a total of $81 million in contracts with three companies to do the work. The new computer, called the Michigan Data Automated System, or MiDAS, turned everything it touched to gold for the state. Unfortunately, the clients of the agency were not so lucky. Governor Snyder and his legislature cut unemployment insurance coverage in the state from twenty-six weeks to twenty, at that time the shortest period in the country. And the agency cut its staff by a third just as the new software was being rolled out in 2013.[15]

What possibly began as a gigantic computer glitch quickly turned into a vicious strategy to gouge innocent people who had applied for or received unemployment compensation. The state realized it had happened on a gold mine, which it harvested despite the havoc it had to know was going to follow.

Kevin Grifka opened a letter from the state one day in December 2014 and found he was being accused—effectively convicted, since there was no due process—of unemployment fraud to the tune of almost $13,000. He is an electrician and the previous summer had been laid off, as he is from time to time. The letter came after he was back at work, and the state immediately garnished his federal tax return, to the tune of $8,500. When he complained, he was told he had passed the thirty-day deadline for appealing. (Snyder's 2011 legislation had also added wages to what can be garnished, raised the amounts reachable from 20 percent to 50 percent, and ended the requirement that the agency seek a court order for garnishment.)[16]

Grifka was able to retain a lawyer and the mistake was rectified on appeal, but only after five months of agony. He had been laid off and applied for unemployment benefits, and then found a new job after a while. What happened was that MiDAS—without any human oversight—spread Grifka's pay from the new job over an entire three-month period. He was still not working during the first part of that calendar quarter and then he was working again. But the computer treated his new wages as though he had been working the whole time while collecting benefits. Again with no human oversight, it concluded he had committed fraud because he was supposedly working when he was actually unemployed. Having "committed fraud," he had not only been commanded to pay back the unemployment benefits he had received, but also been assessed a penalty of four times the amount of the benefits. (Michigan is the only state in the country with such an egregious penalty.) No human being had checked MiDAS's arithmetic.

This happened over and over in Michigan. MiDAS had gone rogue. The "convictions" spewed out of the computer. The era of robo-fraud convictions was on, with a vengeance. Michigan had criminalized unemployment compensation. As Ryan Felton wrote in an excellent story in the *Detroit MetroTimes*, it "is creating fraud, rather than eliminating it."[17]

Since many of the "convictions" were for benefits received a year previously, letters were sent to incorrect addresses and victims found out only when they saw their wages and tax refunds being garnished. Even though they had never received any notice, they were told that their time for appeal had expired. Even people who had been turned down for benefits were declared to have acted fraudulently. People who tried to comply found the computer asking questions they could not understand, and the computer automatically concluded fraud had occurred if the claimant did not answer within ten days or replied in a timely way but disagreed with his former employer, or the computer did not record the claimant's otherwise acceptable response in time. Often the computer spit out multiple determinations, confusing claimants even more.[18]

Michigan had a law from more liberal times that the state

would supply lawyers for appeals from denials of benefits, but the law does not apply to fraud cases. People such as Kevin Grifka, who were able to get legal help on their own, came out all right, because the administrative judges figured out what happened and reversed nearly all of the so-called convictions. But far more people were victimized because they could not afford a lawyer or did not understand what was going on.

Steps the state took to collect included using arrest warrants and pushing people into bankruptcy. Two suicide attempts by unemployment insurance claimants were reported.[19] One local bankruptcy lawyer reported in 2015 that he had nearly thirty cases stemming from the phony fraud convictions. The agency refused to desist in its aggressive collection policies even when they knew the claimant had not received notice of the charges.

The advocacy story here is important. University of Michigan professors, public-interest litigators, journalists, the U.S. Department of Labor, the state auditor, a congressman, and finally the legislature all played a role in fighting back. Even so, it took more than six years of advocacy to obtain a degree of positive response. Pressure from the U.S. Department of Labor in 2015 did not succeed in reducing the number of fraud cases. Nor did the pressure from local media. In early 2016, the Michigan auditor released a scorching report that validated everything the advocates had alleged. In March that year, a federal judge ruled that a case alleging the system was unconstitutional could go toward trial. Nonetheless, the quadruple fraud penalty was still operative along with aggressive collection, the definition of fraud was still bizarrely broad, and the flawed process to give notice to the defendant was still in place.

Congressman Sander Levin involved himself in October 2016 and made the status of the situation public. There had been 62,130 cases during the two years from October 2013 to October 2015, and $68.8 million had been collected in penalties, interest, and overpayments as of October 2014. As of October 2016, 21,956 robo-adjudicated cases had been reviewed, and 93 percent were reversed. Refunds were made in 2,571 cases for about $5.4 million out of the $68.8 million.[20] As of the beginning of 2017, it appeared that more than thirty thousand cases had not been reviewed, and most of those reviewed positively had not yet been compensated.

Some promising steps finally occurred in late 2016. Governor Snyder signed a bill that offered some relief. The law bars computer decisions without human supervision, reduces the power of the state to go after people from six years to three years after the alleged fraud, and bars averaging quarterly wages of claimants to determine fraud (remember Kevin Grifka). The governor also relieved the director of the Unemployment Insurance Agency of her duties. She was apparently the person fingered to take the rap, since many people knew full well about the whole thing, including the governor.

In January 2017, the federal case was settled with a promise by the state to reach out to claimants who had yet to be contacted and to not pursue collection from people appealing from a fraud determination. On the other hand, an accompanying case in state court was still being opposed by the state attorney general. The saga goes on. In May 2017 the *Detroit Free Press* invoked the state Freedom of Information Act and found a 2015 memorandum sent to the governor by a close associate that laid out the problems in the agency, about which the governor did nothing.[21] Shades of Flint.

COLLATERAL CONSEQUENCES

Between 70 million and 100 million people in America have criminal records,[22] including for misdemeanors, violations, and arrests that did not result in a conviction or a trial. Each year 650,000 people are released from prison, and ex-offenders are by far the largest group of people punished in connection with public benefits. Instead of the fraud policies that punish people for something connected to the benefit itself, collateral consequences—typically for a drug-related crime—add further punishment to a previous crime by barring access to public benefits. This added punishment, including the barriers to employment, often turns a sentence of time behind bars into a lifetime sentence of poverty.

Poverty is not only a cause of acquiring a criminal record but also a consequence. One study suggests that poverty over the past thirty-five years would have been 20 percent lower but for mass incarceration and its consequences.[23] By age twenty-three, at least half of African American men have been arrested at least once.[24] Some 45,000 laws impose bans on people with criminal records, including prohibitions on everything from voting to obtaining a license to cut hair.[25] But beyond the tangible barriers are human losses. As Shaila Dewan of the *New York Times* chronicled, children with incarcerated parents, especially mothers, experience more depression, aggression, delinquency, absenteeism, asthma, and migraines, and lower wages and more homelessness as adults.[26]

Nor is the damage merely to individuals and their families. Estimates are that employment gaps because of criminal records cost the gross domestic product up to $65 billion a year, and the cost of mass incarceration tops $80 billion per year.[27] The numbers are hard to measure, but they are definitely very large, especially in relation to federally funded housing. Denial of access to public housing poses the greatest problem, though the impact is difficult to quantify, but a rough analysis suggests as many as 100,000 returning offenders annually (including their families) are turned away from public housing and Section 8 vouchers, plus those who never apply because they know they will be denied.[28]

Together with bars to TANF and SNAP in most states, housing, Pell Grants and other higher education financial aid, and of course collateral consequences relating to employment, any kind of criminal conviction effectively shreds the social safety net, almost always ensuring a permanent state of poverty and often leading to convictions on future crimes that emanate from being poor. Collateral consequences are a major force in the criminalization of poverty.

Housing

Given the widespread use of bans that keep ex-offenders out of public housing and deny them housing vouchers, it may surprise some that most of those bans are not rigidly required by federal law but leave some discretion to the local public housing authorities. Federal law requires the terms of leases and vouchers, which include grounds for eviction, but the local authorities do have leeway in invoking them. Long-standing practice produces enforcement of the conditions in the leases and vouchers, but there is room for local organizing to advocate change in policies.

Federal law requires lifetime bans on only two groups: people convicted for methamphetamine manufacturing on federally owned property, and sex offenders subject to lifetime registration under state law. There is also a mandatory temporary ban for people convicted for a drug-related crime within the previous three years, although this can be overcome if the person completes a drug rehabilitation program. Also, current illegal drug users and alcohol abusers are prohibited.[29]

The other bans reach much further, especially as they are applied. The key in each category is whether the applicant for public or subsidized housing has engaged in a "criminal activity" during a "reasonable" time before applying.[30] This constitutes the "one strike" policy implemented in the Clinton years that is so devastating not only for people returning to the community from a time in prison but also for families currently residing in as well as applying for public or subsidized housing. "One strike" means one event and it does not require a conviction or even an arrest. An entire family can be evicted because of the alleged "activity" of one family member whose behavior is not even known by the leaseholder or the "activity" of a guest who is "under the control" of the tenant.

The "one strike" categories are widely used to exclude people with criminal records even where there is no real basis for believing they pose a risk.[31] Three common application bans used locally include "We do not allow people convicted of felonies to live here," "If it's a drug conviction, that's zero tolerance," and "Anyone who has a criminal record with any sort of violence or drug-related crimes is pretty much excluded from getting housing." All of these criteria, if applied literally (and they are), go even further than federal law says.[32]

Laws enacted in 1988, 1990, 1996, and 1998, coupled with stringent regulations promulgated by the Clinton administration, gave us "one strike."[33] The Supreme Court made matters worse in 2002, holding in *Department of Housing and Urban Development v. Rucker* that it was both constitutional and legally authorized for housing authorities to evict entire households even when the leaseholder knew nothing about the illegal activity in question.[34]

President Obama's secretary of housing and urban development wrote letters to local public housing officials to urge amelioration in the application of the law. One letter stressed the importance of "second chances" and the importance of a place to live to achieving a stable life. The other urged the use of discretion to support family reconnection. After looking at the admissions policies of three hundred housing authorities, the Sargent Shriver National Center on Poverty Law concluded the secretary's plea had fallen on many deaf ears.[35]

A guidance from the federal government in 2015 said flatly that arrest records may not be used in tenancy decisions, but did not abolish "one strike." It reminded the housing authorities that "one strike" is not a requirement and also underlined their obligations to safeguard due process rights of applicants and tenants.

The private housing market also poses serious problems. Discrimination against ex-offenders is rampant. Four out of five landlords do criminal background checks, and applicants who get past the check often get turned down for credit reasons. A few jurisdictions are beginning to respond. The best example is Oregon, which has enacted a fair-chance housing statute. The law requires landlords to give reasons for an adverse response.

Landlords are barred from refusing to rent based on an arrest where there was no conviction or a conviction on certain crimes. San Francisco and now the whole state of California, along with Newark, New Jersey, have taken similar steps.

An important step occurred in 2016 when the U.S. Department of Housing and Urban Development issued a guidance to private landlords about discrimination against applicants with criminal records. The guidance says that disparate impact is the touchstone for liability and that because African Americans and Latinos are arrested, convicted, and incarcerated disproportionately, blanket bans based solely on the fact of a conviction are unacceptable. It further says that arrests cannot be used at all to exclude an applicant, and for convictions the property owner must make an individualized decision and prove that the exclusion is justified by such things as the nature and severity of the crime, lack of rehabilitation, or danger to the community.[36]

As the federal government was offering guidances, civil rights lawyer John Relman sued a large housing development on behalf of the Fortune Society in New York to challenge its blanket ban against applicants with criminal convictions. The legal theory is that the Fair Housing Act prohibits such a ban as applied to African Americans and Latinos because of the disparate and therefore discriminatory effect of mass incarceration on them. The suit says that the landlord of the nine-hundred-plus unit complex must adopt an individualized approach that takes into account such things as evidence of rehabilitation or whether the applicant poses a threat to safety, and places the burden on the landlord to prove its allegations that it is not required to rent to the plaintiff. That theory has now been solidified by the combination of the

Supreme Court's decision in the *Inclusive Communities Project* case and the new HUD guidance, and in this case also the Department of Justice.[37] Altogether, this was a very important step that formally accepts the HUD guidance. John Relman says, "The agency in charge of interpreting the Fair Housing Act agrees with us, and that will have a lot of weight." As of May 2017, the case is still pending.

Employment

Sixty percent of ex-offenders remain unemployed after a year. Not unrelated is the fact that 87 percent of employers utilize criminal background checks when hiring.[38] Commercial screening companies are ubiquitous and information can be gathered at the press of a button. Just three companies did 56 million checks in a recent twelve-month period. LexisNexis has gobbled up other companies, especially ChoicePoint, and now boasts on its website that it has "37 billion public and proprietary records" on "274 million unique identities."[39] Among other problems, this information is rife with errors. There were 400,000 cases of criminal identity theft in a recent year. And there is a great deal of just plain wrong information in the computer data—right name but wrong person, failure to recognize the expunging of a conviction, and old arrests that resulted in acquittals or were otherwise not pursued and not recorded. In 2012, the FBI documented 600,000 mistakes involving accuracy of records.[40]

Lawyers have fought back. In 2005, Community Legal Services in Philadelphia partnered with pro bono private attorneys and gained a pre-litigation settlement with the Pennsylvania State

Police to get them to correct criminal records of people victimized by identity theft, and in 2010 it achieved a similar pre-litigation settlement with the Administrative Office of Pennsylvania Courts on court records. It was part of a litigation team that sued HireRight, which dominates background checking for the trucking industry, for reporting offenses that had been expunged and removed from public databases. The lawsuits were settled for the second-largest amount reached at the time for a Fair Credit Reporting Act case, and HireRight thereafter improved the quality of its background checks.

Not surprisingly, background checks have a racially disparate impact. Half of white applicants with a criminal conviction receive a callback, while only 5 percent of African Americans do.[41] Nor does the pandemic of background data victimize only applicants. In one case, a woman who had killed her abuser twenty-five years earlier, was incarcerated, and then achieved a college and graduate degree in microbiology and worked at high-level positions in research laboratories was fired when her criminal record came to light.[42]

Promising steps are occurring at the state and local levels, as with housing, but are somewhat more widespread. Fair-chance laws have been enacted in thirteen states and seventy municipalities. These typically include "banning the box" (prohibiting questions on criminal records on job applications), prohibiting questions about arrests that did not lead to convictions, permitting applicants to review background checks for accuracy, and allowing applicants to offer evidence of rehabilitation. "Ban the box" is the most visible of the efforts. It has helped some, due to the fact that the employer ostensibly does not know about the criminal record until he has met the applicant. As a result of a multi-prong ordinance, Durham, North Carolina, had a sixfold increase in city hires of ex-offenders, from 2.5 percent to 15.5 percent. "Banning the box" in Minneapolis resulted in half of job seekers with criminal records being hired. In Atlanta, a fair-chance hiring policy resulted in 10 percent of all city hires between March and October 2013 being ex-offenders. Also, Target stores removed criminal history altogether from its job applications.[43]

Public Benefits

One of the most counterproductive collateral consequences is the provision in the 1996 welfare law that slaps a lifetime ban on cash assistance for families (Temporary Assistance for Needy Families) and food stamps for people with felony drug convictions. The law authorized the states to waive or modify the bans, but it was patently obvious that many states would never exercise the power.

The people most affected are women and children. Whether they were selling the drugs or were convicted for possession, poverty was in the picture and continues after incarceration. Finding a job will most likely be difficult and many states bar people with drug convictions from receiving cash assistance or food stamps; more are barred from public housing or subsidized housing. This is not good public policy. The consequences are often homelessness and a kind of desperation in the face of closed-off opportunity that often leads to further illegal behavior.

Heroin and other opioids have recently become popular for more affluent people, so we now hear people saying we need to provide treatment and deal with addiction as a public health matter and not a criminal matter. The situation for poor people has improved some but not nearly enough. In 2011, thirteen states (versus twenty-two in 2001) still had the complete lifetime ban on TANF for drug offenders and nine states still had the lifetime ban for food stamps (now called SNAP). Thirteen states had no ban at all on TANF in 2011 (up from eight in 2001) and sixteen had no ban on SNAP.

The states with complete bans still affect 180,000 women and their children.[44] The states with modified bans do some or all of the following: no ban for people convicted for possession; no ban for people who complete treatment programs; no ban for people who pass drug tests; and no ban after a waiting period following release from prison.[45] California took the biggest step forward when in 2014 its legislature opted out completely from the bans on both TANF and SNAP. Missouri modified its ban on SNAP, exempting people in and after approved drug treatment programs and people who can show they do not need treatment.[46]

Education

Inmates who participate in education while in prison are considerably less likely to reoffend and more likely to find a job. Money spent on prison education saves four to five times that amount in recidivism costs. Nonetheless, Congress in 1995 took Pell Grants away from inmates, and in 1998 it took all federal financial aid for education away from people with misdemeanor or felony drug convictions. There has been some modest walking back. Federal aid is now barred only when a drug offense takes place while the student is receiving aid, and applications for federal student aid no longer ask about criminal convictions.[47]

Other positive steps have occurred here and there. New York State attorney general Eric Schneiderman obtained an agreement with several New York colleges not to ask on applications about arrests and police stops that did not eventuate in conviction or about sealed or expunged criminal records. And the Vera Institute has undertaken a five-year initiative to improve prison and post-incarceration education in Michigan, New Jersey, and North Carolina.[48] Unfortunately, though, admissions and non-federal financial aid policies of colleges and universities regarding criminal records, including the use of background checks, are still overly broad in all too many instances. About two-thirds of a large number of respondents to a national survey stated that they use background checks.[49]

The list of collateral consequences goes on and on. Parents are at risk of losing parental rights, immigrants are subject to deportation, and others risk criminal debt, exclusion from juror service, and more. The shadow of a criminal record is long indeed and is cast disproportionately over poor people.[50]

7

Poverty, Race, and Discipline in Schools: Go Directly to Jail

Jayden (last name omitted at her request), an African American junior in high school in Antioch, California, had been bullied since the fifth grade. She says she is "very short" in stature and "not the fighting type." The schools had never done anything to help and the bullying had gotten worse in high school. One day Jayden arrived early to school and was jumped by two girls she knew. A teacher saw the fracas and tried to break it up. He then alleged that Jayden elbowed him in the chest during the melee.

What happened next happens routinely in schools with disproportionately poor and minority student bodies, especially to African American and Latino children and children with disabilities: Jayden was sent to court for fighting on the school campus and assaulting the teacher, as well as suspended pending total expulsion. Antioch itself is not a high-poverty city, but like many urban schools, its schools have a disproportionate number of poor children: 55 percent of Deer Valley High School's student body is socioeconomically disadvantaged as measured by the California State Local Control Funding Formula.

Jayden's mother was fortunate to find a public-interest lawyer, because she could not have afforded one on her own, and Annie Lee, then a lawyer at the National Center for Youth Law, made all the difference. The Antioch police officer conceded that the school video did not show Jayden elbowing the teacher, and that the only evidence was the teacher's belief that Jayden had elbowed him. Even so, the police and diversion staff were uninterested in the truth and recommended a multi-week diversion program with mandatory anger management and life skills courses (for which Jayden's mother would have to pay). Jayden declined the diversion on principle—she was innocent and had no anger problem—so her case moved from the Antioch Police Department to the Contra Costa County Probation Department, which is the last review before the DA's office.

Like the police, the Probation Department threatened to recommend prosecution unless Jayden completed a diversion program. Jayden's mother, Ms. Williams (she prefers that her first name be omitted), was frightened because the local DA was known for charging students with alleged crimes that occur in school. The program run by the Probation Department was less rigid than the one the police had mandated, and Jayden took it; with Annie Lee's help, the Probation Department did not send the case to the DA. After working toward expungement of the police citation and report for two years, Lee told me in 2017 that they had succeeded in getting her record sealed. This was extremely important since even the police citation could have triggered collateral consequences later on, such as difficulty getting into college, finding jobs, obtaining housing, and obtaining credit.[1]

Jayden had lived in Oakland as a child, but her family had moved to find safer neighborhoods and better schools. Antioch was safer, but Deer Valley High School was not what they hoped for. Jayden said to me, "It's hard to be a black girl in this town." She nonetheless graduated in 2016 and moved on to Diablo Valley College in Concord, California, where she is pursuing performing arts, especially dancing, and her dream is to open an arts school.

Ji Seon Song, a public defender in Contra Costa County, recounts a second case from Deer Valley that underscores what Jayden experienced. According to Song, the school was rife with minor incidents resulting in harsh punishments, including court referrals and probation—a paring knife one student had brought to school to slice an apple, a pocketknife, little fights, and so on. If a child is put on probation, the parents are charged for the supervision, which can mount into thousands of dollars, and collateral consequences are likely to ensue.

Ji Seon Song's client was an African American seventeen-year-old boy with a debilitating and pronounced speech impediment and a mother who is cognitively challenged. The boy was bullied at school and had issues at home. His mother had a drug-addicted, abusive live-in boyfriend who stole the boy's Supplemental Security Income (SSI) money to buy drugs. The boy stayed with his mother to help protect her from the boyfriend as much as he could. The family lived in poverty.

One day the boy exercised exceedingly bad adolescent judgment and did a bad thing: he phoned in two fake bomb threats to school. There were no bombs. But of course he frightened and inconvenienced the entire school. He spent forty-eight days in juvenile hall, and the judge ordered him to make $150,000 in restitution. Why that number? The judge added up the salaries of all of the school's employees and pro-rated them to the time the school was out while searches for the bombs were under way.

A protracted process ensued, and Ji Seon Song argued the restitution down to $23,000; pressure from the school board and the judge's own views kept the amount from going lower. The judge said the boy needed a lesson. The family could not afford to pay the restitution, so the judge put the boy on probation and converted the restitution, which was criminal in nature and could result in incarceration, into a civil debt. He was on probation until 2016.

While he was on probation, the boy transferred to high school in Oakland, where his father lives, and graduated with honors. Ji Seon Song arranged for the boy to plead his restitution case to the Antioch school board. Along with his impressive record, he explained his previous trauma and reported his rapprochement with his disabled veteran father. The school board reduced the restitution debt to $500 and finally forgave it altogether. The boy then graduated from Merritt College in Oakland. This boy had the good fortune to get good free legal representation that the family could otherwise never have afforded.

Many poor children are not so fortunate and end up with criminal records and diminished life prospects as a result of punitive policies related to in-school behavior. Even worse than "zero tolerance" policies that lead to suspension and expulsion for trivial matters, "school resource officers," who are disproportionately posted at high-poverty schools, are empowered to have students arrested and sent to juvenile court for minor misbehaviors that traditionally were handled in the school. At far higher rates than their well-off peers, low-income young people are also routinely sent to juvenile court for truancy, and parents are often arrested or socked with fees for their children's malfeasance or both. Finally and most seriously, a few places—notably Texas—send young people, typically from schools serving mainly low-income children, to adult court for both misbehavior in school and truancy.

Using federal data, the Center for Public Integrity compiled a fifty-state (and District of Columbia) ranking of how many students are sent to court.[2] Virginia had the worst record—15.8 referrals to court per 1,000 students in a school year. African American children were referred at a rate of 25.3 per 1,000, Hispanic children at a 12.1 rate, white children at 13.1, and children with disabilities at 33.4. The national rate was 6 per 1,000, with nineteen states higher than the average. The lowest was the District of Columbia at 1.2 per 1,000.

These statistics are reported by race and disability because the U.S. Department of Education has enforcement power in these areas under federal civil rights laws. Catherine Lhamon, assistant secretary for civil rights in the Obama administration, says that the children sent to court are overwhelmingly from low-income families. The story is one of poverty as well as race and disability, regardless of how the data are kept.

"SCHOOL RESOURCE OFFICERS": CONDUCTORS FOR THE SCHOOL-TO-PRISON PIPELINE

Concern about violence within schools goes back at least to the violence-ridden school in the 1955 film *Blackboard Jungle*, although real life was nothing like what the film portrayed. Schools gradually developed security plans as the years passed, with two-thirds of all big-city senior high schools having professional security personnel by 1978. The National Association of School Resource Officers was founded in 1991. While this might sound like an organization of educational administrators, school resource officers, or SROs, are in reality sworn, often armed, law enforcement officers who are stationed in public schools.

By 1996, about 19 percent of America's public schools had a full-time police officer or some other law enforcement person. In the 1990s, Professor John DeIulio and former Reagan administration secretary of education William Bennett coined the term "superpredator" to describe some juvenile offenders, raising the temperature of an already overheated atmosphere. The Columbine massacre occurred in 1999. Today, there is a police presence in almost half of all public high schools—and a quarter of all public elementary schools—especially those serving poor African American and Latino communities.[3] (And probably none in private schools, except for the Secret Service.) Ironically, the tragedy of white boys murdering white students in suburban schools morphed into the school-to-prison pipeline for poor African American and Latino youth and youth with disabilities.

Since 1999, the U.S. Department of Justice has given $750 million to more than three thousand schools, which has translated to over 6,500 more resource officers, a 38 percent increase. Meanwhile, badly needed mental health personnel were not hired. In 2008–9, New York City had 5,246 law enforcement officers in its public schools and 3,152 guidance counselors.[4] Nationwide, 1.6 million children go to a school that has a school resource officer but no guidance counselor.

The combination of zero tolerance and the omnipresent SROs and other police officers has exacerbated the overzealous enforcement of non-serious offenses, especially when officers are poorly trained and do their jobs badly.[5]

The omnipresence of police in schools has also brought a new (or greatly enlarged) phenomenon that might be called "skip the middle man"—don't bother with school discipline, just send the child to court (or do both). Nationally, in the 2011–12 school year, 92,000 students were the subjects of school-related arrests and 260,000 were referred to law enforcement, according to the U.S. Department of Education Office of Civil Rights.[6]

Jason Nance of the University of Florida did a study that documented what one might suppose. "A police officer's regular presence at a school," Nance concluded, "significantly increases the odds that school officials will refer students to law enforcement for various offenses, including these lower-level offenses that should be addressed using more pedagogically sound methods."[7] Denise Gottfredson of the University of Maryland summed it up: "There is no evidence that placing officers in the schools improves safety. And it increases the number of minor behavior problems that are referred to the police, pushing kids into the criminal system."[8] In her book *Pushout*, social justice scholar Monique Morris adds that school resource officers "blur lines between education and criminal justice, as daily exchanges and interactions with law enforcement expand the surveillance of youth of color and normalize prison terminology and culture in school settings."[9]

Some locales have improved in recent years in their training and the accountability of school resource officers, but many experts continue to believe strongly that their presence is excessive and in need of major reform.

SENDING POOR CHILDREN TO ADULT COURT

Texas is famous and sometimes infamous for its outsized way of doing things. One of the infamous stories involves the state's policy of prosecuting students in adult courts for misbehavior in school and for truancy. Texas is one of just two states (Wyoming being the other) that utilize adult courts, in large numbers, for both in-school behavior and truancy ("failure to attend" in Texas). The story begins in 1991 when the Texas legislature moved a set of misdemeanors involving juveniles from juvenile court to adult courts. The "official" explanation was that this would save expensive juvenile court resources for more complicated cases and that the number of cases moved, including school-misbehavior offenses, would be small.

Beginning in 1995, students who had ten or more unexcused absences within six months were sent to adult court, and schools also had discretion to send to court students with three unexcused absences within four weeks. These were labeled as crimes. Truants were labeled as criminals. The judge could offer community service but could also fine the student and assess costs. The conviction created a criminal record and could mean collateral consequences regarding higher education, employment, and military enrollment. Parents could be fined as well. The stage was set for what followed.

Deborah Fowler of Texas Appleseed doubts the official story of why the misdemeanors were moved and says the reason was that "broken windows" law enforcement and worries of superpredator juveniles were gaining momentum and "zero tolerance" was taking hold. The legislative records of the time reveal a rhetoric of requiring accountability for youth ("if you can do the crime, you can do the time") and belief that young people were shoplifting and the like without suffering any consequences in the juvenile justice system. At the same time, Texas greatly increased the number of school resource officers, especially in districts with large numbers of poor African American and Latino children.

The result was truly amazing—a veritable flood of cases. Deborah Fowler thinks no one knew it would be as bad as it turned out to be. The adult courts that handle these cases essentially have no due process. Under the Texas Family Code, every child in the juvenile court gets a lawyer, which is expensive. But in adult court, there is no real cost for prosecuting—no appointed counsel, no probation, and often no prosecutor in many places unless the child enters a not-guilty plea, which is rare. The school resource officers as well as local police showered a staggering number of tickets on children and youth. Data from the Texas Office of Court Administration for 2009 show that adult courts handled more than 158,000 juvenile cases, mainly involving alleged misbehavior in schools. Truancy violations added 120,000 more cases—in 2012, 36,000 in Dallas County alone. The truancy number was more than twice the number in the entire rest of the country; in every other state except Wyoming these cases are handled in juvenile court.[10]

The fine for either in-school offenses or failure to attend could be as much as $500, plus court costs of up to $70. Many students received multiple tickets in a single year and ended up owing thousands of dollars.[11] So the courts made out well, to say the least, and school districts received a cut of the proceeds as well. The Texas Office of Court Administration told the Associated Press that $10 million was collected from fines and costs in truancy cases in fiscal year 2014.[12] Texas Appleseed found out that in Harris County (Houston), which is the largest county in Texas and the third-largest in the country, the fines and fees from parents were helping to support both the school districts and the prosecutors who brought the cases. And Harris County's student body is 75.5 percent "economically disadvantaged," according to the county's own statistics.

Students who do not pay their fine or finish community service can be arrested and jailed at age seventeen. Texas Appleseed found that 1,238 teenagers were jailed for this reason over the years 2013 and 2014.[13]

Most of the in-school infractions are the vague offenses of "disruption of class," "disorderly conduct," and "disruption of transportation," and also simple assault stemming from student fights and curfew violations (leaving campus without permission). Very few are matters appropriate for sending students (who can be as young as ten) to court. Schools all over the state have abdicated to the resource officers the responsibility to manage behavior in the school building and its environs.[14] As elsewhere, students ticketed are disproportionately poor African American, Latino, and students with disabilities.

School resource officers in many parts of the state lack professional training and use force in schools that includes pepper spray, "stun gun beanbags," guns, and dogs, although it should be noted that a 2015 law required specific training for SROs in the largest school districts.[15] Besides all too often acting inappropriately, school resource officers are expensive.[16]

Texas state senator John Whitmire and a few others began pressing for legislation to get some control over the in-school ticketing of students, but they did not have enough data to support their proposals. Texas Appleseed did three reports on suspensions and expulsions and then wrote an extensive report on sending students to courts called "Texas' School-to-Prison Pipeline."[17]

The report provided the elected officials and other advocates with the data they needed. It garnered wide media attention because the facts were so bad—school police officers writing tickets to ten-year-olds. The attention given the report in turn helped mobilize other families to tell their stories. This all led to the first major reform in 2013. It was a seemingly small thing, but it made a significant difference: Instead of issuing tickets, the officers would now have to file a formal complaint in court. Requiring the resource officers to do this additional work cut the number of cases for in-school behavior in half.

But the remaining cases stayed in adult court, and they were still criminal, and there was still no right to counsel, and the race and ethnic disparities continued. The juvenile judges and the juvenile probation people did not want the cases returned to them. Their caseload was already about 40,000 a year. Taking back these misdemeanor cases as they had ballooned would swamp the juvenile system. Even if they took only half of the in-school cases, that number would still be in the area of 80,000, and the failure-to-attend cases had been 115,000 in 2013, which would make a continuing total of 200,000 total cases. So the juvenile justice people refused to take the cases back.

The best reform measure would be not to use the courts at all except for behavior that anyone would agree is a real crime, while simultaneously overhauling the suspension and expulsion systems. Second-best would be to use the juvenile courts rather than the adult system, but as minimally as possible. Another fallback idea, Fowler says, would be to keep the cases in the adult court but make the cases all civil. So there was much more to do, but the first step—requiring the officers to do more paperwork for each citation—was clever, and helpful.

CRIMINALIZING TRUANCY

In 2015, Texas Appleseed issued another impressive report with jaw-dropping numbers and evocative personal stories about the criminalization of truancy, especially among poor children of color. A homeless teenage boy who sometimes just could not get to school, a teenage girl with clinical depression who achieves success in her academics despite frequent absences, another teenage girl who is home much of the time caring for her mother who has dementia—these students were all convicted as criminals. Often they have multiple convictions and owe tens of thousands of dollars. When they find a lawyer or a lawyer finds them—neither occurs with regularity—the issues can be dealt with and worked out. If not, it does not go well. If they get to be seventeen and still owe money, they can be put in jail, and it really happens.

The best thing in the report is Chief Justice Nathan Hecht's statement in his 2015 State of the Judiciary address to the Texas legislature, quoted in the report's foreword. The chief justice wrote that the truancy and attendance laws, "while intended to keep kids in school, often operate to keep them out." Then, in bold, "But when almost 100,000 criminal truancy charges are brought each year against Texas schoolchildren, one has to think, this approach may not be working." Hecht went on to say that this realization "has led the Texas Judicial Council, a policy-making body for the Judiciary, to call for decriminalizing the failure to attend school."[18]

The bill that passed in 2015 was bipartisan, co-sponsored by Representative James White (R) and Senator John Whitmire (D). The new law ends the criminalization of truancy in Texas and is a significant step forward, although it evidences areas where compromises were made and further change is needed. Adult courts will still handle chronic absentees, but the penalties will be civil, not criminal. The law mandates school policies to help students with the problems that are pushing them away from coming to school. No more crimes. No more criminal records.

Beyond the schools' mandatory truancy prevention efforts, they may not send a student to court until there are ten unexcused absences, and even then they are not required to do so. They may not send students to court if the students are pregnant, homeless, in foster care, or the main income earner for the family, and the courts must divert them back to the school if the schools sent them. Every school system must adopt truancy prevention measures set out by the Texas Education Agency.

For a student referred to court, a truancy prosecutor will decide whether to file a civil case. There will be truancy courts specifically designated to hear the cases. The court can order students back to school, require them to take the GED instead of going back to school (for which parents have to pay), or mandate counseling, community service, or participation in a tutorial. It can suspend a student's driver's license or permit. It has to dismiss a case if the school fails to disclose that the student is receiving special education services or received truancy prevention counseling that was not successful. It may dismiss charges against students who have a mental illness.

The advocates did not get everything they wanted. Parents can still be fined, but only if the school can prove that the absences were the result of the parent's negligence, and the fines are now graduated from $100 at the first offense to $500 for the fifth and subsequent offenses. The court can charge the student a $50 court fee, but only if the family can afford to pay. A student can be held in contempt for disobeying an order of the court, for which the court can levy a fine up to $100 or suspend the student's driver's license or permit. Students younger than seventeen who are found in contempt two or more times can be sent to juvenile probation or to the juvenile court, which can place them in detention. All convictions under the previous law are to be expunged automatically and all records under the new law are to be sealed after the student's eighteenth birthday, but the student must apply to have that done.

Some people predicted the new law would result in more prosecutions of parents, and others predicted that attendance would decrease and dropouts would go up. In fact, the law has had a stunning effect on prosecutions. During the first four months of 2016, truancy filings were 5,000 compared to 60,000 for the same period in the previous year, and filings against parents dropped from 45,000 to 8,200. But while the number of juveniles sent to adult court decreased considerably from the 158,000 of 2009, it is still substantial. In 2015–16 the state Office of Court Administration registered 59,054 non-traffic-related Class C misdemeanor juvenile cases in adult courts, consisting primarily of misbehavior in school.[19]

REAL REFORM

Broward County, Florida, is often cited for having abolished its strict zero tolerance regime, but one of the earliest, most widely cited and emulated efforts to do this was undertaken by Clayton County, Georgia, beginning in 2003, led by Chief Judge Steven Teske of the county's juvenile court. Clayton County, Georgia, is just south of Atlanta and encompasses most of Atlanta's airport. Its population is about a quarter of a million people, two-thirds African American, and almost a quarter of whom have incomes below the poverty line. Teske is a state and national leader in juvenile justice generally and particularly so with regard to zero tolerance and sending children to juvenile court.[20]

Noting national trends of increased use of the courts as well as the similar statistics in the county, Teske convened the county's school superintendent, the chief of police, the directors of mental health and social services, and a community volunteer. His initial goal was to reduce referrals from the county's schools to the juvenile courts. The discussion quickly added a focus on police behavior in the schools, sanctions other than referral to the courts, underlying problems causing disruptions, and positive measures to prevent such disruptions. The group met frequently and came to a number of decisions that were implemented a year later through two agreements, one on reducing referrals to the courts and the second on an integrated services referral plan to get children appropriate help when needed.

The results have been remarkable. The previous situation was woeful. The number of referrals to court had grown by 1,248 percent from 1991 to 2004 and graduation rates had declined by 58 percent. The probation caseload had risen by an average of 150 per probation officer, due overwhelmingly to minor offenses that took officers' time away from high-risk and serious offenders. Following implementation of the new approach, referrals to the court went down 67.4 percent and graduation rates increased by 20 percent. The number of youth of color referred to court declined by 43 percent.

The simultaneity of the increase in sending children to court and the growth in the use of school resource officers is not an accident. In 1993 one student was sent to court. By 2003 1,147 students were sent to court on misdemeanors. Felony referrals peaked at 198 in 2004. The two agreements mentioned above became operative in 2004 and referrals immediately began to plummet. By 2013 the number of students referred to court on misdemeanors had dropped to 154 and the number of felonies was 97.

It is not surprising that Clayton County and Teske are regarded as national models.

8

Crime-Free Housing Ordinances and the Criminalization of Homelessness

Lakisha Briggs is a certified nurse assistant who lives in Norristown, Pennsylvania. When her former boyfriend was released from jail after an earlier episode of domestic violence, she faced a lose-lose situation. Norristown had what was called a nuisance property ordinance, which gave its police department the authority to demand that a landlord evict a tenant who calls 911 three times in four months, in effect criminalizing a person's right to call the police. Briggs had one strike from the earlier domestic violence and had stopped calling the police for fear she would be evicted. Well-meaning neighbors called the police at least twice, which only resulted in the police revoking protection for her altogether. "I had no choice but to let him stay," Briggs said to a reporter. Just days later he cut her head and stabbed her neck with a broken ashtray. She begged her neighbor not to call the police, but the neighbor called anyway, and Briggs was taken by helicopter to Philadelphia for emergency care. The city told the landlord to evict her within ten days or he would lose his license.[1]

Things got better, fortunately. A Legal Aid lawyer to whom Briggs was referred connected her to Sandra Park of the ACLU. The ACLU of Pennsylvania and the Philadelphia law firm of Pepper Hamilton LLP joined as well. Briggs had a lot of law on her side—the Federal Housing Act, the Violence Against Women Act, the First Amendment, the due process clause of the Constitution of the United States, and similar state laws. Even so, Norristown kept pushing back. Finally, though, it settled, and Briggs received $495,000 in damages and attorneys' fees. The city repealed its ordinance totally and committed itself never to pass another version, and the state passed a law banning municipalities from penalizing tenants who exercise their right to contact the police.[2] The federal Department of Housing and Urban Development filed a complaint of its own after the ACLU sued, which was helpful in the case and put the issue on HUD's map for the future. The outcome was a quadrifecta: a big win for Briggs, a new law in the state as a whole, the involvement of HUD, and national press attention for a practice that disproportionately affects low-income women.

Nancy Markham is another person who was victimized first by her ex-boyfriend and then by the city of Surprise, Arizona, which invoked its nuisance ordinance to get her evicted because she had called the police too often. Between March and September 2014, the ex-boyfriend choked her, punched her, and threatened her with weapons. When she called the police more often than they liked, they retaliated by telling her landlord to evict her. She too found her way to Sandra Park, who in turn brought in the state

ACLU and a private law firm that handled the case pro bono. The suit was brought in federal court in August 2015, arguing that the city had violated Markham's First Amendment right to seek police assistance and the Fair Housing Act's ban on gender discrimination in housing. In March 2016, the city entered into a settlement providing $40,000 for Markham and causing repeal of the ordinance.[3]

These problems are illustrative of what is really a national crisis—the surprising number across the country of chronic or "crime-free" nuisance ordinances like the ones that victimized Briggs and Markham. Briggs and Markham are lucky to have found legal help. They are also unusual given the great shortage of lawyers for low-income people. This scarcity affects not just those who qualify for free legal services but also people with somewhat higher incomes who cannot possibly pay market rates for legal help. Briggs and Markham found the needles in the legal haystack and were fortunate enough to get help not only from the ACLU but also from law firms that took on the cases on a pro bono basis. More often low-income people who violate chronic nuisance laws lose their housing even though they have legal rights, because the rights are useless without a lawyer.

The crime of "public nuisance" has been with us from the days of the Pilgrims. It came via the common law of our English forebears and now exists in statutory form in every state. Like disturbing the peace, disruptive conduct, loitering, loafing, and vagrancy, it is a catchall that is limited, if at all, only by previous precedent.

Starting in the 1980s, police forces felt besieged with the crack cocaine epidemic and began looking for third-party help.

Municipalities started enacting chronic nuisance ordinances and disorderly housing ordinances focused particularly on getting rid of crack houses, including conscription of landlords as vigilante deputies. Catchall low-level misdemeanors had moved from the street to the private space of the home. As time passed and police forces found themselves understaffed due to budget cuts, the interest in third-party policing increased even more. Shortages in 911 staffing were a particular challenge and became a centerpiece of many of the ordinances.

Beginning in 1992 in Mesa, Arizona, a new version of the concept came into being—the crime-free housing ordinance. Proponents described a seemingly harmless application of the idea of community policing, which was then becoming popular. They laid out three phases of activity. One, get property managers, police, and tenants to work cooperatively on crime problems. Two, work jointly to provide a safe environment for tenants. And three, get information to tenants so they can help maintain a safe place to live.[4]

Crime-free ordinances and chronic nuisance ordinances caught on and swept across the country. There is no precise count, but observers estimate that around 2,000 municipalities in 44 states have enacted some kind of such ordinance, with more than 130 in Illinois alone, which is the largest number in a single state.[5] And they are not the innocent-sounding idea that was described at the beginning.

Implementation begins with classes for landlords that indoctrinate them in their often unwanted vigilante role. Someone complains to the police about something a tenant is doing. Possibly the landlord complains, but more frequently a neighbor is the complainant, or the tenant herself calls 911. The police get in touch with the landlord. They say, "The neighbors say, 'Your tenant is selling or manufacturing or using drugs.' 'Your tenant or his dog is too loud.' 'There is trash in the yard.' 'Your tenant's kids are skateboarding or playing basketball outside at night.' Your tenant calls 911 too often. We haven't got time to fix the problem. You fix it. You have to abate the nuisance."

Meanwhile, the tenant does not know she is the subject of the "nuisance" complaint. Or worse, she gets wind of it, panics, and leaves on her own, or decides not to chance calling for police or emergency assistance at all anymore. If she stays, "abating the nuisance" generally means evicting the tenant. The landlord does what he is told because he can be fined, jailed, lose his license, have a lien placed on the property, or even see his building condemned or shuttered. There is no due process for the landlord unless he wants to get himself arrested and then try to defend himself in court. It is much easier for the landlord to evict the tenant in a summary way, so the tenant receives no due process, either; the landlord may offer to refund the tenant's deposit if she will leave, or may just change the lock. For the most part, landlords oppose these ordinances as strongly as do the tenants.

Kate Walz of the Sargent Shriver National Center on Poverty Law says, "Nuisance ordinances are criminalizing non-criminal activity. They are creating dire consequences for tenants. Many of the ordinances say essentially, 'anything can be deemed a nuisance.'"

In a surprising number of localities, the law says calling 911 three times in a certain period of time for any reason at all constitutes being a chronic nuisance. Walz says even if the tenant calling is a "victim of domestic violence, has a loved one threatening to commit suicide, or has a kid trying to run away," calling 911 too many times can and does end in eviction. In many places, women (and children) are being evicted by order of the police conveyed to the landlord to implement, because the tenant has made "too many" calls to protect herself from domestic violence. And "too many is as few as one."

Sandra Park of the ACLU describes these laws as victimizing the victim twice: the abuse itself and the eviction for reaching out to get help. For fear of losing their homes, many low-income women endure more violence rather than call the police. Walz goes on to say that landlords in Illinois "are up in arms" about the ordinances and that the Shriver Center "has forged a partnership" with them, although the landlords are understandably more interested in due process for themselves than for tenants. But she says it is hard to find tenant plaintiffs because (apart from the paucity of lawyers) most of the time they do not even understand why they are being evicted.

When lawyers do get involved, they send demand letters to local governments, which usually succeed in evoking immediate rescission of the eviction notices, followed by working with the Shriver Center to change the ordinances. The lawyers find, though, that the municipalities are unwilling to repeal the ordinances wholesale or, if newly considering an ordinance, are unwilling to refrain completely from having one. Instead, as a compromise for now, the Shriver Center asks the jurisdictions to consider factors such as domestic violence, disability, due process, confidentiality rights of minors, and the possibility of homelessness. It will continue to push city councils and states for full protection of the rights of people with emergency needs and beyond that to full repeal. Meanwhile, the Shriver Center's Walz points out that those hit with the ordinances are protected by multiple constitutional and statutory provisions, as was the case with Lakisha Briggs.

The best (and really quite remarkable) research on the incidence of crime-free ordinances was done by Matthew Desmond and Nicol Valdez. Desmond is the author of the powerful book *Evicted*, which follows the housing travails of low-income families in Milwaukee. In working on the book, he encountered the Milwaukee chronic nuisance ordinance. He and Valdez then studied its administration locally and compiled a list of fifty-nine such ordinances around the country, including in the twenty largest cities.

They found that some of the fifty-nine ordinances were quite specific and others were quite vague. Either can be bad. For example, Chicago defines a chronic nuisance property as one that has made three calls for public services within ninety days. On the other hand, several large cities use vague definitions such as that of Dallas: "Whenever a nuisance is found to exist within the city, the city manager has the right to order the owner to abate the nuisance." And fines and other penalties on landlords can be tough. In Seattle, for instance, fines can go up to $500 a day until the chief of police certifies that the property is no longer a nuisance.

The approach to domestic violence in the fifty-nine ordinances is even worse. Only four explicitly exclude domestic violence from the list of nuisance activities for 911 calls, and thirty-nine explicitly include assault, sexual abuse, battery, or domestic violence as nuisances on their list. The other sixteen are open-ended.

Desmond and Valdez's findings in Milwaukee itself are revealing as well. Nearly a third of the citations in the two years studied were for "excessive" use of 911 to report domestic violence. And 57 percent of those citations resulted in eviction, with another 26 percent resulting in threats of eviction by the landlord if there is any further problem. Each of these facts is illustrative of how deeply troubling these ordinances are, over and above the inherent faults in the nuisance idea itself.[6]

Milwaukee revised its ordinance in 2013 to specify that domestic violence cannot be grounds for eviction, almost certainly because of the research of Desmond and Valdez and the public attention it received.[7] And when the Illinois legislature finally got around to it in 2015 due to advocacy from the Shriver Center and its coalition partners, both houses voted unanimously in a compromise to ban counties and municipalities from having limits on 911 calls regarding domestic violence or from people with disabilities (but leaving the rest in place).

The ACLU and the Shriver Center point out that these domestic-violence-specific exemptions are not a solution. They do not adequately protect domestic violence victims, because domestic violence incidents are often not categorized as such in police records. The ACLU and Shriver emphasize that all people in need of emergency assistance should be protected, and Shriver will continue to press for that at the state level in Illinois and throughout the state. Currently, only three states—Minnesota, Pennsylvania, and Iowa—have laws that expressly prohibit municipalities from imposing penalties on tenants who exercise their right to call for any reason.[8]

Meanwhile, litigation continues. An exceptionally ugly ordinance in Maplewood, Missouri, drew two lawsuits in the spring of 2017, the first brought by Washington, D.C., civil rights lawyer John Relman and colleagues and the other by the ACLU's Sandra Park and colleagues from the Missouri ACLU. Maplewood requires an "occupancy permit" to live in the community, and it is a crime not to have such a permit. The city calls it a chronic nuisance if a household makes two or more police calls of any nature—including domestic violence or being a victim of any other crime—and revokes the people's occupancy permit for six months.

The plaintiff in Relman's case, which was brought first, is the Metropolitan St. Louis Equal Housing and Opportunity Council. The important point of that was that there was no individual complainant plaintiff as of then and the willingness of the Equal Housing Council to be the plaintiff made it possible to sue without having to wait for a victim. Sad to say, there is now a case with a victim. Rosetta Watson, the plaintiff in the ACLU suit, experienced exactly what the ordinance threatens, and she was far from the first. She called the police several times to ask for protection to keep her safe from her former boyfriend. They did not protect her and she was attacked by the man, and then she was literally banished from the city for six months (as if she would ever want to come back).

An investigation revealed that 55 percent of those banished in Maplewood were African American even though they constituted just 17 percent of the population. And victims of domestic violence or those with disabilities were also disproportionately sanctioned. Not that these facts are surprising. The whole idea is designed to prey on people who in the city's mind are marginal and not wanted in the community.

Beyond the truly awful ordinance, the participation of the Equal Housing Council as a plaintiff establishes a potentially valuable precedent for suits brought by government entities with the authority to sue in that they need not wait for a plaintiff who has suffered serious injury.

DETERRING DESEGREGATION

City officials also use the police to push out people of color who have moved into majority-white neighborhoods. This is a contemporary version of burning a cross in the lawn of the new resident, sending a message to both them and others that they are not welcome.

Kate Walz sees this firsthand. "With the demolition of a lot of public housing in Chicago, we continue to hear all over the state this perception that all these tenants have moved to their town and they need to regulate their rental housing stock as a result. Skokie had a PowerPoint on its website that said, 'Why are we doing this?' Answer: there was a picture of a partially demolished Cabrini Green high-rise. Except there was no evidence that families from there had moved outside the city. The new residents just represented changing demographics, but the Skokie people perceived they were coming from Chicago public housing."

Walz continues, "Some jurisdictions see that every town around them has a crime-free ordinance, so they're afraid that if they don't have one then they'll get all the 'criminals.' The Illinois

Municipal League says this is just good governance, but if you look through the minutes of city council sessions or at the Skokie PowerPoint, you see the perception that they've had an influx from Chicago public housing. The local governments focus on their federally subsidized housing stock. We don't think that's an accident." This is the reason why localities are reluctant to repeal their ordinances completely.

Criminalizing schoolchildren is another method of deterring desegregation. One example comes from Chesterfield County, Virginia, a suburb of Richmond that has been becoming more racially diverse. Police data showed 1,499 students sent to court in a single year, more than half the 2,548 in all of New York City, which is itself a target of civil-rights complaints about school discipline. More than 50 percent of the referrals to court in Chesterfield County were for simple assault or disorderly conduct. More than half of the students arrested were black, while black students constituted just 26 percent of the student body. And almost half of the students sent to court were fourteen years old or younger. Twenty-seven children under ten were charged with assault, and five under age ten were accused of making bomb threats. One school in the county, Falling Creek Middle School, had a referral rate of 228 children per 1,000, thirty-nine times the national rate. It is difficult not to infer that the push to arrest African American students in school is a message that their families are not welcome in the area.

Antioch, California, a city of about 100,000 people discussed earlier, combined pushing residents out with criminalization of schoolchildren. After the housing crash of 2008, a new cadre of African American residents moved in because affordable housing (and federal housing vouchers) became available in Antioch. The city was already quite diverse—about half white with a mixture of minorities, including Hispanics, Asians, and an already present African American contingent. Nonetheless, the new residents were seen by many as low-income and undesirable, and the city let them know. The city pressured landlords to evict a number of the new residents based on made-up or rumor-based accounts of illegal or inappropriate behavior and pressured the local housing authority to take steps to revoke the housing vouchers of the new residents. The ACLU and a blue-ribbon group of public-interest law firms and private law firms, acting pro bono, sued the city in a class action, which was ultimately settled in 2010.[9]

The criminalization of students went along with the pressure on residents. In 2009 and 2010, the Antioch school district had entered into agreements with the U.S. Department of Education and the ACLU to straighten out the district's disproportionate suspensions and use of the courts for African American students. Lack of compliance in 2015 led to a new lawsuit by the NAACP and others that resulted in yet another agreement, and in 2016 the plaintiffs in that matter then sued the school district for not living up to the last agreement.

Beginning in 2015, John Relman began looking at the racial use of the chronic nuisance ordinances from the perspective of the Fair Housing Act. In June 2015, the Supreme Court somewhat surprisingly restated its support for the disparate-impact provisions of the act—the idea that even without proof of intent to discriminate, a law or policy covered by the act could nonetheless be held unconstitutional if it had a disparate impact on a protected group.[10] Relman saw an opportunity: disparate impact was much easier to prove than intent. Relman had been talking with the Shriver Center and Matthew Desmond and others already, and he asked Desmond to identify a city where the conditions would be conducive to proving that a chronic nuisance was unconstitutional because of its disparate impact.

They selected Peoria. Divided by Martin Luther King Jr. Boulevard, the city is still highly segregated, with an ugly past and a not-so-great present. For example, the police department bought a retired military tank-like vehicle that the locals call "The Armadillo," and they leave it in black neighborhoods overnight, saying they are watching for crimes or nuisances. Not surprisingly, the residents find it intimidating.

Most of the federally subsidized (so-called Section 8) housing in the city is in isolated minority neighborhoods with no services, but some landlords in mostly white neighborhoods have rented to African Americans with housing vouchers. A white city council member has pressed to push the Section 8 tenants out. Among other things, the city created an 8:00 p.m. curfew and then selectively used violations of the curfew to invoke the nuisance ordinance and pressure the landlords to evict the tenants.

Relman used the Freedom of Information Act to get public records on police reports and citations relating to the administration of the nuisance ordinance. The city stonewalled for six months. Meanwhile, Relman and partners met with landlords, the NAACP, other community leaders, and especially the HOPE Fair Housing Center in Wheaton, Illinois. Tired of the city's lack of response, Relman and the Shriver Center made two moves: a federal lawsuit and a complaint to the federal government. Both complaints allege that Peoria is deliberately perpetuating segregation in the city by driving African Americans out of the neighborhood. The lawsuit is the first federal case challenging this kind of housing segregation policy and the Department of Justice investigation is the first of its kind as well. Just as important, the Department of Housing and Urban Development issued a nationally applicable guidance that laid out constitutional and federal statutory issues with crime-free ordinances, citing Shriver's work.

HOMELESSNESS

Crime-free ordinances are ways to push people away from their homes and neighborhoods. The homeless, already without a place to live, are increasingly the targets of ordinances and policies to push them out of entire cities.

A surge in new municipal policies concerning homelessness in recent years has had the effect of further criminalizing the poor, people of color, and people with disabilities. Citywide bans have risen significantly on camping in public, begging in public, loitering, loafing, and vagrancy, sitting or lying down in particular public places, and sleeping in vehicles.[11] Breaking any of these laws can result in a stint in jail. Over the last decade, citywide bans on camping in public space have increased by 69 percent, on loitering, loafing, and vagrancy by 88 percent, and on living in vehicles by 143 percent.[12]

No sleeping, no sitting, no eating in public spaces—add these together and it's clear that many cities just want homeless people to go away. Needless to say, criminalization does nothing to reduce homelessness. The United States Interagency Council on Homelessness said in a 2012 report that "criminalization creates a costly revolving door that circulates individuals experiencing homelessness from the street to the criminal justice system and back." It is not only costly, it is a "vicious cycle," says the Center for American Progress. "If an individual convicted of one of these status offenses is unable to pay fines and fees levied as punishment, he can wind up back in jail for nonpayment. And he ends up with a criminal record, which can make it even harder for him to obtain housing and employment and to get back on his feet. As a result, more than half of the homeless population has a history of incarceration."[13] Homeless people are eleven times more likely to be incarcerated than the population as a whole.[14]

Russell Bartholow epitomized the criminalization of being homeless. During the fifteen years he lived under a bridge in Sacramento, California, he received 190 citations from police, was the defendant in 132 cases, spent 104 days in jail, and was assessed $104,000 in fines. Native American and in foster care as a child and then adopted by his foster mother, Bartholow was a bright student until he sustained a brain injury in a racially motivated attack at school. He was never the same after that. He married and fathered a child but gradually succumbed to drug addiction and paranoia. His wife and son moved away, his mother died, and he ended up living under a bridge. He sought government help from time to time, always unsuccessfully, but was regularly harassed by the police leading to the repeated arrests and incarcerations when he could not pay the assessed fines. It was a vicious cycle.

In 2013 he saw his niece's name—by then she was a legislative advocate at the Western Center on Law & Poverty—in the local newspaper. They had lost track of each other and were ecstatic to reunite. Jessica Bartholow said, "All his teeth were gone. He'd been set on fire and spent months in the burn unit. He had been beat to a pulp several times. He had scars all over this body. And not just like little scars. Big scars. Here's a man who's really no threat. For the most part, his warrants were related to sleeping and camping. He wanted them cleared up. But there was really no feasible way for him to accomplish that." He died of cancer in 2016. There were still thirty-seven warrants for his arrest.[15]

How many people are homeless is not clear, except to say it is too many. According to the annual January Point-in-Time survey, the national number has gone down from 647,258 people in 2007 to 549,928 people in 2016. But Maria Foscarinis of the National Law Center on Homelessness & Poverty says that is a serious undercount. The annual total is considerably larger because some homeless people come and go in the course of a year. Experts think the January figures themselves are undercounts, especially with regard to youth disconnected from their families. The experts also estimate that five times the number actually homeless are at risk of homelessness, living in unstable housing situations. Using that definition, for example, the U.S. Department of Education counts 1.36 million children as homeless or in unstable situations.

And the survey itself causes undercounting. It is done by volunteers, and the cities do it in varying ways. The basic protocol prescribes doing a count of people who are sleeping outside in the middle of the night (as well as those who are in shelters), but the volunteers are told not to venture into any area where they might be at risk. Pervasive criminalization plays a role in the undercounting, too. It keeps the count down because the people who sleep outside tend to locate themselves in places where they will not be seen and arrested.

How we came to where we are now is a long and much-told story. Beginning with the end of World War II, the quality of housing for most Americans improved markedly—but not for all even then. When I was a child in Minneapolis, there were men, largely Native American, who lived mainly outside, huddled in the entrances to office buildings near the train stations. People called them winos. Now we say they are homeless and there are many more of them. They are of all racial and ethnic backgrounds and all ages, although disproportionately people of color. And in too many places, Minneapolis and others, we are not doing as well as we should to help address their needs.

The story of the homeless is a story of what happened to our economy and our public policies. We all know that mental hospitals were closed and community-based mental health services did not follow in sufficiency. But that is only one factor. There used to be affordable single-room occupancy hotels in downtowns—the YMCAs, YWCAs, and the like, including the not-so-nice flophouses—but they are long gone. Downtown development pushed them out and they weren't replaced. Especially with the ascendancy of President Reagan, affordable housing began to disappear and the rent for the depleted inventory shot up. The kind of good jobs that didn't require a high school diploma went away and too many of the new jobs paid awful wages, in many instances not enough to live on. Many among the homeless have such jobs. All of that was the beginning of the homelessness that we now know.

The anti-tax revolution made things worse. Even decent leaders who privately know they should be investing in housing and mental health services but lack the requisite resources have instead taken to punishing the homeless—pushing in multiple ways to make them go away.

Cities have different approaches to the dilemma. Among the bad ones is Orlando, Florida, which simply bans all "sleeping out-of-doors" in a city where 34 percent of the homeless in the area lack shelter beds. Manchester, New Hampshire, makes it illegal to "lounge or sleep in or upon any of the commons or squares of the city" but 12 percent of homeless people there have no housing or shelter options. In Santa Cruz, California, 83 percent of homeless people in the area lack housing and shelter possibilities, but the city nonetheless bans camping in public, sitting or lying down on public sidewalks, and sleeping in vehicles.[16] Dallas issued more than eleven thousand citations to its estimated 600 unsheltered people over a four-year period from 2012 to 2015. Honolulu outlawed sitting or lying in public places and then issued 16,215 warnings and 534 summonses in just two years. In Denver, 73 percent of people seeking emergency shelter were turned away.[17]

According to Teresa Nelson of the Minnesota ACLU, Minneapolis police keep a list of a hundred people who have been convicted of "quality of life" offenses and have been ordered to stay out of downtown. Among other things, this means a person on the exclusion list cannot transfer from one bus to another to get to the other side of the city. Eighty percent of those on the list are homeless and most are African American. The city government clearly wants to keep the city center clear of homeless people (as do many cities). Judge Kevin Burke of the Hennepin

County District Court, who was outspoken in his criticism of the city's police practices in a number of areas, pointed out that the system is ill-equipped to deal with the mental health issues involved. "We need to do something radically different," he said.[18] Given all of that, it is not surprising that Minneapolis forbids use of a "camp car, house trailer, automobile, tent or other temporary structure" as temporary housing throughout the city.[19]

The ACLU and others have fought back with lawsuits attacking the constitutionality of the anti-panhandling and anti-camping ordinances and the seizure of the belongings of homeless people, with mixed success. The ACLU in Hawaii pushed back against Honolulu's punitive laws and achieved a promise from the city to give homeless people forty-five days to retrieve seized belongings and twenty-four hours' notice before clearing sidewalks and parks, and to videotape all seized items.[20] Litigation challenging overly broad anti-panhandling ordinances has succeeded in multiple cities on the ground that they violate freedom of speech. On the other hand, even with the Department of Justice filing a brief, a trial judge upheld an anti-panhandling ordinance in Boise, Idaho. Even though the plaintiffs lost in Boise, opponents of the punitive measures all over the country took heart from the Justice Department's involvement, and the Department of Housing and Urban Development announced that it would disfavor funding of homeless assistance for cities that punish homelessness.[21] It remains to be seen whether the Trump administration will continue this stance.

The opposite of criminalizing poverty is ending homelessness. "What we've learned about homelessness over many, many years," says Steve Berg of the National Alliance to End Homelessness, "is that you have to provide housing, and criminalizing the homeless doesn't keep people off the streets at all."[22]

The Housing First initiative, or supportive housing, changed everything in getting homeless people into permanent housing. Instead of requiring people to demonstrate their sobriety and stability, the insight was to put them into housing first. The goal was always to get people into homes and apartments, but Housing First achieved phenomenal outcomes. Even with the support services that are critical to success, the approach is far cheaper than homelessness with its shelters and hospitals and jails, to say nothing of the pain and sadness of being homeless. City after city has adopted Housing First. Salt Lake City, Utah, is perhaps the highest achiever. Under its ten-year plan beginning in 2005, Salt Lake City reduced chronic homelessness by 74 percent by creating hundreds of permanent supportive housing units and using streamlined assessment and placement at the outset to provide needed services to each person. A national campaign led by the Obama administration to end homelessness among veterans was impressively effective. And Community Solutions, an organization led by Rosanne Haggerty, reported in 2015 that it and its partner organizations had met the goal of their four-year 100,000 Homes campaign of supportive housing for medically vulnerable and chronically homeless people in 186 communities across the country.

The biggest cities—New York and Los Angeles (city and county)—are stories in themselves. New York spends more than $1 billion on homelessness, including $870 million on shelters alone. It spends $34 million on legal services to prevent evictions and $180 million to keep people from being evicted. Its homelessness prevention program provides intensive case management and multiple services, and it both keeps thousands in their homes and saves money for the city.[23] Another consequence is the city's low number of unsheltered people. But it is fair to say that no one is satisfied.

The City and County of Los Angeles spend more than $250 million on emergency housing and services but have not made much headway in reducing homelessness. As of the 2016 January survey, 46,874 people were homeless in LA, and about 31,000 were sleeping in the parks and on sidewalks. Over 167,000 experience homelessness over the course of a year. The contrast with New York City is palpable. Something like a third of people returning from incarceration to Los Angeles become homeless and almost 50 percent of young people aging out of foster care become homeless within six months.[24]

There is movement in the city and the county. City residents voted $1.2 billion in 2016 for funding permanent supportive housing and county voters voted a ten-year quarter-cent sales tax toward ending homelessness, although advocates say that some of the new money is simply replacing funding already in place. Another bright spot is the Inner City Law Center (New York City and other Legal Aid lawyers around the country have counterparts). Led by Adam Murray, in 2016 the center helped more than 3,100 low-income tenants to avoid homelessness and recover more than $1.5 million in rent or relocation benefits, and also represented hundreds of people with other housing issues.[25]

The good things that have been accomplished did not just happen. Responsible public officials, advocates, civic leaders, judges, and others made them happen. They have taken a path that eschews criminalization of the homeless. They know that, as former attorney general Eric Holder said, "the criminalization of the homeless . . . is costly, unjust, and not a solution to homelessness."[26]

A test looms, though. After eight years of strong support from Washington, we have a man running the Department of Housing and Urban Development, Ben Carson, who knows absolutely nothing about the importance of the agency he heads. The challenge for the cities that are pushing ahead to create more housing and decriminalize homelessness is to sustain their momentum until a better day. We shall see.

PART TWO

Ending Poverty

9

Taking Criminal Justice Reform Seriously

Mass incarceration was and still is about race, but it is also about poverty, and especially race and poverty combined. The people locked up have always been disproportionately poor and of color, and for the most part their incarceration has ensured that they would stay poor for the rest of their lives. Mass incarceration has been a political and economic coup. Beginning with President Nixon's "southern strategy," it brought Dixiecrat white politicians into the Republican fold and was so successful that it became a national strategy. The combination of race-baiting without the *n*-word and filling the jails and prisons with black men protected Jim Crow in the South and fueled the Republican Party in the rest of the country. The old guard held on to the white vote and weakened both the emerging black political power and the growing economic strength of the black community. A brilliant move: the beginning of the end of the Second Reconstruction, reconstituted with a modern touch.

The economic value of mass incarceration became even more important with the deindustrialization and globalization of the 1970s. When I was the youth corrections commissioner of New York in the last half of the 1970s and vice chair of the National Child Labor Committee beginning in the 1980s, I saw the growing unemployment crisis among young African Americans and Latinos, although I did not fully understand what it was about. The economy did not need young people, especially young people of color, so if they were not in college, as was the case for many, they were unwanted in the job market until they were twenty-two or twenty-three. If there were not enough jobs, the existing jobs had to be rationed in some way. Intentionally or not, the criminalization of poverty served the needs of the labor market, and served it well.

Mass incarceration became a sorting mechanism. Not only were (and still are) young men and some women, disproportionately people of color, kept out of the labor market while in prison, but they are effectively barred for the rest of their lives from jobs for which they would otherwise be qualified. Not only is the fact of a criminal record (or just an arrest record) a bar or at least a stigma, especially when coupled with the race of the applicant, but the time spent in prison also creates an experiential gap in the ex-inmate's résumé and a loss of networking assets.[1]

We have to end unjustifiable collateral consequences and mass incarceration, but doing so is only part of what we have to do to make things right. The labor market is broken. There are not enough jobs, let alone enough good jobs. We have to begin with an honest discussion about what is wrong, because only then can we fix it. Our goals of improving schooling, helping families, getting more affordable housing, attending to health and mental health needs, investing in childcare, and ending racism all require us to fix the labor market. (The collateral consequence of taking away the right to vote is one way operatives of mass incarceration keep the policy in place.)

EXPUNGEMENT

Where available, expungement, the process of erasing criminal records that can wreck people's lives, negates the collateral consequences of a criminal record far more effectively than ameliorating individual bars to employment, education, and housing one by one. For example, nearly 9 in 10 employers, 4 out of 5 landlords, and 3 in 5 colleges use background checks, which, unless criminal records are expunged, put employment, housing, and higher education out of reach for many people.[2] Broadening the application of expungement will be very helpful, given the 75 to 100 million people with criminal records.

Nineteen states allow some felony convictions to be expunged and twenty-three allow some misdemeanor convictions to be expunged. The trend is positive—twenty-three states and the District of Columbia have expanded their expungement laws since 2000.

As of 2015, for example, Pennsylvania allowed expungement for charges that did not result in a conviction (two-thirds of states do this) and for convictions for summary offenses (such as loitering or disorderly conduct) when five years have passed without further arrest. Also eligible were convictions for underage drinking, and convictions of people over seventy who have not been arrested for ten years. The state also allowed expungement after successful participation in diversion programs. Sharon Dietrich of Community Legal Services and other lawyers in Pennsylvania succeed in getting thousands of expungements every year.

In 2016, Pennsylvania governor Tom Wolf also signed a law that allowed the sealing of some old and minor misdemeanor conviction records. The records will still be available to law enforcement and state licensing agencies but not to the public, employers, or landlords, and the offenders would not have to tell employers or landlords that the records exist. The offenses covered include drug possession, DUI, minor theft, prostitution, and disorderly conduct. The offender cannot have been arrested or convicted for ten years after the original incarceration or probation is completed, and can never have been convicted of an offense more serious than the one for which the person seeks sealing or been convicted of four minor misdemeanor offenses altogether.[3]

This is certainly good news, but Pennsylvania's story also illustrates the difficulty of expanding expungement. Dietrich joined Community Legal Services in 1987 as an employment lawyer. In the early 1990s, she began seeing clients whose complaint was discrimination because they had a criminal record. She and colleagues began taking expungement and other criminal record cases, and a majority of their employment work is now criminal record cases. She and her colleagues and other lawyers in the city, including private pro bono practitioners, obtained 8,500 expungements in Philadelphia in 2015. Statewide the total was more than 90,000.

The total among the local lawyers has gone up substantially in the last few years because of Mike Hollander, who is both a lawyer and a computer genius. Hollander developed a software program, Expungement Generator, that builds petitions quickly. It can analyze criminal dockets for expungement eligibility, and it reduces petition preparation time from around half an hour to about two minutes. Dietrich took me to court to see the process for myself. These cases—and there are plenty of them—involve either no conviction or convictions for very low-level offenses. Even so, the district attorney opposes some of them. In the morning there is a meeting between a DA and the applicant's lawyer (if the applicant has one), to see what motions are uncontested. About 10 to 20 percent of the motions are contested, compared to 40 to 50 percent as recently as 2014. This was "before we established the legal standards for the new expungement judge and the DA got used to its objections being regularly denied," Dietrich said.

We arrived shortly after ten o'clock, when court was supposed to be in session. Bruce the bailiff was there, but the judge was not. There was a crowd, some with lawyers, most without. The ones with lawyers go first.

Mike Lee, a lawyer from a nonprofit called PLSE (Philadelphia Lawyers for Social Equity), said hello to Dietrich. He had the first two cases of the day and previewed the facts. The first was a man with other expungements. The current one was for a 1996 substance-abuse-related arrest. He had no additional arrests, had been clean and sober for twelve years, had a job as a foreman at the city water company, and was a grandfather who helped care for his grandchildren. The case file no longer existed due to a periodic record purge, so the prosecutor had little to nothing on which to base an argument that the motion should be denied. The second was a man whose vengeful ex-girlfriend had accused him of sexual impropriety. The police had searched his house and found nothing. He had no criminal record and the charges were dropped without a trial. Nonetheless, the DA was opposing the motions. Why would the district attorney do that? Dietrich thinks some young prosecutors oppose motions to avoid getting into trouble with their superiors.

At about eleven, the judge showed up. He did not sit down. He walked back and forth behind the bench, seeming rather disengaged. Each side argued and at the end, in each case, without any pause, he said, "Granted." It was unclear whether he would have said more if he denied a motion, but Dietrich said the then-current judge denied motions for expungement only about 5 percent of the time.

Why is a judge necessary? Why not automatically expunge records when people are acquitted or never tried or are guilty of a low-level infraction and do not have another arrest for a period of time? After all, people with nonviolent convictions who do not commit other crimes within four to seven years are no more likely to do so than the general population is.[4]

Dietrich and her colleagues, especially Rebecca Vallas, who is now at the Center for American Progress, have spearheaded a legislative campaign in Pennsylvania that they are calling Clean Slate. Under Clean Slate, minor nonviolent cases would be automatically sealed (still available to law enforcement but not to the public) after ten years if there has been no further felony or misdemeanor convictions. For summary offenses the required crime-free period would be five years. The legislation signed by Governor Wolf was a constructive step, but Clean Slate shows how much more needs to be done.

Clean Slate would save significant time and money and, most important, help far more people. Two hundred thousand felony and misdemeanor cases are initiated in Pennsylvania each year, of which 34 percent do not end in conviction. These cases would be expunged quickly. Many of the remaining 66 percent would become eligible for sealing after ten years if there is no further conviction. Twenty thousand summary cases annually in Philadelphia end in conviction and would be eligible for sealing after five years. Mike Hollander says it "would be an absolutely transformative policy."

The work of Community Legal Services on criminal records occurs on many fronts. In 2000, it and pro bono counsel invoked the state constitution to challenge a lifetime bar on a large group of people with criminal records from working in nursing homes and other health-related facilities, which was ultimately found to be unconstitutional. Dietrich, Vallas, and their colleagues also work statewide and nationally to share their successful strategies. Dietrich counts eighty organizations in thirty-one states that do expungement work across the country.

DECARCERATION

Decarceration, properly done, means not only fewer people incarcerated but also reinvestment of the savings into education, jobs, affordable housing, community strengthening, and anything and everything else that plugs the pipeline to prison. Instead of criminalizing the poor, we need adequate investment in ending poverty.

Decarceration is difficult. Even with crime rates going down and the much ballyhooed involvement of the Koch brothers, Grover Norquist, and Newt Gingrich, jail and prison populations show mixed trends. On the plus side, some thirty states have legislated some sentencing reform and alternatives to incarceration.[5] Nonetheless, about half the states still show annual increases and about half show decreases (most of which are small), although a few states have had quite impressive reductions with little or no adverse effect on public safety. Nationally, state prison populations have dropped only about 3.5 percent since they topped out in 2009 and jail populations have gone down a little over 5 percent since they started down from their peak in 2008.[6] These modest declines occurred after the nationwide state prison population grew 10 percent from 1999 to 2012.[7]

Correctional officer unions, for-profit prisons and associated businesses, prosecutors, and police have political clout. The magnitude of budget savings lags behind the drop in prison populations just about everywhere. Then add in the challenges in achieving reinvestment of the proceeds of decarceration, modest as those may be. Readers of a certain age will remember the peace dividend that some said would appear when the war in Vietnam ended. It did not.

Jack Cowley, a retired prison warden from Oklahoma, told the *New York Times*, "It's hard for me not to be cynical about it. Think about the size of our system, all the judges and lawyers, putting their kids through college, people that make leg irons, Tasers. Crime is driving the train. It's like a business that is too big to fail."[8]

And one highly publicized violent crime can stop the momentum. Arkansas relaxed standards for parole in 2011 to save money. In 2013, a man with many past parole violations and robbery convictions killed a young man in Little Rock. The state board of corrections immediately reinstituted the tougher standards.[9]

But some states have made impressive strides. Connecticut, New York, New Jersey, and California have done well. For them the next level of decarceration—considering more appropriate sentences for serious offenses—is in sight. They give us hope.

CONNECTICUT

Connecticut's prison population began falling from its all-time high in 2008 and as of 2016 had decreased 25 percent. The *New York Times* lauded the leadership of Governor Dannel Malloy, also noting the state's repeal of the death penalty, legalizing of medical marijuana, and enactment of some of the strictest gun laws in the country. In 2015 the governor proposed a "Second Chance Society" package of bills, which passed with bipartisan support. The measures included reclassifying simple drug possession as a misdemeanor, ending mandatory minimum sentences for nonviolent drug possession, expediting parole hearings for people convicted for nonviolent crimes, and simplifying the pardon process. The bills also included body cameras for all state troopers, recruitment of more minority officers, and providing independent investigations of police officer use of deadly force.

Malloy's reforms have paid off. Raising the age of adult criminal responsibility to eighteen from sixteen (then leaving only New York and North Carolina with the age of sixteen as the adult threshold) was followed by a 50 percent drop in incarceration of those between eighteen and twenty-one. Crime is at a forty-eight-year low. And the state has closed three prisons so far.[10]

NEW YORK

New York has seen major declines not only in its state prison population but also in its jail population (remember, a decrease in quantity does not necessarily mean an improvement in quality—think Rikers) and its parole and probation populations—one of the few states with declines in all areas. The prison population dropped 26 percent from 1999 to 2012.[11] These trends stemmed from a big decline in felony crimes and felony drug arrests, substantial reform of onerous sentencing statutes, and an increase in alternatives to incarceration.[12] Why these developments occurred and why they are not even larger are two important questions.

Advocacy is the driver of these declines. The Correctional Association of New York, the Legal Action Center, the Vera Institute, the Brennan Center, the Fortune Society, the Drug Policy Alliance, the Center for Court Innovation, public defenders, bar leaders, academics, foundations, some elected officials, journalists, and many others focused on drug law and enforcement reform and did so over a multiyear effort. The focus was the long-standing and long-criticized Rockefeller drug laws. Driven by the anti-crime frenzy in the 1990s, felony drug arrests in New York City had hit an all-time high of 45,978 in 1998. Major public campaigns—Drop the Rock was one, Real Reform another—went on for a decade-plus until 2009, when the Rockefeller drug laws were finally reformed. Beginning in 1999, polls showed support for reform, with respondents saying they were more likely to vote for candidates who favored reform. At the same time, the New York Police Department moved away from prioritizing felony drug arrests. ("Felony" included possession of small amounts of drugs.) By 2011, the number of felony arrests had dropped to 21,149.[13]

The city's prison population also declined as it expanded diversion programs that offered felony drug offenders alternative dispositions and increased investment in treatment programs. The community courts in the city, led by Red Hook Community Justice Center, played an important role in preventing incarceration; people processed in the regular courts were fifteen times more likely to be incarcerated than those served at Red Hook.[14]

Continuing the trend of decarceration, the New York City Council voted in 2016 to create a civil process for the most common low-level infractions that are within its jurisdiction, including public drinking, public urination, littering, excessive noise, and being in a park after dark. Bicycling on the sidewalk and jumping subway turnstiles had already been made into civil violations. Council officials estimated that a third of the 300,000 offenses that now result in arrests will soon be handled as civil violations.[15]

Still, the crime rates suggest that the incarceration rates should have dropped more. According to New York police records, the incidence of seven major felonies in the city fell from 184,652 to 105,453 from 2000 to 2015, a decrease in excess of 40 percent. Why crime rates went down so impressively is a much debated question in itself, with law enforcement taking credit and others pointing to a new civility in the city after 9/11, and still others not sure what exactly happened.

Why incarceration did not decrease as much is clearer. Laws enacted in the 1990s that lengthened sentences are the major reason. New York lengthened sentences after the 1994 crime bill that President Clinton promoted and signed. The law provided more than $9 billion to states to build more prisons on condition that they enacted so-called truth in sentencing laws that resulted in longer sentences. New York received $216 million under this program, and in the 1990s alone added more than twelve thousand prison beds and increased its prison population by 28 percent. Nationally, the number of state and federal adult prisons grew by 43 percent from 1,277 in 1990 to 1,821 in 2005.[16]

Even as prison populations later declined, prison budgets did not. The annual state Department of Correctional Services budget actually increased from $1.6 billion in fiscal year 1998–99 to $2.5 billion in 2006–7 at the same time as the prisons held eight thousand fewer inmates. No prisons were closed during that period.[17] The corrections union and upstate legislators did not want members and constituents to lose jobs. The budget finally stabilized in 2008, and in 2011 the state closed ten prisons and other facilities.

NEW JERSEY

New Jersey is another relatively large state that accomplished significant prison downsizing, reducing its prison population by 26 percent from 1999 to 2012. A number of factors came together in New Jersey. One ingredient was the substantial drop in crime—violent crime dropped by 30 percent and property crime by 31 percent. Also key was successful litigation in 2001 against the Parole Board for dragging its heels on cases. The settlement of the lawsuit brought a commitment to move more quickly. Parole approvals increased from 30 percent to 51 percent, and have remained at the higher level. The state also reduced the incidence of reincarcerating parolees for technical violations. Further, drug law reform played an important role. A sentencing commission in 2004 caused fairer application of the state's "drug-free zone" law by ironing out racial disparities in its utilization, and the legislature enacted a law to end the mandatory minimum sentences in the school drug-free-zone law. The state attorney general issued guidelines to end prosecution of the lowest drug offenses, and the increased use of drug courts helped to avoid incarceration. Finally, Governor Christie signed a bipartisan bill providing bail reforms that will affect jail numbers and indirectly prison numbers.[18]

The reforms began before Christie took office, but he has been a strong reform supporter, making New Jersey an example of bipartisan cooperation. Federally, the bipartisan leadership of Senator Cory Booker, with Senator Rand Paul, toward decarceration may well stem in part from Booker's New Jersey experience.

CALIFORNIA

California often leads the country in change, sometimes for good and sometimes not. For unique reasons, California has made game-changing institutional progress that has important implications for the entire country.

In 2011, Supreme Court justice Anthony Kennedy got out of bed on the left side one morning and told California that the Constitution required action to reduce overcrowding in its prisons. After Governor Jerry Brown and the legislature responded in a variety of ways, Californians used the ballot initiative process to move more substantially toward decarceration in the historic 2014 Proposition 47.

Not so long ago, California was leading in the other direction, with its "three strikes" law that imposed sentences of twenty-five years to life on people convicted of a third felony no matter how minor (followed by twenty-six other states and the federal government), and lengthening sentences on five occasions in total. In 2006, the state's prison population hit its high mark, at 162,804, with the state having built 22 prisons over a 25-year period. By the beginning of 2016, though, it had fallen to 112,792. Some of the decline was because crime trended down. Violent crime declined by 21 percent and property crime by 13 percent between 2006 and 2012.[19] But there was a lot more to the story, and it is still going on.

In 2007 came an important change in parole policy. Previously, all parolees were subject to the same length of time and restrictions whether their offense was serious or minor. The policy was one of the strictest in the country, and a large number of parolees were returned to prison. The new policy reduced supervision to six months for low-level offenses if the parolee complied with certain conditions. The number of parole revocations dropped significantly.

The first big legislative step was in 2009, when Governor Arnold Schwarzenegger was in office with a solidly Democratic legislature. The legislature enacted the California Community Corrections Performance Incentive Act. Concerned about prison overcrowding, the law sought to reduce the prison population further by lowering the number of parolees revoked by the counties and sent back to prison. Imaginatively, the state offered counties a share of the money saved. By 2011, the revocations dropped 32 percent and saved the state $284 million ($136 million went to local probation and parole agencies). These revocations had been "technical violations"—parole violations that did not involve committing a new crime.[20]

Then came Justice Kennedy's opinion in *Brown v. Plata*.[21] California's prisons had been at 200 percent of capacity for eleven years. The Court ordered the state to reduce capacity to 137.5 percent within two years. By then, Brown was back in office and the state again thought outside the box. The legislature enacted the Public Safety Realignment Act of 2011 ("Realignment").

Realignment had three features. The "non-non-nons" meant that people with nonviolent, non-sex-related, and non-serious offenses could no longer be housed in state prisons, only in county jails. Another was that people with those kinds of offenses not only would have shorter parole periods but also would be supervised by county officials rather than the state. And people with technical violations of probation or parole could be sent only to jail, not prison, and for shorter lengths of time.

To help the counties with Realignment, the state increased funding. The counties were initially terrified and their jail populations did grow, but the combined state and county total went down considerably. Still, even with the additional state support, overcrowding of the jails continued and jails coped for a time by releasing people guilty of misdemeanors before their sentences were fully served.[22]

The next move, after a ballot initiative in 1996 legalizing medical marijuana and another in 2000 requiring treatment instead of incarceration for low-level drug users, was a 2012 ballot initiative,

Proposition 36, which scaled back the "three strikes" law. This led to the release of more than 2,100 people who had been sentenced to life without parole, some of whom had a third strike as minor as shoplifting.[23] Throughout, predictions of crime waves were common, but at every step crime rates continued to go down.[24]

Then came Proposition 47, the Safe Neighborhoods and Schools Act—the biggest step so far. Adopted in November 2014 by a twenty-point margin, it has four provisions, including making California the first state to make possession of any drug, even cocaine and heroin, a misdemeanor. Prop 47 is important in many ways, but the changes in drug possession for personal use are the biggest dents in the so-called war on drugs that we have seen in any state. Incarceration of drug users was a major tool in mass incarceration. Repositioning it as a public health issue is a crucial step, although a responsibility comes with it: to invest in funds for treatment of addiction and funding for community mental health.

The law reclassifies six low-end drug and petty-theft offenses from being chargeable as either felonies or misdemeanors to only misdemeanors, provided the accused does not have a previous conviction for a serious felony. For those who qualify, it means a sentence to jail instead of prison, or a fine, or both, or probation. Thefts of items totaling $950 in value or less are categorized as misdemeanors. About 80 percent of the cases affected are for drug possession for personal use. Around forty thousand people were being sent to prison each year on these offenses, so just changing the rules for those crimes means that every year forty thousand people will be sent to jail instead of prison. Next, the law allows people serving time or on probation or parole for any of the listed crimes to ask a judge for resentencing as a misdemeanor, provided they do not pose an unreasonable risk to public safety.

Further, the reform allows people with a past conviction on any of the six offenses to apply to have it redesignated as a misdemeanor, provided there is not another prior serious conviction. Even though the time has already been served, reclassification as a misdemeanor will reduce but not end all collateral consequences. This will be the largest category of applications, estimated to include a million eligible people.

Finally, savings from reduced prison costs are being channeled to other areas: 65 percent for drug treatment, mental health treatment, and supportive housing, 25 percent for efforts to reduce school truancy, and 10 percent for trauma recovery services for crime victims. There is nothing in the new law that spells out how much money will go to counties and how much to the state.[25] The total saving was originally estimated by the state Legislative Analyst's Office at $100 to $200 million annually, although it has turned out to be less.

Prop 47 is a phenomenal success, but it is only a part of an ongoing process. More funds must be found. Its maximum success depends on more jobs, more mental health and addiction treatment services, and more affordable housing for those who would otherwise have been locked up. Otherwise, the good intentions of Prop 47 will give way to more homelessness, more unemployment, more visible mental health and drug issues, and more reincarceration. That said, it is worth repeating that Prop 47 is a stunning success. Proposition 47 did not come out of nowhere, and its success was not accidental.

Prop 47 was the brainstorm of Lenore Anderson, a well-known and respected lawyer and public policy advocate. She and her staff and partners put together a coalition that included law enforcement leaders and public figures of both major parties. The chairs were the former San Diego chief of police, Bill Lansdowne, and the San Francisco district attorney, George Gascón. The public endorsers included Rand Paul, Newt Gingrich, and B. Wayne Hughes Jr., a conservative philanthropist who made a major gift to the campaign. The coalition included the ACLU, prominent victims' rights advocates, and hundreds of religious leaders. Anderson hired Robert Rooks, an organizer close to the unions, and Ace Smith, a political and communications guru who knew the issues and how to shape a message to pitch it.[26]

Thousands of volunteers were recruited and they in turn contacted more than 300,000 voters and ran more than two hundred voter mobilization events in fifteen key counties by the time they were done. California Calls, a civic engagement organization, and PICO, a nationally respected entity that does community organizing in a faith-related framework, organized a phone bank to get hundreds of spiritual leaders to tell politicians of their support for reform. California Calls and PICO also pursued a civil rights perspective in reaching out to minorities to make sure of their support. Gascón and Lansdowne and other law enforcement leaders spoke out actively and at least caused many people in law enforcement to sit the fight out.[27]

Anderson and her organization are now moving forward. They have funding to give strategic advice to other state-based organizations pushing decarceration in an eight-year campaign using the political process. Of course, other states are far from as blue as California and very few if any have the kind of ballot measure structure that allows change agents to bypass the legislative process. Nonetheless, there is momentum now and this is a timely moment to strike.[28]

The immediate challenge in California is making the most of Prop 47 and pushing back those who continue to express fears of a new crime wave. After a year, crime rates were up slightly in nine of the state's largest cities.[29] Prop 47 advocates point to continuing record lows in San Diego County, among others where crime rates did not change.[30] The violent crime rate in Los Angeles increased 38 percent in 2015 and 2016, but it is still at a historical low, though it is unclear that the rate is related to Prop 47 since the reform did not apply to violent crimes.[31] One study found that counties that invested in innovative approaches to reentry had less recidivism than counties with status quo policies focusing on enforcement.[32] Bottom line, statewide crime rates overall in 2015 were the lowest since 1960.

A rumor among police officers is that misdemeanor arrests are no longer allowed.[33] Another misconception is that Prop 47 is a "get-out-of-jail-free card" because misdemeanor arrests are rendered pointless by short sentences that make the arrests not worth the trouble.[34]

The press played up a young man named Semisi Sina, a meth addict who excelled in committing thefts of property such as bicycles worth less than $950, and carried out his now-misdemeanor crimes with minor consequences at most. But the press failed to point out that Sina already had thirteen arrests and five convictions before Prop 47 kicked in. In fact, the pattern of misdemeanor arrests around the state is checkered, with some counties up quite a bit and others down considerably, suggesting that politics may be playing a role in arrest policies.[35]

Another criticism of Prop 47 is that removal of the "hammer" of a long prison stay, which incentivized drug offenders to choose treatment, will mean that addicts charged with misdemeanors will prefer shorter turns in jail to longer treatment commitments. Censuses are down in some treatment programs, so the programs are branching out in their recruitment policies since there are plenty of addicts who have not fallen into the clutches of the law. Drug court judges are also looking for non-drug offenders whose crime was driven by drug abuse.

Realignment did cause early releases from jails, and critics complain that there were times when a misdemeanor conviction meant doing only sixty days. But after Prop 47 went into effect, narcotics arrests dropped enough in LA city and county to abate the overcrowding in the jail, and inmates now complete 70 percent of their sentences, meaning there is more of a "hammer" than there was for a while.[36] More broadly, we can hope we are finally in a transition toward dealing with drug addiction as a public health matter instead of a law enforcement matter. However, achieving this transition will not occur overnight.

While the critics are still criticizing, others are helping to implement the law. LA county supervisor Mark Ridley-Thomas says that it's "all about implementation" and, not surprisingly, that the state's funding for the tasks the county has to undertake is inadequate. Besides, he said, there is bureaucratic resistance locally to the reallocation of funds among agencies needed in order to fulfill new responsibilities. He is also critical of the rigidity of the implementation process laid out in the initiative, because it is difficult to adjust with experience. He says the process did not allow for a "sufficient road test," and complains that the proponents are "too defensive to acknowledge the need to adjust."

All of that said, Ridley-Thomas and LA County Board of Supervisors member Hilda Solis created two task forces, one to reach out to the large number of eligible offenders who might not know they can apply for reclassification and the other, composed of business, education, foundation, and nonprofit leaders as well as public officials, to develop a strategy to help ex-offenders get jobs and services. Ridley-Thomas points to improved mental services, with the health department taking on new duties that are making a difference. Other officials have pitched in, too. LA district attorney Jackie Lacey convened a task force to expand diversion from jail for the mentally ill, and LA city attorney Mike Feuer, having been handed responsibility for a significantly expanded docket of misdemeanor cases, reached out to city and county agencies to design new approaches to low-level crime.

As of the end of 2016, 519,000 people in LA County were eligible to have their felonies reclassified as misdemeanors, and county officials say it is hard to locate the people who could receive reclassification.[37] Another report said 198,000 felony convictions in the county were downgraded as of the end of 2014.[38] That report contained stories of the efforts public defenders made to find potential applicants, most likely because they do not know of their eligibility. One lawyer said she stays at it because "lopsided sentences inspire [her] to keep going. In one a man had been branded a felon for stealing bales of hay, in another, just a pillow."

Meanwhile, the governor is continuing the decarceration process. As of late 2016 Brown had approved parole for about 2,300 lifers convicted of murder and about 450 lifers sentenced for lesser offenses, in contrast to a grand total of two people receiving such clemency during the entire time Governor Gray Davis was in office (1999–2003). The state also ordered parole hearings for inmates with long sentences for violent crimes committed before they were twenty-three years old, to consider whether their immaturity at the time supports their release.[39]

A significant step occurred in the fall of 2016 when the governor joined a successful ballot measure, Proposition 57, submitted by Lenore Anderson and movie producer Scott Budnick and his organization, the Anti-Recidivism Coalition. The proposition grants early release to nonviolent felons who finish rehabilitative programs and demonstrate good behavior, abolishes statutory restrictions on "good time" credits for good behavior, and allows prisoners convicted of nonviolent offenses to be eligible for parole after serving the base term for their crime. It also allows judges instead of prosecutors to decide if a juvenile should be tried in adult court, with the burden on the prosecutor to prove that a youth should be transferred. The latter in particular will reduce substantially the number of juveniles who are sent to adult court.[40]

The future of Prop 47 is a matter of high stakes. Despite the claims of increased crime stemming from the operation of Prop 47, the recidivism rate for people getting out of prison or jail due to Prop 47 as of the fall of 2015 was 5 percent, against the overall state average recidivism of 42 percent.[41] Among those released after the softening of the "three strikes" law, only about 6 percent were returned to prison, and just 2 percent of lifers paroled committed new crimes.[42] So the prospects are good.

Whether the recidivism rate will hold as the number of people benefiting from Prop 47 increases is a question, and of course the level of recidivism is not the only measure of success. Jobs, mental health and drug treatment services, affordable housing, high school graduation, and other parameters are part of decarceration. Mark Ridley-Thomas reports that one out of three people released under Prop 47 is homeless. A journalist wrote, "Two years after Prop 47 addicts walk free and have nowhere to go."[43] The more people who are out on the street instead of in prison or jail because of Prop 47, the greater the risk there is of more crime if California does not follow up and undertake everything that decarceration requires.

Half a century ago we deinstitutionalized our mental health system, closing mental hospitals with the promise of replacing them with community-based services, but failed to fulfill the promise. If we fail similarly here, we could easily find ourselves opening the prisons again. A huge and highly visible pothole lurks on the road to decarceration: decarceration that does not address the nation's job situation is not going to work out well. We already have an enormous gap for younger workers, and predictably it is young people of color who will be the hardest hit.

Looking beyond the impact of Prop 47, Lenore Anderson of Californians for Safety and Justice says, "The biggest opportunity we have is not just to end mass incarceration. We need to replace it with lifting communities up. I think we are in a moment where we can actually do that, and that becomes our platform for safety. We're not just going to reduce mass incarceration. We're going to clean up the legacy, too."[44]

10

Turning the Coin Over: Ending Poverty as We Know It

Decarceration involves much more than reforming the criminal justice system. It will not succeed if we do not keep people out of trouble, which is an even bigger undertaking. Many people go to prison because they are poor and remain trapped in poverty after they are released. The criminalization of poverty will continue if we fail to address poverty and race directly.

We have to turn the coin over and provide prenatal care for all, child development for all children, first-class education for all, decent jobs and effective work supports, affordable housing, health and mental health, lawyers as needed, safe neighborhoods, no violence on the street or at home, healthy communities, economic, social, racial and gender justice, and justice rather than charity. One can add to the list and elaborate the items mentioned. We want all of this for many reasons, among them that it will reduce the number of people who get locked up.

We know that the targets of mass incarceration come heavily

from just a few zip codes, so the rest of this book is about efforts to narrow the gap among zip codes. It is crucial to focus on the relation of place to poverty as part of a strategy to end the criminalization of poverty. If we move in the right direction, the gap in incarceration between the people who live in lower-income zip codes and those who live in wealthy zip codes will shrink. A real decarceration—a just society—will follow.

For that reason I visited seven programs, largely located in high-poverty zip codes, that with their partners operate on a scale that improves the lives of large numbers. The seven are illustrative, but I could have visited many others that are equally effective and also operate at scale. These entities help children and families and build community strength. Their work accentuates the positive and consequently prevents the negative as well. The work includes advocacy for individual children and families and policies that help more broadly. They exemplify the pursuit of "collective impact," in the terminology now widely heard.

Still, these important programs are themselves only one part of strategies for change. Ending mass incarceration, poverty, and racism require organizing and political action, too.

TULSA, OKLAHOMA: CAP TULSA

A little before eight thirty in the morning on the first day of my visit to Community Action Program (CAP) Tulsa (originally the Community Action Project of Tulsa County), I was standing with Steven Dow, its executive director, watching children and parents streaming into the Skelly Early Childhood Education Center.

The scene was joyous and I felt myself smiling from the top of my head to the tip of my toes.

A woman came up to Dow with a similarly huge smile. She said to him, "I just want to thank you, Mr. Dow. I can't thank you enough. You may not remember me, but you changed my life. I'm a graduate of your Career Advance program and now I've got a great job doing billing for pediatric therapy. I'm a much more confident person now. My kids can see the difference and they want to follow my example." She introduced herself as Jessica Syring and said that she began her educational quest when her son, now eight, was three and in the CAP Head Start program, and now her three-year-old daughter was in the Head Start program.

The encounter with Syring was emblematic. CAP Tulsa is one of the best examples in the country of what are called two-generation or "2Gen" programs that combine child development and family support. The program serves 2,300 children, including 400 infants and toddlers, at nine stand-alone Head Start sites and two sites in churches, plus 350 families receiving home visits and a teen mom program at an elementary school. It keeps a waiting list of 1,200 because children do leave, due to family moves or poor attendance and chronic tardiness. Ninety percent of the children are from families in poverty and the other 10 percent are special cases such as children with disabilities and children in foster care.

CAP has a contract with Family and Children's Services (twenty-seven family specialists and eleven mental health specialists) to help families with financial, health, mental health, legal, and public benefits issues. Social workers welcome the children and parents every day at the start of school, ready to help if asked and noting if something seems amiss that could be a reason for following up. Every family has a support person who is an MA or BA social worker, and Family and Children's Services offers many classes for parents, too. Altogether CAP has a $52 million budget consisting roughly of a third each from federal, state, and private sources.

When we finished the greeting period, Dow took me on a tour of the building, which is gorgeous. All but one of the program's stand-alone buildings are located next to schools so that children get a sense of being in a school-like environment. There are 186 children, so the building is substantial in size. The classrooms are colorful—meant to be warmer than traditional schools, Dow says. The classroom doors are designed so a child cannot catch a finger as a door closes. The toilets are in the classroom, surrounded by a three- or four-foot-wall so the child has privacy but an adult can peek over if necessary. We walked into one classroom where the children were belting out "Oh dear, what can the matter be?" with each child inserting a new "matter."

We sat down with LaToya Nichole Smith, the school leader, or principal. She had started with the program as a Head Start parent and then, acquiring college and graduate degrees, she became a teacher and worked her way up from substitute teacher to teacher to assistant school leader to school leader.

A key part of Smith's job is to identify parents who could be in Career Advance or other programs and then help them get the support they need to succeed, including especially childcare. Some parents are in Smart Singles, a group that helps to identify healthy relationships and educate parents on domestic issues that could be barriers to success. Others are in Healthy Women, Healthy Futures, which is taught by faculty from the University of Oklahoma College of Nursing and helps young women to decide whether to get pregnant and how to handle a pregnancy. About half of the parents are preparing for a job or a better job. Staff members said to me repeatedly that small steps are very important, whether it is getting a GED, studying English as a second language, or even getting a family to keep their house clean.

Smith is also responsible for the attendance policy. No one is turned away for being late, but after three instances of tardiness or two unexcused absences in a month she sits down with the parent or parents to develop an attendance plan. CAP believes strongly that working through such problems early will forestall repeated problems later on, and it succeeds most of the time.

There are constant classroom management issues. Teachers do assessments regularly to divide the children into small groups by level of function. Some children suffer trauma on a regular basis at home, and some suffer a terrible loss that requires bereavement counseling for the children involved, the other children, and the teacher. Still others have disabilities and limitations that need identification and regular consultation or therapy.

Family and Children's Services staff are partners in all of this. They conduct a family needs and strengths assessment with all parents at the outset of a child's starting at Head Start, and check in regularly with them. They also organize and encourage parents to join social groups which result in important friendships and peer education. The mental health team is a vital element of the program and works with about a third of the children, usually in tandem with the parents. The two-generation approach is key to all the work of Family and Children's Services, as it is to CAP as a whole.

Dow was already heading CAP when the Clinton administration decided to allow new applicants to compete against existing Head Start grantees for the first time since the program was created in the 1960s. Backed by civic leaders in the community, Dow applied for and received Tulsa's Head Start grant. The program had been confined to the African American neighborhoods and Dow wanted to reach the entire county. He was held back initially by the fact that the city had only 956 slots (Oklahoma City had 2,500 slots), including just 104 Early Head Start slots, because of the poor condition of the local program when CAP took over.

A crucial turning point occurred in 2005. The now-defunct Fannie Mae Foundation chose CAP as one of fifteen organizations given funding to reexamine their mission and strategy toward finding their own specialty and using partners to get other work done. This grant introduced Dow to Doug Smith, a longtime partner at the McKinsey consulting firm, who became a great friend and continuing adviser. Smith said Dow needed a clear and consistent mission or he would end up being grant-addicted rather than purpose-driven.

Smith told Dow he was all over the place and challenged him to figure out what he could give up if he was going to triple his effectiveness in three years—to identify what he could do and be the world's best at it. CAP was doing asset development, helping people get the Earned Income Tax Credit, and working on affordable housing as well as Head Start. Dow decided to focus on Head Start and early child development, and passed the organization's other functions over to different groups. In something of a miracle, for it was certainly not planned, CAP Tulsa's efforts on early child development did triple over the following three years.

What happened was a combination of a term-limited powerful state legislator and the billionaire George Kaiser, who had a long-standing passion for early child development and was a longtime friend and supporter of Dow and his work. The legislator, who was chair of one of the appropriation committees and wanted to make a mark as he left the legislature, told Kaiser he would put up $5 million in state money if Kaiser would put in $2 for every dollar the state contributed. Kaiser agreed. His outsized match and persuasive argument that this would be a good business investment carried the day, and the legislature agreed. The total in new money for the entire state was $15 million, and a portion of that tripled the program's budget for its early childhood development work.

The $15 million brought new challenges. How would it be spent across the state? How much would be spent on children through age three, to whom both Kaiser and Dow were deeply committed? How much could be used to raise standards and credentials for teachers and get enough high-quality teachers who would then be adequately compensated? What could be done to make programs full-year and full-day as necessary? What could be done to connect family support to the programs?

Dow had been working on these issues since he had taken over the Head Start program. George Kaiser helped in multiple ways. By underwriting the construction of buildings, adding funds to pay teachers and thereby increasing the quality of people hired, supporting teacher training at the University of Oklahoma, and investing in children up through age three, Kaiser and a few others helped CAP look quite different even before the big bump in statewide funding occurred.

Over the years the bump got even bigger, reaching $10 million on the state side and $15 million from philanthropists across the state largely recruited by Kaiser. Even with the state in deep budget trouble, as of June 2016 the state contribution was still extant because of the power of Kaiser and other private donors.

As the expansion of childcare across the state and the filling out of Head Start in Tulsa took place, Dow was also worrying about economic well-being for parents, a concern that eventuated in Career Advance. He had obtained advice from national experts and received pilot funding from George Kaiser for fifteen students headed toward healthcare jobs when the Affordable Care Act came along. They were at the right place at the right time. They received federal funding for five years beginning in 2010 and were beginning a second five years when I visited. They began with the nursing sector and the career path leading up to it and added other parts of the health care workforce as time went on. Of course the election of Trump puts everything up in the air.

It turned out, though, that many of the people interested in a health-related job were not remotely ready to do community college work. CAP had to back up and develop what turned out to be a four-tier developmental education system, with the largest group being at elementary school levels in English and math. Each person who is accepted for Career Advance receives an academic coach, a career coach, a financial coach, and a life family coach, to be mobilized as needed. Over the first five years, after winnowing down the large number who expressed interest, the program produced 376 people who achieved at some level. Of this group, 271 obtained health care jobs, 39 completed remedial education, and 66 finished an ESL program. The goal for the second five years is for 588 people to complete training, with 435 in health care sector jobs.

Dow took me to a Career Advance graduation. The group of five graduates was small enough to allow each one to be feted with a congratulatory speech by a staff member and make a short talk as well. There were streamers and balloons and big families there to cheer the graduates on, and all of the top staff of CAP Tulsa, too, with cake and punch afterward. The graduates included a registered nurse, two technicians, an associate technician, and a physical therapy assistant.

Next was a meeting with the team that runs the program's substantial home visiting program. Unlike some of the public portrayals of home visiting as a panacea, the conversation was sophisticatedly nuanced. They said it is especially helpful for some and of no apparent value to others. Recruiting families is difficult and there is a high dropout rate, but there is a critical mass who benefit greatly. Needless to say, the team believes deeply in the importance and efficacy of its work.

The program, Learning at Home, has 350 families at any one time, with seventeen staff members, including three team leads and fourteen parent educators. There is little staff turnover, so there is valuable continuity. The team does ninety-minute home visits every two weeks for families who have children up to three years old. They spend about a third of the time in child interaction with the parents—reading, singing, and playing with the children—and the rest of the time with the parents, providing developmental information and addressing issues of family well-being. Each new family receives a series of screenings to determine where the child is on a developmental scale and offer appropriate resources.

Dow asked the team for success stories. Jackie Marshall noticed a misalignment in one child's eyes, so she pushed the mother to take the child to a physician. The mother broke two appointments but finally went and the boy now has glasses. Marshall's prodding also resulted in a physician finding a heart murmur. One of Arianne Betancourt's team was working with a family that had an extremely dirty home. The parent educator convinced the parent to make small goals toward a clean house, and step by step the parent made great progress. Carolyn McCulpin organized a social group of her parents, which resulted in three of the parents sharing that they had been abused as children.

I met a number of families who told me how important CAP had been. One was definitely a "2Gen" story, starting with Learning at Home. The family came to the program because Parker, their eighteen-month-old second son, did not speak at all except to say "Mommy" and "Daddy." Kyden, a year older, was a chatterbox. The program started with home visiting mainly to pave the way for getting Parker a spot in a center when he turned two. Once he was given a place, he cried when his mother left him there for the first time. Four days later he couldn't stop talking at the center, and two weeks later his father heard him counting to twelve in the bathtub.

Then Dad blew out his knee at his job. They owned their home but were on the verge of having it foreclosed on even though Family and Children's Services had been advising them on their financial problems. Family and Children's Services regularly helped tenants on the verge of eviction but this was new. Nonetheless, it found an organization that worked with people at risk of foreclosure, and they helped the family with a payment plan they could afford. The parents also benefited from mental health counseling from Family and Children's Services.

Dad had a second knee surgery and was now getting workers' compensation and Mom was now working outside the home. They were back on track toward college for their boys.

Looking to the future, Dow had me sit in on a strategic planning meeting with a hundred central office staff, which was a key step toward a new ten-year plan. A core writing team had already conducted an extensive listening campaign, gathering feedback from families, teachers, donors, and others, and pulled together a draft for comment.

Dow is data-driven, research-driven, and evidence-based. Community Action Program has an Innovation Lab, a data collection team, and evaluation consultants, and Dow is in constant touch nationally with the leading researchers, practitioners, and policy experts. The strategic planning is an integral feature.

A key challenge in the new plan is to tackle the number of children who do not keep pace and are not ready for the third grade and further schooling. The program had played a role in making education available down to the pre-K level, and now Dow thought it had to find a role in staying with children as they go beyond third grade. The program is not going to run schools itself, so the question, a big one, is what it can do to work with the families to help them keep their children on pace.

There are four areas of success to be achieved going forward:

child success, family success, organizational success, and community success.

Child success includes redesigning the front door—being clearer with families about what the program will do and what families are expected to do, and being more alert for early warning indicators that might show up at age two and possibly foretell problems that will manifest at age six.

Family success entails an individualized at-home curriculum that helps parents to be confident, financially secure, and emotionally and physically healthy, and extends to families on the waitlist and those whose children have already graduated from Head Start.

Organizational success means a commitment to continuous improvement, especially in light of state budget cuts, so that CAP will continue to be a highly desirable place for talented people to want to work. The program will have to play an outside role in advocating for the state budget not only for early child development but also for adequate funding for kindergarten through third grade schooling, and an inside role to become a professional learning community even more than it is now.

Community success requires partnering with other nonprofits about needs of families and children that are not met by CAP itself and with national organizations that it can learn from and help as well, including research groups that can help it do better.

The children and families in CAP Tulsa's care are in good hands. If the program has its way, it is only going to get better.

CHICAGO: LOGAN SQUARE NEIGHBORHOOD ASSOCIATION

Logan Square Neighborhood Association is more than half a century old. It has grown with the times, both in the composition of its clientele and in the breadth and sophistication of its work. In the 1960s, Logan Square was an Eastern European neighborhood and the program was basically a settlement house. Its constituency now is mainly Latino and its work is cutting-edge.

Monica Espinoza epitomizes the organization. She came to the United States when she was seventeen after a difficult childhood in what she describes as a "somewhat dysfunctional family." She married, went to work, and had children, but she says, "I never thought of having goals or aspirations." She was working in a factory making plastic parts for computers and her first child was starting kindergarten when someone told her she should apply for the association's signature Parent Mentor program. She remembers vividly that she was asked at her interview what her skills were. She thinks she "may have said I was not good at anything."

She was sure she would not be chosen, but she was wrong. The experience was wonderful. She learned "to be a second set of eyes, ears, and hands for the teacher." She loved her teacher and by the end of the year, she says, "the kids had become my kids, too."

Now, eleven years after starting out, with her son now a high school honor student, she is a parent mentor coordinator organizer. The Monica Espinoza of today organizes in the neighborhood and goes to the state capitol to lobby for funds for the Parent Mentor program and bring a parent voice to support the teachers in her community. She was afraid at the beginning but her experience over the years "built strength in me so now I am not scared to talk to legislators. I say to them, 'You asked our community to vote for you. Now we need your vote.'" When she encountered legislators who said their hands were tied, she found herself saying, "We'll help untie them." "Knowledge is power," Espinoza says. "Going to Springfield—that is where you get multiplication, where you get leverage."

With its partners and others, Logan Square works on immigrant integration, protection and expansion of affordable housing, opposition to gentrification, restorative justice and violence prevention, adult education and after school programs, connecting people to health services and coverage, civic engagement and legislative advocacy, and parent engagement, which encompasses the Parent Mentor Program that was the reason for my visit. The numbers of people touched are impressive and the political visibility is impressive as well.

The association has 51 member organizations of one kind or another in the neighborhood, 225 partner organizations, and a budget of about $3 million, about half from foundations and corporations and half from grants and contracts from all levels of government. Though it has about fifty funders, staying solvent is a constant challenge, especially at a time when an ideological Congress cuts the federal budget for helping lower-income people and the people of Illinois elected a governor who has a similar attitude.

My guide for the visit was Joanna Brown, a longtime education organizer. In 1993 she was leading a campaign to get more schools in the area when the principal of Frederick Funston Elementary

School, the poorest school in the poorest area of the community, suggested what became the Parent Mentor program. She thought it would help in her school and also help nonworking mothers to further their education and find jobs. It has been replicated elsewhere in the state and around the country, and deserves to be spread even further.

The heart of the program involves having these mothers spend two hours a day in the classroom working with children directly. "That two hours gets you hooked into everything," Brown says. "It's a life changer."

The process begins at the start of the school year by recruiting mothers (and a few fathers) who are parents of children in the school in third grade or lower. Those in the Logan Square area are generally immigrants who typically (but far from all) have not been working outside of the home and are not active in the community, and most come from Spanish-speaking homes. They are definitely low-income. Almost all of the children in the schools are eligible for free or reduced-price lunches.

Next comes a week of training. The parents are partnered with a teacher and assigned the task of being a tutor or a coach, so they work one-on-one or in a small group. The teachers often put them with children who have special needs. Many of the children have language issues. (They are never assigned to their own child's classroom.)

Each of the nine Logan Square area schools (with about a thousand children each) has fifteen to twenty-five parent mentors. They are required to work one hundred hours during the semester—fifty days at two hours a day—plus a workshop on Fridays to build leadership skills, although most stay longer than the two-hour minimum each day. When they complete their one hundred hours they receive a stipend of $500. Some mentors stay on for a second year, but the program tries to have 50 to 60 percent new people each year.

The program has created a successful ladder of opportunity. About two thousand mentors have gone through the program since 1995 and they have done well. Some become coordinators in the program itself or get other jobs with Logan Square. Many get jobs in the schools as cafeteria workers and bus monitors or other career positions. Others start small daycare centers, work in community centers, or do something else in the neighborhood. Many get GEDs. The ones Joanna is most proud of have become teachers through the Grow Your Own Teachers program, which they created in partnership with a coalition of community organizations.

Getting the program started was difficult. Traditionally, teachers could not even conceive of having parents in their classrooms, let alone having them offer academic support. Principals feared turf issues. But the program was highly structured. Existing parent mentors who know their neighbors do the recruiting and the principal interviews every candidate. The program utilizes contracts, timesheets, and supervisors. The teachers have become the best supporters and advocates for the program.

It has worked. The parents become partners with the teachers. They have a degree of ownership, as do the students. Parents become more important to the educational system; schools engage students more successfully and student achievement increases.

The program is a leadership development strategy, too. Logan Square gets the mothers involved in public issues, especially issues of direct interest to their community. The mothers have testified frequently in the legislature on such issues as in-state tuition and driver's licenses for the undocumented, as well as state funding for the expansion of the Parent Mentor Program and affordable housing for the neighborhood, and they have invited legislators to visit the schools that received funding when the legislature enlarged the program. They have gone to Washington to lobby for immigration reform, too.

Joanna Brown calls the program "transformative." She says it has done incredible things for immigrant families. Some women have left their extended families in their home countries and are isolated here in the United States, sometimes just with their nuclear families and sometimes without their husband and some of their children. The program becomes their second home. They meet other women who have similar stories and they find community. Then many of them get involved in community issues, such as trying to save a school from being changed into a military school (a Mayor Rahm Emanuel idea), opposing demolition of public housing that the city wants to replace with a mixed-income development with many fewer units for low-income people, or any of a raft of other issues. Parent mentors are ambassadors in their neighborhoods for many purposes, including voting and making presentations about foreclosure prevention and President Obama's DACA (Deferred Action for Childhood Arrivals) and DAPA (Deferred Action for Parents of Americans) immigration programs, as well as telling people about opportunities for their children to play on athletic teams and get academic help for their children. Admittedly biased, Joanna says that Parent Mentors is "the best immigration program for low-income families."

The Southwest Organizing Project, also in Chicago, replicated the program in 2005 in eleven neighborhoods in its part of the city, adding diversity to the program. Now, with state support, the program is in seventy schools around the state, run by sixteen community organizations. Logan Square Neighborhood Association and Southwest Organizing created a Parent Engagement Institute that trains more than six hundred mentors a year who provide support to six hundred teachers and bring additional personal attention to fourteen thousand low-income students. The results of the program are proven. Schools that were in the program saw an increase of 35 percent in scores on state tests over ten years compared to other children, and dropouts went down by 61 percent.

Joanna took me to a training for new coordinators who will be the trainers and supervisors of parent mentors in the state-funded program. The highlight was lunch with a dozen longtime coordinators who were doing the training for the day, almost all of whom had started as Parent Mentors themselves. Not surprisingly, most of them were longtime friends, and two of them, Leticia Barrera and Silvia Gonzalez, had recruited most of the others as mentors before they became coordinators.

Gonzalez is a great role model for the other women. She started as a parent mentor in 2002 while going through a depression caused by her special-needs son's serious health issues. She went on to be a parent tutor, took a seat on the local school council, then accepted a part-time job at Logan Square, and finally became a parent mentor coordinator. Now she is a grandmother and studying for a college degree. She says Logan Square turned her life around.

I asked Gonzalez what she thinks are the most important things the program has accomplished. She said, "Self-esteem. You find the leader within you. You learn to think on a community level. You ask how you can build a better community and how you can build a better future for yourself. The program gives you the tools. As a coordinator, you are a mother hen. You become friend, psychologist, and mentor. You are someone who believes in the parent mentors. They feel powerful."

Barrera is a good example, too. She had been a teacher in Mexico but did not speak English and so was working a factory job in Chicago. When her first son started kindergarten in 1998 at James Monroe School she was sad that he was going inside and she had to stay outside. (He was in college when I visited.) A woman was handing out flyers and told her about being a parent mentor. Barrera understood that the program would allow her to be in school with her son. She signed up without really knowing what she was getting into.

She is now the parent mentor organizer for the nine schools in the Logan Square area—hiring the coordinators, communicating with the principals, and working with each school to select the new parent mentors. Meanwhile, she joined Logan Square's Grow Your Own Teacher program and is steadily working toward a bachelor's degree at Chicago State University so she can become a teacher. That is her dream. She says her husband, a catering truck driver, has supported her all the time to make her dream possible.

Then there is Tami Love. After hearing just one sentence from her I knew she was a big personality. People listen to her. Love is another pioneer of the Parent Mentor Program and now divides her time between housing and the Parent Engagement Institute. The thing that is a bit different for her living in Logan Square is that she is African American. She came to the neighborhood in 1994, when she had to find a place to live she could afford. She found a three-bedroom apartment for $450 a month. She was on welfare and had time on her hands, and she kept seeing signs saying the school wanted volunteers.

Then Love saw a sign for a meeting at the school, and she went. She could not understand the conversation, which was in Spanish, but she saw that the parents there felt very emotional about whatever it was about. She came to understand the mentoring idea and also that they would knock on doors in the community. "Unheard of!" Love says now. She signed up, and she and the other parents gradually found ways to communicate. Her work now is to get parent mentors into schools around the city and follow up to make sure everything runs well. She also works on housing issues and participates in the annual fight in Springfield to keep the state funds going.

To Nancy Aardema, Logan Square Neighborhood Association's executive director, the group's initials could also stand for "Leaders Shaping Neighborhood Action." A conversation with her dramatized the constant challenges the organization faces, both in tackling new issues in the community and in the ups and downs of finding the money to keep things going. It is hard enough to keep funding programs to serve people, but Logan Square also does organizing and advocacy, and finding funding for those activities is even more difficult. Foundation grants and public funding do go up and down, but Logan Square perseveres and is a major presence in the community.

The association's work is guided by a holistic plan that is based on the strategy of a comprehensive development approach to creating a strong community. They redo the plan annually, and their fifty member organizations come together twice a year as key stakeholders in the community to look at what is going well and what they need to do better.

Bridget Murphy, who set up my visit in the first place, concluded the visit by saying, "We're having a sea change. We have several new independent progressive elected officials on the North Side. So this part of the city is leading in many ways, and the Logan Square Neighborhood Association will play a big role in all of it. On the other hand, it's so hard with gentrification. The neighborhood will look very different very soon." On top of everything on the existing agenda, the next challenge is to make gentrification their friend, creating an economically and ethnically integrated place that makes everyone a winner.

MINNEAPOLIS: THE NORTHSIDE ACHIEVEMENT ZONE

Minneapolis is perplexing. It has a very low unemployment rate overall and nonetheless an African American poverty level of over 40 percent citywide and an unemployment rate of about 14 percent. The Northside Achievement Zone is one of the Promise Neighborhoods created by President Obama's administration to improve outcomes for children and families in neighborhoods of concentrated poverty. NAZ, as everyone calls it, is in North Minneapolis, concentrated mainly in a thirteen-by-eighteen-block segment that is 79 percent African American; 73 percent of the families here earn $19,000 or less, and the area experiences high unemployment, coupled with extensive violence.

What is particularly disturbing about the high unemployment is that North Minneapolis is very close to downtown. One can see the tall buildings from there, but it might as well be a thousand miles away. It reminded me of Alcatraz, where the inmates could see San Francisco with no possibility of getting there.

This segregation and poverty did not just happen. The neighborhood's African American population grew substantially beginning in 1967. The city's civil unrest after the death of Martin Luther King Jr. took place in North Minneapolis. It caused white flight among residents and business owners, especially in the Jewish community. At the same time, the tiny African American community in North Minneapolis grew thanks to a new migration, mainly from Chicago, of people seeking a better life and perhaps drawn to the neighborhood by the low housing prices. (Somalis came, too, but they came to South Minneapolis, also a fraught but different story.)

Minnesota was a leader in civil rights through the 1970s in both housing and education desegregation. Developers built enough affordable housing in the suburbs to cause noticeable increases in diversity. In the 1980s, however—perhaps because of an infusion of new African American families into the city—a new set of public officials and developers had a different view, one chronicled by Myron Orfield of the University of Minnesota, a nationally respected expert in the relation of race to place.[1] These officials caused new affordable housing—limited as it was during the Reagan administration—to be located heavily in the inner city. At the same time, public officials and education leaders who had advocated metropolitan school desegregation gave way to others who up to this day continue to stifle constitutionally permissible options for desegregation.

Families that might have moved out of North Minneapolis found it much harder to do so. With a segmented housing market in the area due to segregation, slum landlords took advantage of the low-income clientele, and rents soared.[2] In a world of low-wage jobs and no jobs for too many—people who still encountered discrimination in hiring, especially for those with criminal records—rents ate up paychecks and welfare and disability checks. People using subprime loans bought homes beginning in the late 1990s only to lose them in the wave of foreclosures, and then saw lending dry up. Over 55 percent of mortgage applications in the neighborhood were rejected between 2009 and 2012, the highest rejection rate in the region.[3]

Schools underwent a parallel disaster. The good public schools I attended growing up in Minneapolis in the 1950s disappeared and African American children, stuck in the neighborhood, experienced too much bad teaching. They dropped out in large numbers, often pushed out by repeated suspensions and expulsions. Beginning in the 1990s, charter schools became a good option for some, but they are of uneven quality and mainly segregated as well. The Northside Achievement Zone's business plan says that the neighborhood's schools have the second-worst achievement gap in the country.[4] The police made matters even worse. Over a period from 2012 to 2014 African Americans in the city were nearly nine times as likely as whites to be charged with low-level offenses.[5]

North Minneapolis was a perfect site for one of President

Obama's Promise Neighborhoods. Organizations were doing good work in the neighborhood, but there was no ecosystem pulling them together. Now there is one in the Northside Achievement Zone. It is far from showing the outcomes of a mature and successful entity, but the staff know what they are doing, and parents think it is worth the time to participate.

The heart of the Zone's mission is to improve educational outcomes for its children, but its theory of change is based on families. The organization knows that parent participation is vital and that all of the supports a family might need—housing, jobs, community safety, and more—are equally vital to children's success. There are 5,500 children under eighteen living in the Zone, and about 20,000 live across the Northside. The program has reached its goal of serving 2,500 of them directly, and is now working to reach a larger pool outside the immediate neighborhood.

Antoinette Whiteside and her family are illustrative of the tangible outcomes the Zone has had. The Zone has not reduced poverty in the neighborhood as a whole, but many people like Whiteside have benefited individually. She had three high school and college-age children and significant issues with her work, her housing, and two of her three children. A year connected to NAZ made a big difference.

Whiteside was definitely skeptical at the outset. Andre Dukes, the Zone's family education and engagement director and a pastor and longtime youth worker, was her family coach, a role at the heart of the Zone's method. The initial challenge was that Whiteside's daughter, then a senior in high school, had moved out to live with her boyfriend. Whiteside had had two children by the time she was twenty-one and was deeply worried that her daughter was on the same path. The staff stressed their belief that the daughter was not going in that direction. The key event was convincing Whiteside not to show up at the prom as she had threatened to do, which they told her could have lifelong effects. Staying away from the prom proved to be the righting of the relationship between mother and daughter, and with the Zone's help the daughter went on to community college.

Whiteside's son had problems in high school and had been sent to vocational school, which was not a positive step. The Zone coaches worked with him, and as of the fall of 2016 he was on track to graduate. Whiteside herself had had a series of dead-end jobs and Dukes pushed her to meet with a job coach and get help on rewriting her résumé. Whiteside procrastinated but finally got around to it, and that same day happened to hear from the job coach about a job that was exactly what she wanted. Whiteside was hired with a higher wage, a convenient shift, and people she liked.

Finally, Whiteside had been continually harassed by maintenance workers from the public housing authority coming to her apartment unannounced. Dukes advocated for her and received a letter stating that the housing authority would come only with her permission. Now that the family had stable housing, the daughter and son were doing well, and the mom had a better job, Dukes said, he expected to "graduate" the family from the Zone.

The heart of NAZ is the great care that was taken to create a sophisticated and family-friendly structure. The family coaches are like home visitors, in that they recruit families initially and continue to visit them at home and in the neighborhood. They are also located at partner schools and early childhood centers. Their responsibility is to connect families with outside support and informal counseling. The coaches connect families to various Zone specialists (depending on the need) who have expertise in education, parenting, childcare, housing, jobs, or financial literacy.

The entire approach of the Zone is two-generation, including parent involvement in strategies for children, services directed at parents, classes at the Family Academy, getting hired on as staff, and the emphasis on parents as leaders. The classes at the Academy track the age of the children. First comes College Bound Babies (three and under), then Ready to Succeed (ages four and five), and after that College Bound Scholars (kindergarten through fifth grade), with a class called Family Academy Foundations for all parents.

Achievement Zone staff do not tell parents how to parent, but rather offer a toolbox of strategies. All of the courses are evidence-based, with curricula prepared by experts. They are eight or twelve weeks long, and the Zone offers stipends for participating. No one can take more than two classes at once, but parents can take a class a second time if they think it would be useful.

One dad said he was learning a "different way of parenting, a different way of bringing your kids up, better communication with the kids." Another said this was his third class and added he had learned "new ways to communicate," that "how you say it" is important. He went on, "How I grew up was whupping. I've realized there are other ways." He also reads with his four children and helps with childcare. A third dad, who was the custodial parent, said he had learned "new ways to help his kids." He said he had never had a father himself and then said he had learned to use his words in communicating with his children. He was ecstatic because he had just been hired as a housekeeper at a hotel.

Other parents said things like, "You need to be clear in what you are telling the children to do," "I need to keep in mind what I am teaching the children with the way I talk to them," "Always help each other out," "Do the do. Don't say what not to do. Say what to do," "Make it positive," "Make the consequences fit what happened. Warn first. Be clear. Be consistent," "They do everything I do," "Think about the consequences of hitting," "I got whupped all the time. Everything I learned then, now I've learned something else," and "Praise them. Reinforce the good things."

Sondra Samuels, NAZ's president and CEO, is a longtime civic leader in the city and resident of the Zone. Her husband, Don, was for twelve years the council member for their part of the city. Samuels took me on a windshield tour of the Zone and some of the area around it. In place of Beth El synagogue, where I often went for youth meetings when I was growing up, is an impressive new federally supported community health center. I remembered the stores and small orthodox synagogues on Plymouth Avenue as we drove by, and seeing homes in the middle-class part of the North Side brought back memories of girls my friends and I dated in that neighborhood.

In the Achievement Zone neighborhood, I remembered that low-income neighborhoods in smaller Midwest cities (and in Los Angeles as well) do not look like low-income neighborhoods in Chicago or the East. Houses in the Zone are largely single-family (or were built as single-family). Tree-lined streets contribute to a superficially pastoral appearance. As we drove by, Samuels pointed out places where gang murders, shoot-outs with the police, or home invasions had taken place; many of the parents with whom I spoke also talked about violence. It was unnerving to think of the difficult lives of the parents who are trying to do the right thing for their children in these challenging circumstances.

As she drove, Samuels pointed out the path of a big tornado in 2011. The process of rebuilding, she said, had had an unexpected side effect: positive community-building. She talked about the slumlords, the violence, the sex trafficking, and the campaign to shut down convenience stores that are nothing but a front for drug sellers. We saw new mixed-income housing that was beautifully designed. We also saw an apartment house that houses a hundred undocumented people in terrible conditions; the city does not shut it down because it does not know what to do with the people. And we saw an area where the former NBA basketball player Devean George, a native of Minnesota, is developing affordable housing and a food co-op.

The staff who work with families are all residents of the neighborhood who have struggled themselves or know others who have tough life stories. They all stressed that the "change has to be within the people themselves," as Rebecca Nathan put it. "You have to work on the ground with the people," she added. She is a college graduate who also experienced homelessness, and at thirty-nine, after a series of jobs that were not right for her, found NAZ—and it found her. She started as a coach at one of the anchor schools and when I met her she had become a facilitator, which is part curriculum writer and part teacher at the Family Academy.

The parents I spoke with underscored the value of the help they had received, and they raved about their coaches, who in many cases had come to be dear sisters and friends. Calahena Merrick is a college graduate and has a good job in human resources at the state Department of Transportation. Her two children, eight and four, were her concern. Her coach ("very responsive") found her a mentor for her older child and a scholarship for an early childhood program for the younger one. Merrick had taken two classes at the Family Academy, too. She said she "came from a culture of whupping" and had "learned much more about parenting" from the classes, which were "very interactive" and have given her "tools to become a better parent."

Amy Suchi said she was "apprehensive at first" about the organization but "they really come through." The Zone got three of her children into early childhood programs and helped her with housing, and she took classes at the Family Academy. The Family Academy, she said, "opens you up for different ways to punish." She made a particular point of praising the partners and emphasizing that she would most likely not have found them if the Zone did not exist. She had lived in Birmingham and East Chicago and she said there are more opportunities in Minneapolis but the violence is worse. "I've got to keep my boys alive," she said.

In just a few years NAZ has matured, nurturing and supporting a group of strong partners with knowledge and capacity that would be impossible to create within a single organization. It has already made a tangible difference for hundreds of families. The challenges the Zone faces going forward are formidable, though. There is the challenge of continued funding as its Promise Neighborhood grant ends, especially in the Trump administration. Another issue is how to bring about improvement in the neighborhood schools when they are controlled by the city's school system central office. Other problems are the job situation and the shortage of housing. Getting many more residents hired requires a strategy of advocacy and organizing that the Zone is building but has not perfected.

The city and its power brokers should be ashamed of what they have allowed to happen. Jobs and especially good jobs are a major problem. The police are a big problem. Affordable housing is a significant problem. Mass incarceration is a huge problem. Racism is a continuing and malignant force. The Northside Achievement Zone and all of its partners are operating within a formidable context of structural problems. Nonetheless, the Zone is making an identifiable difference in the lives of many poor people, even if the organization has not yet been able to affect the overall poverty in the neighborhood as a whole.

BROOKLYN: COMMUNITY SOLUTIONS AND THE BROWNSVILLE PARTNERSHIP

Rosanne Haggerty makes no small plans. She has been a leading practitioner and advocate for ending homelessness in our country for a long time. Her work to renovate historic hotels in New York City and make them available to people who had been homeless brought her honors and awards, capped by her selection as a MacArthur Foundation Fellow.

Some years ago, though, she began to feel that housing alone was not enough. Housing needs to be situated in healthy and safe neighborhoods and people need to be able to pay the rent. She began asking what a real end to homelessness would require, and began looking at how homelessness might be prevented in the first place. In 2011, she left her prodigious work at Common Ground that had housed four thousand homeless people in New York City and created Community Solutions to pursue these broader questions. Community Solutions led a successful national campaign for Housing First supportive housing and began to work more holistically on the ground, focusing on the Brownsville neighborhood in Brooklyn, New York, and on Hartford, Connecticut, two neighborhoods of deep poverty where becoming homeless was a common experience.

Brownsville is tough, for sure. In a neighborhood of 88,000 people, 36 percent have incomes below the poverty line and 44 percent of working-age residents are out of the workforce altogether. Eighteen public housing and otherwise subsidized developments make up the largest concentration of such housing in the country. The neighborhood has the highest homicide rate per capita of any precinct in the city, and a total number higher in some years than the entire borough of Manhattan. The homicides are largely a youth activity, with perpetrators as young as twelve and thirteen. An indictment in 2012 brought in forty-three members of two gangs all at one time to be tried for murder, conspiracy, and related crimes. And the victims of the killing include babies.

Haggerty did a reconnaissance and found that many public agencies and nonprofit organizations serve neighborhood people, but in pieces, not as whole people and whole families. She asked herself, "Can we find a way to connect local residents to the agencies and organizations and get them to serve people comprehensively?" Her answer came in the form of the Brownsville Partnership.

The heart of Haggerty's work in Brownsville began as homelessness prevention—catching people before they become homeless. She was looking upstream to find out what was causing all the homelessness that was showing up downstream. Haggerty and her staff started by focusing on preventing evictions. Using tips from various social service agencies and going door-to-door, they would find people on the edge of eviction and coordinate the resources of various partners to help keep the people in their homes. Whether the key to preventing an eviction is a lawyer, public benefits, a health or mental health professional, a job, a charity, or all of the above, Haggerty and the Partnership prevented more than 800 evictions and connected more than 350 residents to job training and jobs, preventing human catastrophes and saving millions of dollars.

With this experience, Haggerty realized that the heart of the problem is a lack of jobs. So she and her staff embarked on a campaign to find five thousand jobs by 2018 for residents of Brownsville as a central element of the Partnership. The 5,000 Jobs Campaign, as it is called, aims to close the gap between employment rates in Brownsville and the citywide average. As of the end of 2016, 1,670 Brownsville residents had been placed in jobs.

The Gregory Jackson Center for Brownsville, a beautiful new site built to be the hub for the Partnership, also houses some of the other organizations that are part of the network. Greg Jackson was a hero in Brownsville, a local boy who played basketball for the New York Knicks. He returned home after his basketball career and devoted himself to the young people of the neighborhood. He was the first director of the Partnership, but a heart attack took him at the age of sixty. The building is a fitting memorial.

At a Monday morning staff meeting, the first item on the agenda was a performance review of the previous week's deliverables. This was followed by a discussion of how time consumed by some of the other projects of the Partnership could be "optimized" so as to have more time for the jobs campaign. The aim was not to stop other efforts, including current health promotion activities to improve nutrition and promote active and safe living, but to do the work more efficiently. Sustaining a youth market selling fresh fruits and vegetables, doing cooking demonstrations in four bodegas and in senior centers and community centers, creating a walking trail, and campaigning to get better crosswalks at intersections—all of these were important and had to be kept. But how? The job campaign entails passing out flyers, expanding outreach, helping people to write résumés, staffing tables, recruiting and organizing volunteers, and working on office norms and protocols. Who should do what? How many hours should be assigned to each task? What else should be considered?

The meeting ended, as did all staff meetings here, by repeating three times: "Where's Hope? Inside Brownsville 11212."

By 2016, the Brownsville Partnership had largely shifted from direct services to more of a switchboard function, serving as a hub for the partner groups. Eviction issues were now addressed by new partners, notably an organization called Legal Hands, located on the ground floor of the Greg Jackson Center. Overall, a more integrated partner communication system is now in place, with core partners meeting monthly and coordinating the various elements of the work. Some partners are place-related, focused on promoting public safety and neighborhood amenities: improving public housing blocks, restoring the century-old Betsy Head Park, and reclaiming Belmont Avenue, the neighborhood's historic market street, which had become blighted and dangerous. Others focus on specific issues, including jobs, food systems, early childhood supports, and a local "youth corps" to involve teens in improving public spaces and solving community challenges.

Haggerty is especially excited about new developments, including more work on the real estate side. Community Solutions, the parent organization of the Partnership, is attempting to acquire several sites that would provide space for partners such as a tech incubator and new mixed-income housing. Another is a collaboration among the community, the police, and mental health professionals toward reducing harms to children exposed to violence and assisting volatile families. A third is improvement of financial services. The most immediate is a free tax preparation site at the Greg Jackson Center, but longer-term steps will include finding a financial service partner to collaborate in improving sources of credit and improving financial literacy.

Particularly good news was the commitment from the City's Department of Small Business Services to bring a branch of Workforce 1, its largest job placement program, to the area. Physical accessibility will have an important positive effect on neighborhood employment outcomes. And Starbucks became an employer partner, too, and is working to provide soft skills and customer training for young people.

All of that said, there are difficulties and challenges. The most serious problem stems from the fact that the 5,000 Jobs Campaign is committed to serving people in deep poverty and chronic poverty—people with barriers that make them unlikely to succeed without extra attention. There is little demand among employers for the tough cases, and getting people the help they need is expensive. To work through the barriers—lack of a GED, low literacy, addiction, mental health issues, ex-offender status, and so on—requires a more costly investment than public funding typically makes available for job training programs. Publicly funded workforce development organizations generally get paid by the placement and often by retention as well. Taking the cream off the top is what the programs that fund those organizations are designed to do. As Haggerty says, "Everyone in the city believes there is a job system that is supposed to be accessible, but those who need help the most find it difficult to actually access it."

The notion of a coordinating and integrating role seems to some funders to be a frill. The effort to connect to the high schools in the area and to the nearby community colleges is coming along at a maddeningly slow pace; the latter cite budget issues. The Brownsville Partnership needs many more employers to hire Brownsville residents and more partners to help with education and training, health and mental health and addiction issues, domestic violence, housing issues, and criminal justice. These are big challenges.

Two of the Partnership's partners deserve special attention. One is a very important building block for the Partnership, and the other a wonderful young man who is not dealing with a large number of people but is especially notable. The first is the Brownsville Community Justice Center, an indispensable institution in Brownsville. The Justice Center is a project of the Center for Court Innovation, which operates innovative initiatives throughout the city. But for ugly local politics, the Justice Center would be a full-fledged community court like Red Hook in Brooklyn, which is nationally acclaimed and has been replicated in five other sites in the city. Red Hook and its clones are multidimensional in what they do; among other things, they have the authority to handle low-level misdemeanors in ways that do not end in jail. Unfortunately, a local Brooklyn councilwoman has blocked a full-fledged community court in Brownsville, at least for the time being.

Even so, the Justice Center is doing a great deal to help young people avoid a criminal record and all of the difficulties that ensue from a conviction, so it is a vital asset for the Brownsville Partnership. Lisa Bernard, the Justice Center's youth and community programs coordinator, grew up in Brownsville and went to Long Island University. The Justice Center started in 2011 and now has nineteen full-time staff, mostly working with young people out in the community. Even without status as a full-fledged community justice center like Red Hook, it does important work. As of the summer of 2015, a person arrested for a low-level misdemeanor is sent to the Kings County Criminal Court. Those from Brownsville who are between eighteen and twenty-four and have no previous felony can then be diverted to a program at the Brownsville Community Justice Center.

The judge sets the parameters—community service, case management, anger management, and so on. When the individual completes the requirements that the judge has stipulated, the judge can dismiss, grant an adjournment in contemplation of dismissal, or continue the diversion with volunteer or internship requirements. Some participants ask to continue their connection with the Justice Center and can, for up to two years. The Justice Center offers paid internship opportunities in fashion, sports journalism, music, and media, among other things; they had 250 interns in the summer of 2015.

In 2015, the Justice Center was allowed to take a step further and start Project Reset, under which a young person with a first-time arrest can skip going to court altogether and be sent instead straight to the Justice Center, an option that culminates in dismissal of the matter on completion of the stipulated conditions. The Justice Center also started the Brownsville Youth Court. where it trains teenagers from fourteen to eighteen years old to be judges and attorneys who handle about a hundred cases a year involving very low-level offenses. Participants complete their sanctions in the Justice Center's offices.

Bernard's staff also works with young people in the community. The staff has pulled in some of the most dangerous young people to help reduce violence in the Belmont Avenue area, which had become a shooting range. Mostly court-involved, the young people cleaned up, painted street murals, painted over graffiti, and set out chairs, tables, and umbrellas for events. Their broader aim is to work toward peace, and to that end the staff do home visits and send out about fifty people every day with purple shirts to walk around the neighborhood to promote the Justice Center. Bernard said they do succeed in bringing young people together, although too often the camaraderie goes away after they disperse.

A major limitation in the Justice Center's work is that it cannot reach young people who are arrested on felony charges. Getting more felonies reduced to misdemeanors, as California was able to do in Proposition 47, and including current felonies in the center's work are major goals on which they and others are working now.

Quardean Lewis-Allen, a lifelong Brownsville resident known

simply as "Q," is the founder/director of Made in Brownsville, a youth-engaged partner project that trains young people in design and tech skills to increase access to design fields. Q wanted to be an architect from the time he was eight years old, and he studied architecture at SUNY Buffalo and the Harvard School of Design. He then worked in Nigeria designing ecofriendly housing, followed by a period studying social housing in Paris with the renowned architect Anne Lacaton. In graduate school he realized that he wanted his work to contribute to economic stability, especially in Brownsville.

During Q's last semester of graduate school he worked for the Brownsville Partnership doing creative work on large contracts for which he had been commissioned. That experience taught him that if he could find the money, he could create a system to employ people as an investment in the community.

That insight ultimately resulted in Made in Brownsville, which challenges attitudes and violence in the neighborhood through peacemaking, community vision making, and empowering young people to make change. In the summer of 2015 the group employed a full-time landscape architect, an advocacy coordinator, two junior graphic designers (who had gone through the Made in Brownsville program), and a summer intern. Q believes that if everything else is failing for someone, an opportunity to work can be the stabilizing aspect of life. His door is open, he has financial resources, and he has space where a young person doesn't have to be on the street.

One of Made in Brownsville's graphic designers at the time was a talented tattoo artist who had taken every studio class the organization offers (product apparel design, 3-D printing, prop design, and urban design). He also had "significant system involvement," as Q put it—he had been on probation for five years and had five years to go. He "tries to do his best to stay on path," Q said. The young man was coming to work when he could, and he knew that Made in Brownsville would not constrain him by a "need for statistics and outcomes."

Q mentioned two projects. One, a contract from the City of New York's Small Business Services, involved a needs assessment for the area around Belmont Avenue to determine why it was vacant and to create a plan for revitalization. He was able to hire five interns for the yearlong project, to conduct surveys, create maps, and do time-lapse videos of the area.

The other was a commission from Marcus Garvey Village, which is made up of low-rise privately owned multifamily row houses with some Section 8 residents. The communal space in the back of the houses had become unsafe, leading the property owners to restrict its use, which meant that residents could not barbeque or sit on their own stoop. Q worked with fifteen young people ages fifteen to twenty, all of whom were under the supervision of and paid by the Brownsville Community Justice Center. They developed a "safety map" of what measures would make it possible for residents to walk safely around the development. They suggested that there be a basketball court, a community center, and entrepreneurial space, and they created a plan and architectural renderings.

Q took the young people, some of whom had never been to Manhattan, to present their plan to Kenneth Frampton, a well-known professor of architecture at Columbia University, and his students. The architect and the young people exchanged questions and comments on the decisions the young people had made about the use of the space. It was a life-expanding experience for them. The center then brought the plans to the developer that manages the village.

Q has a vision. He hopes to have an industrial design and manufacturing facility with a shop, a 3-D printing facility, and innovation space. He would have a for-profit side and a nonprofit side, and it would be both the largest employer in Brownsville in total and the largest nonprofit employer as well.

The Brownsville Partnership and the 5,000 Jobs Campaign are an important developing initiative, grappling with the right issues and building a sensible framework. Their eyes are focused on what needs to happen for the people of Brownsville if they are going to succeed in surmounting barriers including insufficient childcare, educational and skills gaps, mental health issues, addiction, and criminal records. Equally, they know precisely the partners they need to add to the excellent list of existing partners. They are going in the right direction.

NEW HAVEN: THE NEW HAVEN MOMS PARTNERSHIP

Most innovative organizations emerge from the leadership and entrepreneurship of a remarkable individual. Megan Smith, an assistant professor of psychiatry, child study, and public health at Yale's medical school, and the New Haven MOMS Partnership she founded is no exception. Nationally, 20.6 million children live with a parent with mental illness, and the incidence is disproportionate for children in low-income families. Coping with the serious stresses of daily life that come with poverty or near-poverty takes an enormous toll. Those daily struggles do not necessarily spell psychosis for the adults involved, but they make life miserable, and that misery often spills over onto children, with long-term implications. Major depressive disorders are commonplace as well, along with trauma, issues of parenting and executive function, and more.

The heart of the program Smith set up consists of stress management groups. Using multiple strategies of community outreach, Community Mental Health Ambassadors recruit mothers to enroll in the groups, which meet twice a week in two-hour sessions over a period of eight weeks. The staff starts by assessing needs; moms are then assigned to classes depending on their measure on the depression scale. Each class is run by a clinician (there are three of them) and cofacilitated by an ambassador.

The groups focus on cognitive behavioral therapy, using a curriculum developed with the Clifford W. Beers Guidance Clinic, a renowned mental health organization in New Haven that specializes in children and families. The classes are decidedly down to earth, and they provide babysitting. Not only do they offer the mothers techniques to manage stress and take time for themselves, but they also tell the mothers about resources in the community. Participants who live in public housing get $20 Walmart gift cards for each session they attend. Others receive a basic needs bag that, to the extent possible, contains items that the moms ask for.

The MOMS Partnership also offers job readiness classes, but

these are not about résumés and interview training—they are mental health oriented, focusing on the stresses and fears that relate to the job-seeking process. A former participant can come by one of the Partnership's sites any time she is stressed or needs to talk. A clinician is available not only to talk but also to direct her or her child to other services in the community, especially in relation to mental health.

An experimental social networking app connects new mothers around the common experience of childbirth to deal with the isolation and internal depression that often come from that experience. The new moms in the experimental group received cellphones with the apps that promote continuing communication. A control group was given cellphones but without the app. All of the mothers received the cellphones at no cost for eighteen months but then had to begin paying the monthly fees. The initial purpose of the app was to help with postpartum depression, but the further purpose was to promote relationships. Very quickly the moms began exchanging information, advice, tips—really, building new friendships. They went from being isolated with no friends to having a group of friends. Someone would post, "I'm feeling stressed. I'm crying." Other moms immediately offered support—"Call me," "Do you need me to come over?"

Part of the experiment was to send out challenges to the moms—little activities they could do with their baby out in the community, maybe for one mom to meet another at an art museum. When the mom did so she would receive a certain number of tokens, and an accumulation of those could be cashed in for Walmart cards. Counselors would be available to help with emotional issues the moms were having, and for a biweekly screening for depression. The overall purpose was to decrease postpartum depression.

A smoking cessation app, Momma Live Long, is designed to decrease the chances of a mother returning to smoking after delivery. Each mom receives an iPhone 5 and a sensor for carbon monoxide that can be read remotely by a technician. Moms who don't smoke get monetary rewards; if they crave a cigarette, they can press "I crave" and they get a supportive quote and social support from other mothers on the app.

Another research project follows mother and child pairs over time. With saliva samples and blood-spot tests, the clinicians look for biomarkers of stress and morbidity as well as connections between experiences mothers are having and biological reactions. The moms come in and answer forty-five minutes of questions about experiences, and their clinicians do the physical measurements and collect blood spots. They are looking for premature aging due to toxic stress by examining the length of telomeres found on the ends of chromosomes (among other markers). These connections between stress and health are in the literature, but finding them in the lab is new. The hope is that if precursors are identified, things can be done in response to mitigate their effects.

The stress management and job readiness groups are obviously not the solution for every problem people have, but participants in the stress management groups say they are now better parents and better spouses (if they have a spouse), and the smaller number who experience the job readiness sessions also say they made a positive difference. Of course, such problems as the lack of jobs, basic skills, affordable childcare, and affordable housing, as well as issues of mass transit, domestic violence, addiction, and so on, do not go away magically, but those who have participated in the groups say they have benefited.

Kimberly Streater and her six children have surmounted some serious personal trials. Her children's father is a violent person who eventually went to jail for his violence. One of her sons had such anger about what had happened that he became violent at home, so violent that she signed him into the child welfare agency, where he fortunately received the help he needed; now he is in college. Streater worked for a number of years at AT&T, but during her prolonged difficulties she had no job; her only income was food stamps and medical coverage, and occasional help from her mother. She applied for TANF and she was told she had exhausted her eligibility at some earlier time.

Streater found her way to a pilot version of the stress management program. She quickly found that it was not an academic class but rather about learning to deal with her stress and that it was okay to take time for herself. She says that "it helped me to feel more like a mom again, not to feel so guilty, to manage time, and to do things with myself."

Megan Smith not only hired her but did it in a considerate way—starting Streater at ten hours a week, which finally brought some income into the house, then eight months later going to twenty hours a week, and finally full-time. "It helped me and my family tremendously," Streater said. "I never thought I could get a job that could work around my kids' schedule. As a single mom who does everything, there was a point in my life where I didn't even think I could . . . no money, no income coming in, and it's the hardest struggle of your life. You can't pay for everything."

Streater jumped right into the work. "Soon as I hopped out we were out in the community—knocking on doors introducing myself to the moms to see if they would be interested in participating, stopping moms to tell them about the program. We engage with moms where they are—at the playground, on the bus. We just engage with moms everywhere. I like to be in the community. It's a good feeling. We still have moms who are finished with the program and they call us to check in. A lot connect with me because I went through a severe domestic violence situation, and I have no problem sharing that story, and I can really relate."

Cerella Craig is a lifelong New Haven resident and has been a Community Mental Health Ambassador for three years. Her mother is a clinical technician at Yale New Haven Hospital, and Craig says nurturing and caring run in the family. She was fortunate enough to receive a scholarship to a private school, and she completed a bachelor's degree in 2009 at the University of Connecticut in public health with a focus on health and social inequalities. She has been at MOMS almost from the beginning. When she started, the program was much simpler. The work was doing the stress management classes in the public housing complexes with the outreach being largely door-to-door. Craig reports that MOMS has grown greatly with the establishment and expansion of the hubs, the major shift in the scale of the work, more people filtering in, and classes constantly ongoing. "It's a good thing," she continues. "When we initially started we were only in housing, and now we can reach out to more people in different places and have transportation not be as big of a barrier. It was everybody's vision to reach as many people as possible."

Natasha Rivera-LaButhie was one of the first moms to complete the MOMS Partnership needs assessment. She started to work for the Partnership as an ambassador and as of 2015 was the site coordinator for a branch inside a large grocery store. She had experienced rough times, but she had strong family support over the years. As Rivera-LaButhie was growing up, her mother was in and out of the family, and her grandfather, who had a work-related injury, became the stay-at-home de facto parent while her grandmother worked outside the home. Rivera-LaButhie became a certified nursing assistant in her senior year of high school and worked at Yale New Haven Hospital until her grandfather had a liver transplant, when she quit the job to be his caregiver. After he recovered, she had twins and then went back to work. Her husband gets laid off pretty often, she says: "If I don't work, with my husband always being laid off, I know it's on me."

Until Rivera-LaButhie and MOMS found each other, things were up and down. "I was always one emergency away from flat broke but one penny too high to get any assistance," she says. "I've never gotten cash assistance. Food stamps, yes, and Earned Income Tax Credit once, which went toward paying for all the things I was ignoring all year round."

Walk-ins as well as graduates of the class come to the grocery location, and Rivera-LaButhie's challenge is to make sure moms know of the services and actually use them. She draws on her own life experience, her health services experience, and her sales experience with Avon. The moms she sees are at different places in their lives and have different individual problems, and she needs to figure out what kind of help each person needs.

Stacy Downer is also an ambassador. She brings a particular interest in connecting mothers with work and teaching them financial literacy. "I was never taught credit," she says. "I was going through life making choices that diminished me." She was working at a check-cashing place doing tax refunds and started having conversations about the importance of saving and investing. "I would see people with their refunds and people were hood rich," she went on. "They would get their money and a guy would get sneakers here and shoes there, and a month later the $8,000 was gone. They had this lump sum of money but they didn't know what to do with it."

Downer heard about MOMS and said to herself, "Why are we poor? Why can't we get ahead? I just wanted to get to the moms and say, 'Listen, you got to take a good look at how you're living. Just because you don't have money doesn't mean you have to be poor.'"

She had a baby when she was fifteen. She had a lot of cashier jobs and wasted a lot of money buying things she saw on television. At one point, she was a single paycheck from being homeless. Now she co-facilitates both a stress management class and a job readiness class and goes around the city doing outreach. She has also put together a financial curriculum for moms—education on how to manage funds. The day I met her she had been to Job Corps and had breakfast with the students and a men's council, which resulted in ten phone calls from the women in their households.

Rose is a satisfied customer, really satisfied. She was a new mom with two toddlers. She had worked her way up to be a store manager at a Walgreens, but when her husband found a higher-paying job they decided she would stay home rather than have childcare eat up a huge chunk of her salary. She realized she "had a little bit of an issue" when she yelled and screamed at her kids and bruised her hand hitting it on the refrigerator, essentially because the kids were tired and were crying and whining. Her husband came home one day and found her sitting on the kitchen floor in tears. Her hair had started falling out and her food tasted "nasty because there was no love in it." She realized that if she couldn't take care of herself, she couldn't take care of her family.

She found the MOMS Partnership at the Stop & Shop, and she signed up without expecting a lot. She says, "You don't even know what frustrations you're dealing with until you're confronting them. I learned different ways to communicate and how the slightest miscommunication could change your entire thought pattern. These ladies really taught me how to stop, take a breath, reevaluate, and think about how you're dealing with the stress of everyday life, and of your own children. With my kids, I didn't realize that my stress level has an effect on them. The group really helped me put everything in perspective. It made me stop and realize that some of the unhealthy things I was doing to myself really had an effect on my kids and on my marriage. I was taking it out on my husband, who was doing his best to be a good dad and good provider. He would come home, tired, and just wanted to relax, and I'd flip out on him for taking his shoes off in the living room. I was yelling at my kids all the time. My stress was toxic not only to me but to them, and the more stressed I was, the more toxic it became.

"My husband noticed a huge difference after the course ended. Now I start to notice when I get angry or stressed out—I take a five-second deep breath and relax. Now I take ten minutes for myself, because if we can't take ten minutes for ourselves, we can't take care of others around us. They taught us breathing exercises, how to take a walk, imagine all your stress in a little bubble and pass it away. I'm smiling a lot more, less frazzled. My cooking has improved, since I put more love and care into what I'm doing. It taught me to reevaluate the importance of the things I thought were massive.

"I ended up losing about fifteen pounds since I started writing in the journal, doing more breathing, walking, noticing things I didn't notice before. I went from smoking a pack of cigarettes a day to maybe five. And back on my way to quitting again.

"I see the girls from MOMS almost every day. I can talk to them and actually feel like they're listening to me and giving me advice, and I'll bring the girls over and they'll play and laugh. The fact that you have these ladies there is absolutely amazing. If it ever came to it, if I needed someone to talk to, if I was about to have a massive breakdown, I know these ladies could give me someone I could talk to. That personal factor is amazing. This is an amazing program. I really wish I had found it years ago."

Rosalyn Forant, a grandmother, saw an ad for the class, went, and found it "something special." She had not realized how stressed she was. She brought the ideas from the class to her job, and now leads some of the breathing and movement techniques at their morning meeting. She learned about all kinds of stressors, some good and some bad, and gained information about how to manage the bad stressors. She was raising her grandson, and from the class she realized that she was buying his love instead of appreciating him without rewarding him. She could appreciate him by using words and affection. She learned how words hurt: "If you tell him he's next to nothing, it affects him. Words can change behavior. You don't have to say, 'If you do this, I'll get you the sneakers.' You can tell him positive things: 'I know you can do it! I love you!' That's what they taught me," she concluded.

Then the plot thickened. Her grandson's mother, who lived in a poorer side of town, had been shot, and the grandson decided he needed to go back to living with her. She had to deal with that. Her husband (not the boy's maternal grandfather) and the boy began to clash as the boy got closer to adolescence. She saw it as a fight for her love, and she had to deal with both of them. The manual for the stress management group told her to find a quiet place where she could just take deep breaths and lose herself in herself. It told her to take time for herself. She said that now "I pray every morning, in my bathroom, my quiet spot, because of what this group taught me. I never did that because I could never take time for me."

As with many poor people, Forant had a multitude of problems to contend with. Her daughter had been raped two months prior to our conversation. Her husband was about to go through chemo. She said in conclusion, "If it wasn't for this class, I wouldn't even know how to deal with stress. I'm an ex-addict. I've been in recovery for many, many years. I haven't picked up a drink or used drugs through all of it. I would tell the world about MOMS."

SAN LEANDRO, CALIFORNIA: ALAMEDA HEALTH CONSORTIUM

Community health centers were and are one of the most important components of the 1964 legislation we called the War on Poverty. To say that the program is alive and thriving today is an enormous understatement. In 1975 community health centers served a then-impressive 2 million low-income people. They now serve about 28 million people in 1,300 health center organizations with a total of 9,200 delivery sites. The program has had strong bipartisan support almost throughout its existence, perhaps because it saves something like $24 billion in national health care costs every year.

Community health centers are a model of partnerships among organizations, and the Alameda Consortium in Oakland, California, headed by Ralph Silber, is an outstanding example of a partnership. In Alameda County the consortium has eight centers with seventy-five clinic sites, and in 2014 it served 184,000 people.

Silber pulled together a meeting with staff from a group of school-based health centers to show me how partnerships work to help children and families. Three of the eight centers were represented, each of which runs multiple school-based clinics, and Kimi Sakashita, a senior official from the county health department, was there, too. In all, there are 160 school-based clinics in the county. Each has base funding of $113,000 secured from a ballot measure, a share of a tobacco lawsuit settlement, and local taxes, which leverages additional funds by a multiple of five to ten from Medicaid and other sources. Staffing of each school-based clinic is anywhere from three to ten people. All offer medical, dental, and behavioral health services, health education, and youth development. This is a far cry from the school nurse of my childhood.

The approach is holistic and systematic. A student who comes in for first aid is often testing the waters about the clinic's other programs, and a visit for first aid generally leads to broader participation. The Consortium's aim is that all students should graduate healthy and ready for college academically, physically, socially, and emotionally. Thus, each school-based clinic also strives to change policy and atmosphere in the school and help families outside of school. The volume of their work is large. For example, of the eight school sites run by La Clinica de la Raza, just one handles 25,000 individual visits annually.

Trauma that students have experienced constitutes a major theme of the work. The La Clinica school sites, Ruth Campbell said, conduct a universal screen for depression, substance abuse, and trauma on students who come into the clinic and then offer ten-week group sessions and one to three individual sessions with a master's level licensed clinician for parents and children who want to participate. The staff also offers training for the teachers—"Trauma 101," they call it—to help them understand what trauma looks like and how to respond in non-punitive ways. The incidence of trauma is widespread: a study of twenty-three students found that nineteen had experienced at least one traumatic event, and the average was four.

Mizan Alkebulan-Abakah, also at La Clinica, talked about their gender-specific culturally based healing circles. Boys and girls of African descent and girls of Latino descent benefit the most, she added. They start with a daylong retreat that begins with sharing the trauma they have experienced, then identifies the similarities among them, and finally sets standards for how they will interact. This creates a safe space for resolving situations, using a restorative justice model to analyze what harm has been done and how to repair it. As a consequence, disciplinary actions have decreased over the four years they've been doing this work. Suspensions at the Wilson Middle School, one of La Clinica's eight sites, are down from about three hundred annually to about thirty.

Of particular note are the medical-legal partnerships that La Clinica has begun with the East Bay Community Law Center. In this initiative, which is funded by the Kresge Foundation, lawyer Rosa Maria Loya Bay rides circuit among four of the school-based health centers and even makes house calls when needed. When a student comes to the school-based clinic, the health professional asks questions to ascertain if the student or his or her family have legal issues. The health professional might uncover education or juvenile justice issues facing the student, or housing or immigration problems that the family may have.

The clinic staff then refers the matter to Bay.

There is a steady flow of students, often because of behavior in school that results in arrest but stems from trauma. A growing category of referrals is for immigration problems. Bay may represent the youth or their families or refer the case to her colleagues or other attorneys. A student younger than eighteen needs permission from a parent to undertake a full intake and be represented. The organization also runs general legal civil clinics and immigration clinics every two weeks at each school, which parents can attend.

Bay's work encompasses systemic work on policy as well. Her advocacy and that of others have brought about the elimination of the "pay to stay" policy in the county's juvenile system. As is ubiquitous in other California counties and nationally, youth (really, their families) are charged for GPS monitoring and other procedures, which are usually run by a private company, and for room and board itself. If the fees are not paid, the family can be subject to a civil judgment and the garnishment of wages. The clinic's efforts have resulted in the rescission of all of that except for restitution for the crime itself, which remains subject to a civil judgment.[6]

The Native American Health Center represents similar breadth. Alameda County has the largest Native American urban population in the country and the center has nine school-based health centers in the East Bay. They take all comers but have a special focus on Native American youth that introduces them to their cultural traditions. Atziri Rodriguez told me about a Unity Council program for young Latino men and boys at three sites, a sort of rite of passage to manhood that focuses on cultural healing and leadership and prevention of alcohol and drug abuse, teen parenthood, and violence. Nova Wilson described a student health navigator program that promotes informed and healthy decision-making and educates students about available services. The student navigators, who are paid $200 each semester, learn about clinic operations, minor consent law, contraception technology, peer counseling, and stress management. The ultimate benefit is to connect young people to the job market in the health sector.

Preethi Raghu and Delia Zaragoza described the integrated behavioral health services of the school-based clinics associated with Tiburcio Vasquez Health Center. They employ peer advocates who receive small stipends and letters of recommendation.

They always put together a diverse group so they can reach the different demographics in the school. With a focus on social justice, peer advocates along with relevant professional colleagues engage the students in discussions about current issues in the school and the broader community, and conduct contraceptive education for all ninth graders. At any given time sixty peer advocates and 1,500 students participate. The school clinic also runs discussion groups for parents on topics including college admissions, drug and alcohol awareness, and issues with police and the law.

Opened in 2015, the Trust Clinic fills a service gap in downtown Oakland—health and behavioral health care for adults on general (state-financed) assistance who have a disability and/or are homeless with no other health care home. Its clientele is 70 percent male and 70 percent African American. The clinic is aimed at helping people with bad health outcomes, who are very expensive for the system. It offers a high level of support: one case manager for every fifteen to twenty recipients. The population has unique needs and requires concentrated and specific care. Investing in these types of clinics produces better outcomes and costs less by redirecting money to proactive services as opposed to reactive services. People in the target population can just walk in or call to get an appointment. It is meant to be easy access, open-door.

What is particularly special about this clinic is its emphasis on trauma. The behavioral health care services are set up to prioritize helping people with diagnoses of bipolar disorder and schizophrenia who have also experienced trauma. The facility is very user-friendly. Food and coffee, tea, and water are available all day, and people can sit in the lounge as long as they like, reading and playing board games and cards. There is a shower for anyone who wants to use it.

The county housing office is upstairs, and the clinic helps with SSI benefit applications. It can refer clients to any of more than sixty clinic sites in the county that may offer a particular service that is not available at Trust. It also connects people to the county workforce development system when that is indicated.

The location of the Trust Clinic was not an accident. Around the corner is the Harrison Hotel, which, like the hotels in New York City that Rosanne Haggerty rehabilitated, now constitutes supportive housing for eighty people. Homelessness and a disability are required to live there, and residents are required to pay a third of whatever income they have in rent. Typically, residents have issues of substance abuse, mental health, a debilitating chronic physical ailment, or long-term illness. It is not a clean and sober building: people can move in even if they are still struggling with substance abuse.

The overall aim is to create a healthy milieu in the building. The city funds a restorative justice organizer, and the staff has reached out to local colleges with social welfare programs and a college of the arts. One result has been a colorful mural on the wall done by residents depicting a scene of the neighborhood. Interns from the social work schools offer classes about mental illness and how to cope with it, put on socials to get residents to interact with one another, and sponsor lunch-and-learn programs.

Mary Ann, who is a resident, says flatly that the Harrison Hotel is terrible and that she does not want to be there in the first place.[7] She said the place was set up for failure and that the residents shouldn't all be previously homeless. She doesn't trust anyone, which she realizes may stem from being sexually molested as a child.

Dave, another resident, said he was currently depressed because his niece had attempted suicide.[8] Referring to the group of residents as a whole, he said some will ultimately die there, while others will struggle but get up, go out to work, and come back smiling. Still others get jobs and earn enough to move out. Earning enough to move out has gotten harder and harder, though. Oakland is gentrifying and rents rose 40 percent in the previous year, to levels where rents typically take up 70 percent of an individual's earnings.

Dave told me he has bad times but reads spiritual books. He was homeless for nine years and lived under a bridge and had his clothes stolen. Here he has electricity, heat, water, and counselors. All in all, he said he feels blessed to be there. He sees a counselor once a week and he knows that there is someone out there doing worse than he is, so he is grateful.

Dave went on to say that maybe he should stop beating himself up and try to do some things outside. The downside, he said, is that the system puts you back in the very place you tried to escape. If you earn too much, it may affect your housing eligibility and you might not be able to afford the rent outside. You can only go to school part-time and you can't get financial aid (this suggests that he was incarcerated at some point). His last full-time job was in 2005. He said employers have no use for him because he is too old.

But, he said, people are resilient and they do survive. He

remembered running into a woman who had been shot several times and lived on the streets near the county morgue for ten years. She came to the Harrison in 2009, while she was caught up in drugs, but she turned things around and had been living independently in her own apartment for the previous six years. She would say, "I try to walk with the Lord every day," and she would talk about her dad. Dave concluded that people embrace their lives despite all the difficulties. Perhaps it goes without saying, but the Trust Clinic and the Harrison Hotel are keeping people out of prison.

The Spot, an outpost of the Asian Health Services Community Health Center, is a youth center in downtown Oakland, and is co-located with Banteay Srei, a safe space that empowers young Southeast Asian women and their communities, especially women who are at risk of or engaged in the underground sex trade.

Kimberly Chang is a family physician with Asian Health Services who focuses on teens and on human trafficking. She runs a teen clinic on Wednesday evenings and, along with colleagues, began noticing substantial numbers of young women on the streets of Oakland, and the commercial sexual exploitation of which it was a manifestation. One particular incident spurred her to advocate for policy changes: a young woman (a minor) with a high temperature and other serious symptoms came to her teen clinic but refused to go to the hospital because of an earlier health care experience. Chang eventually learned that when the young woman had been previously hospitalized for a miscarriage, the admission process had somehow revealed a bench warrant for her arrest because she had not appeared in court on charges of solicitation. After she left the hospital she was sent to jail—criminalized for being a victim of trafficking.

Chang and others continue the work in Oakland to serve women who are at risk of or engaged in the underground sex trade. At the same time Chang participates in efforts to improve policies in Alameda County and nationally, and works to involve other health centers in caring for trafficking victims. Along with colleagues she founded a network of health care professionals to organize around the issue. They also developed a screening tool for trafficking and undertook to teach health care professionals to recognize its signs and clinical indicators. They are also moving forward with publishing their research on the role of community health centers in efforts to stop human trafficking.

All along, the staff at Banteay Srei has addressed the root problems that lead to trafficking. Nkauj Lab Yang, the program manager, says that lawyers and mental health providers have become involved along with physicians, but what is missing is addressing the social determinacy—the force that is pushing or pulling the young women into sexual exploitation. Many have come from a war-torn background. Their parents were refugees and had to survive. They often worked long hours and were not present in the house while their children were growing up as Americans. Some of the girls and young women looked for love in unhealthy places and found, besides the ersatz love, what seemed to be an easy way to earn a hundred dollars.

Banteay Srei offers a space to empower young women in a positive way, teaching them how to recognize sexual exploitation, how to be in control of their reproductive health, and how to envision positive dreams for the future. In order to address the girls' lack of connection with their elders, the organization developed a cooking and storytelling program, with matriarchal elders who cook for the young women and tell stories about being refugees and resettled. The food and the stories connected the girls and young women to their identity, history, and culture. It produced healing in the elders, too, who had felt disconnected. Banteay Srei continues the relationship through a case management program and sustains its continuity in significant part through its alumnae, who recommend it to others.

Mike Tran talked about The Spot and its programs for boys and young men. The center began by surveying five hundred young people who said they needed jobs and a place where they could get a variety of resources in one place. The Spot, located in Chinatown, was the result. One challenge was gangs, but the broader question was how to find a space for young men to find themselves individually.

The programs at The Spot begin with bonding—getting young men to get past the fear that their vulnerability will be used against them if they open up. The program on violence uses men who had been in gangs and involved in violence but have become positive forces in the community. They include construction workers, a school site security guard, an assistant principal, and a barber. The barber, Mac Sheldon, had been a drug dealer and a pimp. Another program confronts violence by teaching the young men about nutrition and how to cook. The program leader, a man named Haivo who works on a farm and is a gifted cook, conducts a workshop series in which every class comes with a meal and a lesson. He teaches a healthier version of Vietnamese cuisine and concludes the workshops with a community crab feast. The young men, many of whom have never seen a crab let alone eaten one, prepare and cook for the group.

In the East Oakland neighborhood that residents call the killing fields, The Spot is a vitally important effort to reduce the violence.

LOS ANGELES: YOUTH POLICY INSTITUTE

Dixon Slingerland, the Youth Policy Institute's executive director, came to Los Angeles in 1996 after working in Washington, D.C., for David Hackett, who was Robert F. Kennedy's best friend. What he has achieved in twenty-plus years is remarkable.

The Institute, now one of President Obama's Promise Neighborhoods, is all about families and especially young people, and the Enciso family is illustrative of the thousands it has served successfully over the years. Immigrants in the 1990s, the family was doing all right economically, with the father, Julian, working as a mechanic, when they suffered the ultimate tragedy of losing their thirteen-year-old daughter to illness. Her younger brothers, then ten and six, were hit especially hard and lost their motivation to do much of anything positive. The despondency and lack of purpose continued for a long time until their mother, Sylvia, convinced them to participate in programs offered at the Youth Policy Institute.

Julian Jr. enrolled in the Institute's GEAR UP program, a federal initiative that supplements the classroom for middle and high school students. The program turned Julian around and now, in his early twenties, he is in college, works with his father, and has a child. The change in his younger brother, Luis, was even more dramatic. Luis was getting D's when he finished ninth grade, but the next year an Institute staffer noticed his artistic skill and involved him in painting a mural at his school. With that boost in his confidence, Luis became an honor student, was elected to a student body office, and created a tutorial program for ninth graders. He has since graduated from high school and is studying computer science in college.

Noemi Valdez was always smart but had a difficult time when her family left Mexico when she was nine. In high school she was a high achiever but had no idea what was actually possible for her. Youth Policy Institute's College Ambassador and Cash for College programs opened the door to the very best colleges, and she ended up at Harvard on a full scholarship. The first in her family to go to college, Noemi's goal is to one day teach at the college level herself.

Anthony Chavarria spent four years in juvenile hall, dropped out of school, and at twenty was homeless. His life changed by way of an Institute youth center, where he received help to get a GED, create a résumé, and obtain job interviews. As of 2015 he had a job at UCLA Medical Center and was in college studying music technology at night.[9]

More broadly speaking, the standardized test scores of schools affiliated with the Institute have gone up steadily. For instance, in late summer 2016 the STEM Academy of Hollywood achieved a 38 percent improvement in the English Language Arts test, achieving 81 percent proficiency and becoming the sixth-highest-rated school among all high schools in the school district, one with a student body that is 98 percent qualified for free or reduced lunch. Sixteen of the eighteen Promise Neighborhood schools increased their test scores in 2015–16.

The Institute also runs family centers outside schools and offers job training programs, and it has opened three charter schools as well as directly managing two Los Angeles Unified School District schools. The Institute has nearly sixteen hundred employees now, of whom more than three hundred are full-time, and it has a total yearly budget of almost $50 million. It has 137 program sites and annually serves more than 115,000 children and adults.

Slingerland has long pursued a place-based saturation strategy, understanding that success is possible only if education, health, and employment are addressed simultaneously. The heart of the work is child-centered and nested in a family-centered frame.

"There is no silver bullet," he says. "You have to do it all and do it well, do it with partners both in schools and elsewhere, track it well, and measure outcomes for children and families in combined ways. It's enormously complex. We have to spend a lot of time on relationships." He says the Institute runs schools only when necessary; they partner with more than a hundred schools and have at least five staff members in each. They have a full-service community schools coordinator, a family advocate, tutors (before and after school and in the summer), college and career advisers in the high schools, and instructors who come in for specific subjects. They provide resources that the school district cannot provide and help support the priorities of each principal.

Slingerland is also passionate about structural change, always thinking and acting big. In 2015, he and others in the nonprofit world started the wheels turning for a state ballot measure for

2016 that would have brought in $7.7 billion annually for a raft of programs to ameliorate child poverty, including prenatal care, home visiting, childcare, full-day preschool for all low-income three- and four-year-olds, an enhanced state Earned Income Tax Credit, job training, and more. It would have been financed by a 1 percent surcharge on the $3 million–to–$5 million portion of assessed value of all real property in the state. In March 2016, various forces convinced the authors not to pursue the proposition in that year. No doubt they will be back. The plan now is to have it on the ballot in 2018.

MOVING FORWARD

The new criminalization of poverty is a calamity. It entangles and victimizes large numbers of people, and too many of us did not begin to understand what was going on until Ferguson. Sad to say, we currently lack the will to act as a nation to rectify those problems, and the situation deteriorated further with the election of Donald Trump as president. New directions and transformation require a different politics from what we have now, and to make that happen we need a new wave of organizing and a concomitant commitment to act individually and collectively in communities for the common good, outside of what governments do. It is heartening how many people and organizations are fighting back—far more in number than the remarkable people highlighted here. If we are to achieve an improved politics, we have to start from the bottom and work up.

National politics aside, there are some state- and local-level movements that have had some success, or at least raised consciousness. To date the successes have been mainly in blue states, and though there have been a few success stories in red states, the pattern of successes reflects a continuing slide into two countries under one flag that has been going on for decades.

In the quest to address poverty in our wealthy nation, the very public and successful fight to raise the minimum wage gives hope. Fast food workers walked off the job in 190 cities in 2014, and in the same year Walmart workers held the first retail sit-down strikes since the 1930s. In April 2015, low-wage workers in fast food, home health care, hotel housekeeping, airports, and chain retail stores struck in five hundred cities.[10] The people in the street led to success in ballot initiatives and legislation, producing benefits that will double the income of millions of people and do more to reduce poverty than any single legislative action in half a century. Despite Trump's narrow national victory in the fall of 2016, I believe strongly that the effective organizing and the popular support for improving the minimum wage at state and local levels will see continued success.

The movement for decarceration is gathering momentum, too. Its tangible results are visible so far mainly in California and New York City, plus a few smaller states. Nonetheless, whether they find mass incarceration unconscionable or not, people across political lines have come to understand that the amount of money being wasted by our current punitive system is unsupportable. No doubt the Trump Department of Justice will push back, but criminal justice takes place primarily at the state and local level, and we are seeing a growing list of judges, attorneys, elected officials, and academics who are calling for reform, and lawsuits are proliferating across the country. Most important, Proposition 47 in

California has led the way to broad participation among people in general, which is critical to moving ahead at an accelerated pace.

The Black Lives Matter movement, born from the shock of millions of people of all races at the wholly unjustified killings of African American men, is vitally important and in the light of the 2016 election returns is moving more in a direction of focusing its organizing on achieving concrete policy outcomes. This work must continue and grow.

Success in rolling back the criminalization of poverty depends on changing our national attitudes about both poverty and race. The criminalization of poverty is built on the pillars of racism and antipathy to low-income people generally. Organizing for better wages and decarceration has a direct effect on the decriminalization of poverty, and we can hope that these movements will continue to grow, but we need to do better.

The forces now in place will effect changes primarily in responsive states. The glimmers of hope and progress are good, but when it comes to more far-reaching outcomes, there is not enough momentum as yet to attack either poverty or racism frontally. Perhaps a book like this will help expose even more the extent to which criminalization causes and perpetuates poverty and the continuing discrimination against people of color, and therefore add a brick to the structure of the struggle for justice in all senses of the word.

In 2017 we are seeing the awakening of the most important movement of all—the crucial movement to defeat the power that upended the governance of our nation. Adding a brick to the struggle for justice means nothing if the whole edifice is crumbling. Millions of Americans took for granted their right to vote in 2016 and allowed our country to fall into the hands of people who stand only for their own interests and emphatically oppose the justice—economic and racial—for which so many of us have struggled for so long. We will return to that path. But we will do so much sooner if all of us who believe in justice stand up and work with every ounce of energy to turn back what we allowed to happen. That is what we must do. That is the overarching movement we need now.

Afterword

Since this book was first published in the fall of 2017, national awareness of the criminalization of poverty has increased, and more advocates, legislators and other public officials, judicial leaders, and journalists are working on the issues with notable results.

Perhaps the biggest achievements are reforms of money bail going on across the nation. The successes did not come by accident, but rather through synergism among all of the players. Journalists and advocates repeated the story until it finally resonated. Officials running for reelection had to pay attention, and people running for office had to prioritize money bail reform. Lawyers sued and were successful. Legislators began to legislate. Their joint effort produced much more than any one actor could accomplish alone.

The most significant success stories took place in Harris County (Houston), Texas, and the state of California. With an initial court win in Harris County in 2017, people accused of misdemeanors but stuck in jail for lack of bail began to be released in droves and not held on bail at all. Lawyers led the way—including Alec Karakatsanis and the Civil Rights Corps, the Texas Fair Defense Project, the law firm of Susman Godfrey, the federal judge

Lee H. Rosenthal, and then the judges of the Fifth Circuit. Judge Rosenthal's powerful 193-page opinion contains the stunning reports that hearings typically took about one or two minutes per person and set bail for only four people below $500 out of nearly 51,000 cases in which bail was used. These and other facts led to her decision that the county's bail practices were unconstitutional, which, as of July 2018, had prevented almost 13,000 people from being detained on bail in just one year in that one county. Nonetheless, in the fall of 2018, it was still possible that the judges of the Fifth Circuit would take the win away.

However, politics recently entered the game and made a huge difference. The highly publicized election in 2018 of seventeen African American women judges in Harris County opened the door to the crucial final litigation step on reforming money bail. The new judges played an integral role in dropping an appeal to overturn the bail reform injunction, and began an effort toward settlement. This resulted in an agreement in early 2019 to allow 85 percent of misdemeanor defendants to be released on cash-free bail immediately after arrest. The remainder would get a robust hearing promptly at which judges would consider releasing them on the least restrictive non-monetary conditions possible. The political dimension took the matter to the goalposts, and the reform in Houston is now almost in the end zone—which could ultimately mean pretrial release for almost 20,000 arrestees a year who would have been detained just two years ago.

The fight in California has become more complicated and the story is still unfolding. A habeas petition filed by Civil Rights Corps and the San Francisco public defender in the state courts started the saga with a ruling that the state's entire money bail system was violating the Constitution.

This time, however, politics made the road rockier. The legislature hurriedly enacted a statute, but the product showed the mischief of the politically connected judges and district attorneys. Although the new law eliminated cash payments as a condition of release, infuriating the for-profit bail bond industry, it also gave judges considerable discretion to detain far larger numbers of arrestees, and it allowed prosecutors to delay any bail hearing at all for as much as two weeks in the large number of cases that the new law made eligible for no-bond detention. Civil liberties advocates are fearful the degree of discretion will actually lead to even higher numbers of pretrial detentions of minority and low-income defendants than before. The ACLU denounced the bill as a sellout and opposed it. Nonetheless, Governor Jerry Brown signed it in August 2018.

Almost immediately, the bail bondsmen and insurance companies that sell the bonds spearheaded an effort to place a referendum on the 2020 ballot to get the statute repealed. They raised $3 million from bail agency businesses and private equity firms that own bail-bond companies, the biggest of which was an Oregon entity called Endeavour Capital, which gave almost $800,000. The initiative, named Californians Against the Reckless Bail Scheme, obtained almost 600,000 signatures, which put it on the ballot. This is a big business, with 3,200 bondsmen and 7,000 employees altogether in the state.

The momentum is still good, but the California story illustrates that the opposition does not go away, and even a legal victory does not ensure that the system will not reproduce the same injustice in a different form.

Fines and fees and related work are different from money bail reform. Fines and fees issues are more scattered across the states and require a different strategy. State legislation and court rules can definitely accomplish things on a wholesale level, but much of the work involves individual localities, especially in rural areas.

The Fines and Fees Justice Center is a welcome arrival in this arena. Its founders, Lisa Foster and Joanna Weiss, are nationally respected experts. They are working intensely in two states—Florida and New York—and serve as a national clearinghouse to disseminate information and a national reform hub to help strategize more effectively. This is an important asset whose impact is already visible.

A local gem is San Francisco's Financial Justice Project. Started in the office of the city's treasurer, it identified unacceptable policies such as charging for probation services, and worked with the court and legal services advocates to develop ability-to-pay guidelines for people owing court debt. The project's work has been emulated quite widely. For example, Chicago has launched its Fines, Fees & Access Collaborative, which aims to unite elected officials, academics, advocates, and city departments to make reform recommendations on fines, fees, and court collections.

Missouri is an example of both accomplishment and how much more there is still to do. On the plus side, the 2016 ArchCity Defenders and Civil Rights Corps lawsuit against the city of Jennings won a settlement of $4.75 million for people who had been jailed in debtors' prison and has become a national exemplar as the city's jails sit mostly empty now. On the other hand, the city of Ferguson is only just going to trial for the damage its debtors' prison caused for tens of thousands of people. The facts had been unearthed five years earlier, but Ferguson stonewalled until recently.

In late 2018, the Missouri legislature took steps to lower fines and fees, and the chief justice of the state supreme court created a Municipal Court Work Group that wrote a 140-page report recommending a multiplicity of improved procedures. Eric Schmitt, the new attorney general who was appointed in early 2019, immediately spoke out against debtors' prisons. Tony Messenger of the *St. Louis Post-Dispatch* is a ball of fire, with thirty articles on debtors' prisons and related subjects between the fall of 2018 and early 2019. Matthew Mueller at the state public defender's office is another powerful force. He works full-time on fines and fees all over the state; as of early 2019 he had six cases pending in all three of Missouri's appellate courts on behalf of indigent clients who were wrongly charged on jail fines and related debt fees.

This is good progress and change has occurred, but it's hard. In rural Missouri, issuing exorbitant fines and fees is only a fraction of the problem. "Pay to stay," or charging for room and board, is rampant, as is for-profit probation and more. A pending case illustrates this. George Richey in Warrensburg, Missouri, has a monthly income of $600 from disability payments. He was first assessed $116.50 in court costs and then was hit with $3,165 in "court costs" for room and board to cover his ninety-day sentence for being unable to pay his initial debt. When he fell behind again, he was hit for $2,275 more. Calling the debt "court costs" instead of civil debts, the judge treats them as criminal and demands monthly hearings in person for "payment review dates."

Mr. Richey lives in the next county and has no driver's license. Most of the time he can't get to court and he can't pay on his payments anyway, so the judge adds more to the "court costs." It can go on and on.

Representing Mr. Richey, Matt Mueller is arguing that the debt should be civil and not subject to the monthly hearings and ever-mounting "court costs." Making things worse, the judge unconstitutionally also fails to consider Mr. Richey's ability to pay. The story repeats in rural counties all over the state, and they continue even though prosecutors and judges in urban and suburban counties have condemned the practices.

In contrast to the difficulty of smoking out issues in rural places, the issue of driver's license suspensions has become more visible nationally. California, the worst offender in this realm, had four million licenses suspended at one point but now has enacted a series of laws that have largely ended license suspensions for unpaid court debt and for juvenile court fees. Litigation in Tennessee, filed on behalf of over 250,000 low-income people who had licenses suspended for failure to pay court debt from traffic tickets, resulted in a preliminary injunction in the fall of 2018 that allows all of those people to apply for reinstatement. Federal judge Aleta Trauger wrote a 116-page opinion, bound to become a national model, finding that the statute was unconstitutional on grounds of equal protection and due process. Following that suit, the Southern Poverty Law Center filed suit against Alabama for license suspensions.

Virginia is also fighting against license suspensions for unpaid fines and fees. Charlottesville commonwealth's attorney announced he will stop prosecuting individuals for driving on a license suspended for unpaid court fines. A federal judge in Virginia issued a preliminary injunction ordering the DMV to reinstate three plaintiffs' driver's licenses that were suspended for failure to pay fines and fees. And the governor announced he would seek to repeal a statute mandating license suspensions for unpaid fines and fees, although he was rebuffed in the legislature in 2019.

Likewise, the newly elected district attorney of Boston, Rachael Rollins, has implemented a campaign promise to stop prosecuting individuals driving on a suspended license due to unpaid fines and fees. Mississippi, Maine, and the District of Columbia have all taken steps to reduce suspensions and, in some instances, have reinstated licenses. And in Montana, Florida, and Arkansas, the ACLU is preparing new bills to end suspension of licenses for court debt.

With respect to the practice of penalizing low-income women who call for help in response to domestic violence, Maplewood, a St. Louis suburb, reached a settlement with Rosetta Watson, a survivor of domestic violence who was evicted for calling 911 just twice and then banished from the city for six months according to the terms of the local ordinance. The settlement included overhauling the stunning ordinance as well. Sandra Park of the ACLU not only represented Watson, but with others is making progress nationally on this disturbing problem. Iowa, Indiana, Illinois, Minnesota, Nevada, Pennsylvania, and California now have laws protecting residents from being penalized for calling 911 and preventing the police from ordering landlords to evict the tenants.

The past two years have also seen major developments in three related areas. In a phenomenal success for democracy, 2018 brought a successful ballot initiative in Florida to restore voting rights for well over a million people who have returned from prison. Notable, too, is the First Step Act in the federal system, which reduced some sentences and promises to improve prison conditions, which in turn has induced new reform legislation in a number of states. And third, the nation saw not just Rollins in Boston, but a wave of newly elected local prosecutors promising to reduce jail populations, end cash bail, and move forward on other issues disproportionately affecting the poor and people of color. Since Larry Krasner's highly publicized election as district attorney in Philadelphia in 2017, other reform candidates became DAs in Dallas, Chicago, Kansas City, and many more.

While most of these developments represent positive outcomes, progress is not always linear. The opposition hasn't disappeared and some who have a victory find themselves coping with new attacks. And because it's a big country, even important gains look spotty on a national map.

So, even with all the added people power, much, much more is still needed. We need lawyers in every relevant role. The superb nonprofit full-time lawyers need more funding and additional partner organizations. Public defenders, who make a vital contribution, are understaffed and in some locales are contract lawyers in thrall to a local judge. Pro bono lawyers, doing great work on big cases, need to ramp up further. Legislators, chief justices, and journalists, both national and local, are already engaged in reform work, and need to enlist many more colleagues. And, of particular interest to me, we need to recruit law students who, among other tasks, would help identify the unjust judges, prosecutors, and sheriffs and hold them accountable for their behavior, working to get them out of office if they don't improve.

Most challenging, with all of the enlarged personnel and the wider understanding of the issues, there is still nothing like a national movement—something with the dimensions of the fight against mass incarceration, which is instructive and inspiring. We need the same public awareness and political activism in the struggle against the criminalization of poverty. We should feel good about what has been achieved in recent years, but there is a long way to go before this nation can truly say that it is not a crime to be poor.

Acknowledgments

This book would not exist without Diane Wachtell and all of the great people at The New Press.

That one was easy. After that it gets complicated because so many helped in so many ways. There are the friends who read the draft at various stages, the people who have been treated unfairly and the people who have been helped, the lawyers, judges, public officials, journalists, organizers, and others who are fighting back, the many who help families and build stronger communities, the students at various law schools who took notes as I visited around the country, and the wonderful research assistants at Georgetown Law Center. Thank you to all. And a special thank-you to Dean Bill Treanor for the sabbatical year that made an enormous difference.

The readers: David Birenbaum, Jeff Shesol, Allegra McLeod, Mark Angney, Mark Greenberg, David Super, Jonah Edelman, and Betsy Kuhn.

The lawyers and other advocates, the public officials and judges, the journalists, and the resistance: Sharon Dietrich, Danny Engelberg, Adrienne Watt, Alec Karakatsanis, Thomas Harvey, Jonathan Smith, Sarah Geraghty, Sam Brooke, Jack Muse, Rebecca Vallas, Luke Shaefer, Kate Walz, Annie Lee, Ji Seon Song,

Jon Wool, Judge Steven Teske, Jill Webb, Mike Herald, Senator Robert Hertzberg, Los Angeles Supervisor Mark Ridley-Thomas, Sandra Park, Nusrat Choudhury, Myron Orfield Jr., Lauren-Brooke Eisen, Marc Schindler, Tim Murray, Deborah Fowler, Elisa Della-Piana, Susannah Karlsson, Steve Gray, Nina Revoyr, Rosa Bay, Vicki Turetsky, Chris Albin-Lackey, Rachel Cicurel, Teresa Nelson, Maria Foscarinis, Hallie Ryan, Vanessa Hernandez, Mike Brickner, Joe Shapiro, Kate Rabb, Hannah Benton, Kate Weisburd, Carrie Graf, Maren Hulden, Miriam Aukerman, Rick McHugh, John Philo, David Socolow, Andrea Marsh, Jenny Egan, and Mary Bauer.

The community and family builders: Steven Dow, Rosanne Haggerty, Sondra Samuels, Dixon Slingerland, Megan Smith, Nancy Aardema, Ralph Silber, and all of their colleagues.

My terrific research assistants: Ben Shaw, Joshua Gillerman, Olivia Jerjian, Lauren Kelleher, Austin Davidson, Madeline Meth, Naomi Iser, Greg Carter, Julianne Cozzetto, Rebecca Williams, and Rachel Smith.

The great law school students who took superb notes at my field visits (with profuse thanks to Caroline Fredrickson and her colleagues at the American Constitution Society): Emily Lekahal, Matthew Roloff, Priscilla Ankrah, Ranit Patel, Anne Easton, Kate Azevedo, Julia Waterhous, Misha Guttenberg, Olevia Boykin, Lindsey Croasdale, Tony Wadas, Sonia Housany, Mark Hartman, and Cybil Rajan.

Special thanks to David Udell and Melissa Ludtke for keeping an eye out for new material, and to Ellika and especially Zoe Edelman, who never failed to ask how the book was coming along.

And most of all, thank you to the people who told me how they had been victimized by high fines and fees and bail they could not afford, the lawyers who helped, and the organizations I describe in the last part of the book.

Notes

Introduction

1. Alicia Bannon, Mitali Nagrecha, and Rebekah Diller, "Criminal Justice Debt: A Barrier to Reentry," Brennan Center for Justice, 2010, 2, 28.

2. Alexes Harris, *A Pound of Flesh* (New York: Russell Sage Foundation, 2016), 51.

3. See United States Department of Justice, Civil Rights Division, *The Ferguson Report: Department of Justice Investigation of the Ferguson Police Department* (New York: The New Press, 2015).

4. Douglas Evans, "The Debt Penalty: Exposing the Financial Barrier to Offender Reintegration," Research and Evaluation Center, John Jay College of Criminal Justice, August 2014, 7; Council of Economic Advisors, "Fines, Fees and Bail," Office of the President, December 2015.

5. See Ruth Marcus, "Policing by Fleecing, in Ferguson and Beyond," *Washington Post*, March 6, 2015.

1: Ferguson Is Everywhere

1. See Mathilde Laisne, Jon Wool, and Christian Henrichson, "Past Due: Examining the Costs and Consequences of Charging for Justice in New Orleans," Vera Institute of Justice, New York, 2017.

2. Jessica Feierman, Naomi Goldstein, Emily Haney-Caron, and Jaymes Fairfax Columbo, "Debtors' Prisons for Kids? The High Cost of Fees in the Juvenile Justice System," Juvenile Law Center,

Philadelphia, 2016; Eli Hager, "Your Child Is Jailed. Then Comes the Bill," *Washington Post*, March 3, 2016.

3. *Bearden v. Georgia*, 461 U.S. 660, 668 (1983).

4. Alicia Bannon, Mitali Nagrecha, and Rebekah Diller, "Criminal Justice Debt: A Barrier to Reentry," Brennan Center for Justice, 2010, 21.

5. Ibid., 22.

6. *Fuller v. Oregon*, 417 U.S. 40 (1974).

7. "State-by-State Court Fees," part of the special series "Guilty and Charged," National Public Radio, May 19, 2014.

8. Bannon et al., *Criminal Justice Debt*, 7.

9. Ibid., 12.

10. John Pfaff, "A Mockery of Justice for the Poor," *New York Times*, April 30, 2016.

11. United States Department of Justice, Civil Rights Division, *The Ferguson Report: Department of Justice Investigation of the Ferguson Police Department* (New York: The New Press, 2015), 19, 84.

12. Joseph Shapiro, "As Court Fees Rise, Poor Are Paying the Price," *All Things Considered*, National Public Radio, May 19, 2014.

13. Arianna Pickard, "Jail's Revolving Door: Thousands Arrested Every Year for Failure to Pay Court Costs," *Tulsa World*, September 28, 2015.

14. Ibid.

15. Ibid.

16. Barbara Hoberock, "Fees to Increase Friday as New Oklahoma Laws Take Effect," *Tulsa World*, July 1, 2016.

17. Casey Smith and Cary Aspinwall, "Jailed for Failure to Pay," *Tulsa World*, November 3, 2013.

18. See Douglas A. Blackmon, *Slavery by Another Name* (New York: Anchor Books, 2008), 1–2. Continuing into the twentieth century, men in the South (mainly African American) were convicted of "vagrancy," sentenced to hard labor, and turned over to a private company such as U.S. Steel, which subjected the convicted men to unimaginably horrible conditions.

19. Chris Albin-Lackey, "Profiting from Probation: America's Offender-Funded Probation Industry," Human Rights Watch, New York, 2014, 33.

20. Ibid., 3.

21. Karen Dolan with Jodi L. Carr, "The Poor Get Prison: The Alarming Spread of the Criminalization of Poverty," Institute for Policy Studies, Washington, DC, 2014, 17.

22. Shapiro, "As Court Fees Rise."

23. Albin-Lackey, "Profiting from Probation," 33.

24. Ibid., 36.

25. Bannon et al., *Criminal Justice Debt*, 1, 7.

26. Ibid., 7.

27. Ibid., 2.

28. See Laisne, Wool, and Henrichson, "Past Due."

29. Class Action Complaint, *Cain v. City of New Orleans*, No. 15-4479 (E.D. La. Sept. 17, 2015).

30. Joseph Shapiro, "How Driver's License Suspensions Unfairly Target the Poor," *Morning Edition*, National Public Radio, January 5, 2015.

31. Marc Levin and Joanna Weiss, "Suspending Driver's Licenses Creates a Vicious Cycle," *USA Today*, February 21, 2017; Amanda Whiting, "75 Percent of All Suspended Drivers in Virginia Are in a Debtor's Prison Scenario," *Washingtonian*, July 21, 2016.

32. Western Center on Law and Poverty, Lawyers Committee for Civil Rights of the San Francisco Bay Area, East Bay Community Law Center, A New Way of Life, and Legal Services for Prisoners with Children, "Not Just a Ferguson Problem: How Traffic Courts Drive Inequality in California," 2015, 4.

33. Rebekah Diller, "The Hidden Costs of Florida's Criminal Justice Fees," Brennan Center for Justice, 2010, 1.

34. Fla. Stat. § 322.34 (2011).

35. Mike Riggs, interviewed by Michel Martin, "Reconsidering Driver's License Suspensions as Punishment," *Tell Me More*, National Public Radio, March 10, 2014.

36. Bannon et al, *Criminal Justice Debt: A Barrier to Reentry*.

37. Ibid.

38. Joseph Shapiro, "Can't Pay Your Fines? Your License Could be Taken," *National Public Radio*, December 29, 2014, http://www.npr.org/2014/12/29/372691960/cant-pay-your-fines-your-license-could-be-taken. In January 2017, Alec Karakatsanis of Civil Rights Corps and others sued the state, contending that the licensing suspensions of people unable to afford the underlying fines were unconstitutional. Class Action Complaint, No. 3:2017cv00005 (M.D. Tenn., Jan. 4, 2017).

39. Shapiro, "As Court Fees Rise"; Council of Economic Advisors, "Fines, Fees and Bail," Office of the President, December 2015, 3.

40. Shapiro, "As Court Fees Rise."

41. Douglas Evans, "The Debt Penalty: Exposing the Financial Barrier to Offender Reintegration," Research and Evaluation Center, John Jay College of Criminal Justice, August 2014, 3.

42. American Civil Liberties Union, "In for a Penny: The Rise of America's New Debtors' Prisons," October 2010, 30.

43. Feierman et al., "Debtors' Prison for Kids?"

44. Amy Silverstein, "Dallas Bills a Dead Jail Inmate for an Ambulance Ride," *Dallas Observer*, April 27, 2015.

45. Shaila Dewan and Andrew W. Lehren, "After a Crime, the Price of a Second Chance," *New York Times*, December 12, 2016; Shaila Dewan and Andrew W. Lehren, "Alabama Prosecutor Sets the Penalties and Fills the Coffers," *New York Times*, December 13, 2016.

46. Shapiro, "As Court Fees Rise"; Council of Economic Advisors, "Fines, Fees, and Bail," 10.

47. Steve Mills and Todd Lighty, "State Sues Prisoners to Pay for Their Room, Board," *Chicago Tribune*, November 30, 2015.

2: Fighting Back

1. United States Department of Justice, Civil Rights Division, *The Ferguson Report: Department of Justice Investigation of the Ferguson Police Department* (New York: The New Press, 2015).

2. Class Action Complaint, *Fant et al. v. City of Ferguson*, Case No. 4:15-cv-253 (E.D. Mo. Feb. 8, 2015); Class Action Complaint, *Jenkins et al. v. City of Jennings*, Case No. 4:15-cv-00252, (E.D. Mo. Feb. 8, 2015).

3. Campbell Robertson, "Missouri City to Pay $4.7 Million to Settle Suit over Jailing Practices," *New York Times*, July 16, 2016.

4. Consent Decree, *United States v. The City of Ferguson*, Doc. No. 12-2, Case No. 4.16-cv000180-CDP (E.D. Mo. Mar. 17, 2016). The consent decree was approved by Judge Catherine Perry on April 19, 2016.

5. Clyde Woods, "Les Misérables of New Orleans: Trap Economics and the Asset Stripping Blues, Part 1," *American Quarterly* 61, no. 3 (September 2009): 790.

6. Meghan Ragany, Rose Wilson, and Jon Wool, "Racial Disparity in Marijuana Policing in New Orleans," Vera Institute for Justice, New York, 2016, 6.

7. "A Waiting List for Justice in New Orleans" (editorial), *New York Times*, January 22, 2016.

8. John Simerman, "Orleans Criminal Court Judges Turn Over Documents Detailing Lavish Life-Insurance Benefits," *Times-Picayune*, April 17, 2013.

9. Micah West, "Financial Conflicts of Interest and the Funding of New Orleans's Criminal Courts," *California Law Review* 101, no. 2 (April, 2013): 521–52.

10. Campbell Robertson, "Suit Alleges 'Scheme' in Criminal Costs Borne by New Orleans's Poor," *New York Times*, September 17, 2015.

11. Ibid.

12. Class Action Complaint, *Cain v. City of New Orleans*, No. 15-4479 (E.D. La. Sept. 17, 2015).

13. Alexes Harris, Heather Evans, and Katherine Beckett, "Drawing Blood from Stones: Legal Debt and Social Inequality in the Contemporary United States," *American Journal of Sociology* 115, no. 6 (May 2010): 1753–99.

14. American Civil Liberties Union of Washington and Columbia

Legal Services, "Modern Day Debtors' Prisons: The Ways Court-Imposed Debts Punish People for Being Poor," February 2014.

15. Ibid., 6.

16. Ibid., 7.

17. Complaint for Declaratory and Injunctive Relief, *Fuentes v. Benton County*, 15-2-02976-1 (Wa. Super. Ct. Oct. 7, 2015).

18. Texas, a major offender in the world of high fines and fees, is beginning to wake up. Chief Justice Nathan Hecht pointed out in his 2017 State of the Judiciary address that in the prior year 640,000 defendants were jailed for fines on misdemeanors that do not allow incarceration. This was the worst aspect of a revenue-amassing machine that totaled seven million such cases that resulted in collections of more than $1 billion. State Representative James White, chair of the House Corrections Committee, added, "We've got constitutional issues, cost issues, common sense issues and compassion issues here." Sam DeGrave, "Texas Supreme Court Justice, House Corrections Chair Want to End 'Unconstitutional' Practice of Debtors' Prison," Texas Observer, February 23, 2017. See Texas Appleseed and Texas Fair Defense Project, "Pay or Stay: The High Cost of Jailing Texans for Fines and Fees," February 2017.

19. Chris Albin-Lackey, "Profiting from Probation: America's 'Offender-Funded' Probation Industry," Human Rights Watch, 2014, 18–19.

20. Ibid., 44.

21. Ibid., 17.

22. Michelle Willard, "Probation Violations Help Fill County Jail," *Murfreesboro Daily News Journal*, October 2, 2015.

23. Ibid.

24. Class Action Complaint, *Rodriguez v. Providence Community Corrections, Inc.*, No. 3.15-cv-01048 (M.D. Tenn., Oct. 1, 2015), 18.

25. Complaint, *Thompson v. Dekalb Cty.*, No. 1:15-cv-00280 (N.D. Ga. Jan. 29, 2015).

26. Settlement Agreement, *Thompson v. Dekalb Cty.*, No. 1:15-cv-00280 (N.D. Ga. March 18, 2015).

27. Class Action Complaint, *Edwards v. Red Hills Cmty. Prob.*, 1:15-cv-67 (M.D. Ga. April 10, 2015).

28. Debra Cassens Weiss, "Court and Probation Company Are Running 'Extortion Racket,' Alabama Judge Says," *ABA Journal*, July 16, 2016.

29. Sarah Stillman, "Get Out of Jail, Inc.," *New Yorker*, June 23, 2014.

30. Amended Complaint, *Cleveland v. City of Montgomery*, 2:13-cv-00732 (M.D. Ala. Nov. 12, 2013).

31. Class Action, *Mitchell v. City of Montgomery*, 2:14-cv-186 (M.D. Ala. May 23, 2014).

32. Lee Romney, "A Frenzied Start for State's Traffic Ticket Amnesty Program," *Los Angeles Times*, November 14, 2015.

33. Marcus Nieto, "Who Pays for Penalty Assessment Programs in California," California Research Bureau, February 2006.

34. Ibid., 6, 9–10.

35. Western Center on Law and Poverty, Lawyers Committee for Civil Rights of the San Francisco Bay Area, East Bay Community Law Center, A New Way of Life, and Legal Services for Prisoners with Children, "Not Just a Ferguson Problem: How Traffic Courts Drive Inequality in California," 2015, 6.

36. Caroline Chen, "California Drives Up Traffic Fines with Fees Earmarked for Projects," Center for Investigative Reporting, September 25, 2013.

37. Darwin BondGraham and Ali Winston, "OPD Still Appears to Be Targeting Blacks," *East Bay Express*, February 4, 2015.

38. Western Center on Law and Poverty et al., "Not Just a Ferguson Problem," 6, 12.

39. Ibid., 6–7.

40. Ibid., 16.

41. Ibid., 17.

42. Daniel Denvir, "How a Dragnet Snagged Philly's Poor," *Philadelphia City Paper*, October 16, 2014.

43. John Gibeaut, "Get Out of Jail—but Not Free: Courts Scramble to Fill Their Coffers by Billing Ex-Cons," *ABA Journal*, July 1, 2012.

44. Suzanne Young, "A Successful Campaign in Philadelphia to Eliminate Unsubstantiated Criminal Debt," *Talk Poverty* (blog), September 11, 2015.

45. Denvir, "How a Dragnet Snagged Philly's Poor."

46. Gibeaut, "Get Out of Jail."

3: Money Bail

1. Jennifer Gonnerman, "Before the Law," *New Yorker*, October 6, 2014.

2. Ram Subramanian et al., "Incarceration's Front Door: The Misuse of Jails in America," Vera Institute for Justice, 2015, 7.

3. Ibid., 4–5; "Bail Fail: Why the U.S. Should End the Practice of Using Money for Bail," Justice Policy Institute, 2012, 1, 15.

4. "For Better or for Profit: How the Bail Bonding Industry Stands in the Way of Fair and Effective Pretrial Justice," Justice Policy Institute, 2012, 46.

5. Lorelei Laird, "Court Systems Rethink the Use of Financial Bail, Which Some Say Penalizes the Poor," *ABA Journal*, April 1, 2016.

6. Nick Pinto, "The Bail Trap," *New York Times Magazine*, August 16, 2015, 41.

7. Christopher Mathias, "1,500 Rikers Island Inmates Have Been Behind Bars More than a Year Without Being Convicted," *Huffington Post*, April 14, 2015.

8. "What Is Happening at Rikers Island?" (editorial), *New York Times*, December 15, 2014.

9. Pinto, "The Bail Trap," 45.

10. Ibid., 42.

11. Margaret Talbot, "The Case Against Cash Bail," *New Yorker*, August 25, 2015.

12. Ibid.

13. Ibid.

14. Laird, "Court Systems Rethink"; Risk Assessment, Arnold Foundation, "LJAF Research Summary, Developing a National Model for Pretrial," 2013.

15. Shaila Dewan, "Judges Replacing Conjecture with Formula for Bail," *New York Times*, June 28, 2015; Laird, "Court Systems Rethink."

16. Lisa W. Foderaro, "Mercy vs. Risk as New Jersey Cuts Cash Bail," *New York Times*, February 7, 2017.

17. Ibid.

18. Laird, "Court Systems Rethink."

19. Ovetta Wiggins and Ann E. Marimow, "Maryland High Court Revamps State's Cash-Based Bail System," *Washington Post*, February 8, 2017.

20. Robin Steinberg and David Feige, "The Problem with NYC's Bail Reform," Marshall Project, July 9, 2015.

21. "Ending the American Money Bail System," Equal Justice Under Law, http://equaljusticeunderlaw.org/wp/current-cases/ending-theamerican-money-bail-system.

22. Jonah Owen Lamb, "SF Won't Defend 'Unconstitutional' Bail System in Lawsuit," *San Francisco Examiner*, November 1, 2016.

23. Michael Hardy, "In Fight over Bail's Fairness, a Sheriff Joins the Critics," *New York Times*, March 10, 2017.

24. Eli Rosenberg, "Judge in Houston Strikes Down County's Bail System, Saying It's Unfair to the Poor, *New York Times*, April 30, 2017.

4: The Criminalization of Mental Illness

1. Julie K. Brown, "Behind Bars, a Brutal and Unexplained Death," *Miami Herald*, May 17, 2014; Julie K. Brown, "Prisoner: I Cleaned Up Skin of Inmate Scalded in Shower; Human-Rights Groups Call for Federal Intervention," *Miami Herald*, June 25, 2014; also see reporting by Brown in *Miami Herald*, May 17 and June 25, 2014, and May 28, 2015.

2. Eyal Press, "Madness," *New Yorker*, May 2, 2016.

3. Brown, "Behind Bars."

4. Judith Weissman et al., "Serious Psychological Distress Among Adults: United States, 2009-2013," Centers for Disease Control and Prevention, 2015, 2–3.

5. Brandon Vick, Kristine Jones, and Sophie Mitra, "Poverty and Severe Psychiatric Disorder in the US: Evidence from the Medical Expenditure Panel Survey," *Journal of Mental Health Policy and Economics* 15, no. 2 (2012): 83–96.

6. Robin E. McGee and Nancy J. Thompson, "Peer Reviewed: Unemployment and Depression Among Emerging Adults in 12 States, Behavior Risk Factor Surveillance System, 2010," *Preventing Chronic Disease* 12 (2015): 3.

7. KiDeuk Kim, Miriam Becker-Cohen, and Maria Serakos, "The Processing and Treatment of Mentally Ill Individuals in the Criminal System," Urban Institute, 2015, 12.

8. Dean Aufderheide, "Mental Illness in America's Jails and Prisons Toward a Public Safety/Public Health Model," *Health Affairs Blog*, April 1, 2014.

9. Jenny Gold, "Report: Jails House 10 Times More Mentally Ill Than State Hospitals," *Kaiser Health News*, April 8, 2014.

10. E. Fuller Torrey et al., "The Treatment of Persons with Mental Illness in Prisons and Jails," Treatment Advocacy Center, 2014, 101.

11. Aufderheide, "Mental Illness."

12. "Callous and Cruel: Use of Force Against Inmates with Mental Disabilities in US Jails and Prisons," Human Rights Watch, 2015, 3, 11.

13. Ram Subramanian et al., "Incarceration's Front Door: The Misuse of Jails in America," Vera Institute for Justice, 2015, 12.

14. "Callous and Cruel," 20.

15. Matt Ford, "America's Largest Mental Hospital Is a Jail," *Atlantic*, June 8, 2015.

16. Subramanian et al., "Incarceration's Front Door," 12.

17. Ford, "America's Largest Mental Hospital is a Jail."

18. CBS News, October 31, 2014.

19. Stephen Rex Brown, "City Settles for $3.8M in Rikers Island

Inmate's Soap-Swallowing Horror," New York *Daily News*, November 17, 2015.

20. Greg Dober, "Corizon Needs a Checkup: Problems with Privatized Correctional Healthcare," *Prison Legal News*, March 15, 2014, 1.

21. Paul Von Zielbauer, "As Health Care in Jails Goes Private, 10 Days Can Be a Death Sentence," *New York Times*, February 27, 2005.

22. Dober, "Corizon Needs a Checkup," 1.

23. Rhonda Swan, "Time for State to Be Done with Corizon Health," *Sun-Sentinel* (Orlando), December 4, 2015.

24. Timothy Williams, "A Psychologist as Warden? Jail and Mental Illness Intersect in Chicago," *New York Times*, July 31, 2015.

25. Ibid.

26. Ibid.

27. Lisa Schenker, "New Cook County Clinic Aims to Keep Mentally Ill out of Jail," *Chicago Tribune*, November 1, 2016.

28. "Cook County Jail Population Down About 700 people," *Daily Herald*, January 3, 2017.

29. Eric Peterson, "Preckwinkle Addresses Role of King's Legacy in 2017," *Daily Herald*, January 13, 2017.

30. Class Action Complaint, No. 2016CH13587 (In the Circuit Court of Cook County, Illinois, County Department, Chancery Division, Oct. 14, 2016).

31. Williams, "Psychologist as Warden?"

32. Ian Lovett, "Los Angeles Agrees to Overhaul Jails to Care for Mentally Ill and Curb Abuse," *New York Times*, August 6, 2015.

33. Ibid.

34. Department of Justice, "Justice Department Reaches Agreement with Los Angeles County to Implement Sweeping Reforms on Mental Health Care and Use of Force Throughout the County Jail System," press release, August 5, 2015.

35. Ibid.

36. Cindy Chang and Joel Rubin, "After Years of Scandal, L.A. Jails Get Federal Oversight, Sweeping Reforms," *Los Angeles Times*, August 5, 2015.

37. Associated Press, "Former LA County Inmates File Action over Treatment of Mentally Ill Prisoners," CBS Los Angeles, September 28, 2015.

38. Frank Stoltze, "LA Sheriff, US Dept of Justice Announces New Reforms Protecting Mentally Ill in Jails," KPCC, August 5, 2015.

39. Maya Lau, "L.A. County Supervisors Vote to Expand Sheriff's Mental Health Teams," *Los Angeles Times*, January 11, 2017.

40. Devin Browne, "LA County's Plan to Keep Skid Row's Intoxicated out of Jail and the ER," KPCC, January 2, 2017.

41. Maya Lau, "After Scandals, a Group of Civilians Ushers in a New Era of Oversight for the L.A. County Sheriff's Department," *Los Angeles Times*, January 26, 2017.

42. Julie K. Brown, "Prosecutors Find No Wrongdoing in Shower Death at Dade Correctional Mental Health Unit," *Miami Herald*," March 17, 2017.

43. Disability Rights Florida, "Department of Corrections Sued over Inmate Abuse at the Dade Correctional Institution," September 9, 2014.

44. Disability Rights California, "Under Proposed Settlement, Fresno County Prisoners Will No Longer Be Denied Adequate Health Care," May 28, 2015.

45. ACLU of Florida, letter to Attorney General Eric Holder calling for investigation of Florida prisons, June 25, 2014, https://aclufl.org/resources/letter-doj-investigation-fl-prisons.

46. CBS Miami and Associated Press, "US Investigating Florida Prisoner's Death In Scalding Shower," May 20, 2015.

47. "Callous and Cruel," 64.

48. Jennifer Gonnerman, "A Lawsuit to End Abuse at Rikers," *New Yorker*, December 19, 2014.

49. Ibid.

50. Michael Winerip and Michael Schwirtz, "Rikers: Where Mental Illness Meets Brutality in Jail," *New York Times*, July 14, 2014.

51. Gonnerman, "Lawsuit to End Abuse at Rikers."

52. Jillian Jorgensen, "City and Bharara Reach Settlement in

Federal Lawsuit over Rikers Island," *Observer* (New York), June 22, 2015.

53. Preet Bharara, United States Attorney, letter to the Honorable James C. Francis IV, June 22, 2015, https://www.justice.gov/usao-sdny/file/479956/download.

54. Benjamin Weiser, "Deal Is Near on Far-Reaching Reforms at Rikers, Including a Federal Monitor," *New York Times*, June 19, 2015.

55. Bharara letter to Francis.

56. Ibid.

57. Michael Winerip and Michael Schwirtz, "New York City to End Contract with Rikers Health Care Provider," *New York Times*, June 11, 2015.

58. Michael Schwirtz, "New Officers Add to Hope for Reform at Rikers Island," *New York Times*, December 5, 2015.

59. Florence Finkle, "How to Really Fix Rikers," *New York Times*, June 19, 2015.

5: Child Support

1. Due in part to the plummet in Temporary Assistance for Needy Families (TANF) and recent legislation, 95 percent of child support payments goes to families and just 5 percent goes to federal and state governments. Office of Child Support Enforcement, Administration for Children and Families, "FY 2015 Preliminary Data Report," DCL-16-07, April 16, 2016.

2. Fathers account for about 20 percent of custodial parents, and a significant number of parents share custody.

3. Flexibility, Efficiency, and Modernization in Child Support Enforcement Programs, 81 Fed. Reg. 93492, 93493 (Dec. 20, 2016).

4. Melissa Boteach and Rebecca Vallas, "3 Facts You Need to Know About the Obama Administration's Proposed Child Support Rules," Center for American Progress, June 18, 2015.

5. Frances Robles and Shaila Dewan, "Skip Child Support. Go to Jail. Lose Job. Repeat," *New York Times*, April 19, 2015.

6. Tonya L. Brito, "Fathers Behind Bars: Rethinking Child

Support Policy Toward Low-Income Noncustodial Fathers and Their Families," *Iowa Journal of Gender, Race and Justice* 15 (2012): 634–59.

7. Elaine Sorensen, Liliana Sousa, and Simone G. Schaner, "Assessing Child Support Arrears in Nine Large States and the Nation," Urban Institute, 2007.

8. Ibid.

9. Robles and Dewan, "Skip Child Support."

10. Mike Brunker, "Unable to Pay Child Support, Poor Parents Land Behind Bars," NBC News, September 12, 2011.

11. Robles and Dewan, "Skip Child Support."

12. *Turner v. Rogers*, 564 U.S. 431 (2011).

13. Brito, "Fathers Behind Bars," 622–31.

14. Flexibility, Efficiency, and Modernization in Child Support Enforcement Programs.

15. Project to Avoid Increasing Delinquencies, Office of Child Support Enforcement, Administration for Children and Families, U.S. Department of Health and Human Services, Child Support Fact Sheet Series, Number 4, "Realistic Child Support Orders for Incarcerated Parents" (2013).

16. Ibid.

6: Criminalizing Public Benefits

1. Kaaryn Gustafson, *Cheating Welfare* (New York: New York University Press, 2012), 668, 708; Karen Dolan with Jodi L. Carr, *The Poor Get Prison: The Alarming Spread of the Criminalization of Poverty* (Washington, DC: Institute for Policy Studies, 2015), 7.

2. Bryan Lowry, "Bill Tightening Restrictions on Welfare Recipients Advances in Kansas," *Wichita Eagle*, April 1, 2015.

3. *The Daily Show with Jon Stewart*, "GOPsters Paradise," April 9, 2015.

4. Ife Floyd, LaDonna Pavetti, and Liz Schott, "TANF Continues to Weaken as a Safety Net," Center on Budget and Policy Priorities, October 27, 2015, 6.

5. Neil Abernathy and Rebecca Smith, "Work Benefits: Ensuring

Economic Security in the 21st Century," National Employment Law Project and Roosevelt Institute, January 2017, 14.

6. David Super, *Public Welfare Law* (St. Paul, MN: Foundation Press, 2017), 957.

7. Alexandra Sirota, "How to Build an Economy That Works for All: Support Jobless Workers' Connection to Work and Careers," North Carolina Justice Center, Budget and Tax Center, Oct. 2016.

8. "Media Release: North Carolina's Unemployment Insurance System Offers Too Little for Too Few Workers for Too Short a Period," North Carolina Justice Center, Workers Rights Project, April 7, 2016.

9. Rachel West et al., "Strengthening Unemployment Protections in America," Center for American Progress, 2016, 39.

10. Jason Taylor, "MO Lawmakers Consider Reducing Unemployment Benefits," *Ozarks First*, January 30, 2017.

11. Chris Otts, "Bevin Administration to Pull Workers from 31 Ky. Employment Offices," WRDB, January 11, 2017.

12. Kristin Seefeldt, "We Need to Fix the Social Safety Net, Not Shame Those Who Need It," *PBS NewsHour*, February 2, 2017.

13. Wisconsin Office of the Governor, "Governor Walker Approves Rule Requiring Drug Testing for Unemployment Insurance Recipients," press release, May 4, 2016.

14. Juliet M. Brodie, Clare Pastore, Ezra Rosser, and Jeffrey Selbin, *Poverty Law, Policy, and Practice* (Frederick, MD: Wolters Kluwer Law & Business, 2014), 561–62.

15. Ryan Felton, "Criminalizing the Unemployed," *Detroit Metro Times*, July 1, 2015.

16. H. Luke Shaefer and Steve Gray to Gay Gilbert, Administrator, U.S. Department of Labor, memorandum, "Michigan Unemployment Insurance Agency: Unjust Fraud and Multiple Determinations," May 19, 2016, http://democrats.waysandmeans.house.gov/sites/democrats.waysandmeans.house.gov/files/documents/Shaefer-Gray-USDOL-Memo_06-01-2015.pdf.

17. Felton, "Criminalizing the Unemployed."

18. Ibid.

19. Ibid.

20. "State Falsely Penalizes Thousands for Unemployment Benefits Fraud. Now Victims Want Their Money Back," Michigan Radio, January 11, 2017.

21. Paul Egan, "Aide Warned Mic. Governor Rick Snyder About Jobless Agency Leadership," *Detroit Free Press*, May 13, 2017.

22. Rebecca Vallas and Sharon Dietrich, "One Strike and You're Out: How We Can Eliminate Barriers to Economic Security and Mobility for People With Criminal Records," Center for American Progress, 2014, 1.

23. Robert H. DeFina and Lance Hannon, "The Impact of Mass Incarceration on Poverty," *Crime and Delinquency* 59, no. 4 (2013): 562–86.

24. Marie Gottschalk, *Caught: The Prison State and the Lockdown of American Politics* (Princeton, NJ: Princeton University Press, 2015), 243.

25. Shaila Dewan, "The Collateral Victims of Criminal Justice," *New York Times*, September 6, 2015.

26. Ibid.

27. John Schmitt and Kris Warner, "Ex-Offenders and the Labor Market," Center for Economic and Policy Research, 2010.

28. Human Rights Watch was specifically told by some local public housing authorities that they actually keep no data on these matters. There are four thousand public housing authorities around the country, but many either do not even keep data or do have it but do not report nationally. A government study estimated 49,000 applications were denied for public housing due to criminal activity and 9,000 residents were evicted. But the government does not report data on Section 8 vouchers, which account for more than half of federally supported housing. Human Rights Watch, "No Second Chance: People with Criminal Records Denied Access to Public Housing," November 18, 2004, 31–34; Government Accountability Office, "Drug Offenders: Various Factors May Limit the Impacts of Federal Laws That Provide

for Denial of Selected Benefits," GAO-05-238, September 28, 2005. See also Afomeia Tesfai and Kim Gilhuly, *The Long Road Home: Decreasing Barriers to Public Housing for People with Criminal Records*, Human Impact Partners, May 2016.

29. Human Rights Watch, "No Second Chance," 3.

30. The three categories are drug-related criminal activity, violent criminal activity, and criminal activity that would adversely affect the health, safety, or right to peaceful enjoyment of the premises by others. Marie Claire Tran-Leung, "When Discretion Means Denial," Sargent Shriver National Center on Poverty Law, 2015, 7–9.

31. Human Rights Watch, "No Second Chance," 3.

32. Tran-Leung, "When Discretion Means Denial."

33. Ibid., 28–31.

34. *Dep't of Hous. v. Rucker*, 535 U.S. 125, 130–31 (2002).

35. Tran-Leung, "When Discretion Means Denial," iii.

36. Mireya Navarro, "Federal Housing Officials Warn Against Blanket Bans of Ex-Offenders," *New York Times*, April 4, 2016.

37. *Texas Dep't of Hous. and Cmty. Affairs v. Inclusive Community Project, Inc.*, 576 U.S. ___, 135 S.Ct. 2507 (2015).

38. Society for Human Resource Management, "Background Checking—the Use of Criminal Background Checks in Hiring Decisions," July 19, 2012, slide 3.

39. "Data, Analytics & Technology—Data," LexisNexis.com, http://lexisnexis.com/risk/abpit/datasource.aspx.

40. Vallas and Dietrich, "One Strike," 14.

41. Christopher J. Lyons and Becky Pettit, "Compounded Disadvantage: Race, Incarceration and Wage Growth," *Social Problems* 58, no. 2 (2011): 257.

42. Fredrick Kunkle, "Woman Who Killed Man She Says Abused Her Can't Escape Felony Past," *Washington Post*, March 30, 2015.

43. Vallas and Dietrich, "One Strike," 12.

44. Half in Ten and Sentencing Project, "Americans with Criminal Records," Poverty and Opportunity Profile, 2015, 2.

45. Vallas and Dietrich, "One Strike," 22–25; Marc Mauer and Virginia McCalmont, "A Lifetime of Punishment," Sentencing Project, 2015, 2.

46. Vallas and Dietrich, "One Strike," 24.

47. Ibid., 26–27.

48. Ibid., 28.

49. "Use of Criminal Histories in College Admissions Reconsidered," Center for Community Alternatives, 2010, i.

50. Amy Hirsch et al., "Every Door Closed: Barriers Facing Parents with Criminal Records," Center for Law and Social Policy and Community Legal Services, 2002.

7: Poverty, Race, and Discipline in Schools

1. A searing report done in 2016 by the Juvenile Law Center in Philadelphia showed that all or parts of states impose high fines and fees in juvenile courts across the board along with those imposed in adult courts. Jessica Feierman, Naomi Goldstein, Emily Haney-Caron, and Jaymes Fairfax Columbo, "Debtors' Prisons for Kids? The High Cost of Fees in the Juvenile Justice System," Juvenile Law Center, Philadelphia, 2016, 20.

2. Susan Ferriss, "Virginia Tops Nation in Sending Students to Cops, Courts: Where Does Your State Rank?," Center for Public Integrity, April 10, 2015.

3. Emma Brown, "Five Eye-Opening Figures from the U.S. Education Department's Latest Civil Rights Dump," *Washington Post*, June 7, 2016.

4. "The Facts About Dangers of Added Police in Schools," Sentencing Project, January 2013.

5. Monique W. Morris, *Pushout: The Criminalization of Black Girls in Schools* (New York: The New Press, 2016), 76.

6. U.S. Department of Education Office for Civil Rights, "Civil Rights Data Collection: Data Snapshot; School Discipline," March 2014, 7.

7. Kari Dequine Harden, "Dealing with the School-to-Prison-Pipeline," *Louisiana Weekly,* April 27, 2015. See Jason P. Nance, "Students, Police, and the School-to Prison Pipeline," *Washington University Law Review* 93 (2016): 919.

8. Erik Eckholm, "With Police in Schools, More Children in Court," *New York Times,* April 12, 2013.

9. Morris, *Pushout,* 76.

10. Deborah Fowler, Rebecca Lightsey, Janis Monger, Elica Terrazas, and Lynn White, "Texas' School-to-Prison Pipeline: Dropout to Incarceration (2007) 18, 76.

11. Ibid., 5.

12. Associated Press, "Texas Law Decriminalizes School Truancy," *New York Times,* June 21, 2015.

13. Fowler et al., *Texas' School-to-Prison-Pipeline,* 71.

14. Ibid., 1, 6, 67, 79–80, 88.

15. Ibid., 8, 44, 58, 119–40.

16. Ibid., 48.

17. Ibid.

18. Deborah Fowler et al., "Class, Not Court," Texas Appleseed, 2015, ii.

19. Texas Appleseed and Texans Care for Children, "Dangerous Discipline: How Texas Schools Are Relying on Law Enforcement, Courts and Juvenile Probation to Discipline Students," 2016, 4, 58.

20. Donna St. George, "Judge Steve Teske Seeks to Keep Kids with Minor Problems out of Court," *Washington Post,* October 17, 2011.

8: Crime-Free Housing Ordinances and the Criminalization of Homelessness

1. Eric Eckholm, "Victims' Dilemma: 911 Calls Can Bring Eviction," *New York Times,* August 17, 2013.

2. Sandra Park and Michaela Wallin, "Local Nuisance Ordinances: Penalizing the Victim, Undermining Communities?," *Municipal Lawyer Magazine,* May/June 2015, 9.

3. ACLU, "Nancy Markham v. City of Surprise," last modified August 27, 2015, https://www.aclu.org/cases/nancy-markham-v-city-surprise; Settlement, *Markham v. Surprise*, 2:15-cv-0169 (D. Ariz. Sept. 2, 2015).

4. International Crime Free Association, "Crime Free Programs Instructor Workshop," Waco, Texas, October 19–21, 2016.

5. Nicole Livanos, "Crime-Free Housing Ordinances: One Call Away from Eviction," *Public Interest Law Reporter* 19 (Spring 2014): 107.

6. Matthew Desmond and Nicole Valdez, "Unpolicing the Urban Poor: Consequences of Third-Party Policing for Inner-City Women," *American Sociological Association* 78, no. 1 (February 2013): 117–41.

7. Eckholm, "Victims' Dilemma."

8. Bryce Covert, "When Calling the Police on an Abusive Partner Leads to a Victim Losing Her Home," Think Progress, August 27, 2015.

9. Rachel Swain, *Renting While Black—Antioch Tenants Charge Police with Campaign of Intimidation* (American Civil Liberties Union of Northern California, 2008); *Williams v. City of Antioch*, 2010 WL 3632197 (N.D. Cal. Sept. 2, 2010).

10. *Texas Dep't. of Hous. and Cmty. Affairs v. The Inclusive Community Project, Inc.*, 576 U.S. ___, 135 S. Ct. 2507 (2015).

11. "Housing Not Handcuffs: Ending the Criminalization of Homelessness in U.S. Cities," National Law Center on Homelessness and Poverty, 2016, 9–10; "No Safe Place: The Criminalization of Homelessness in U.S. Cities," National Law Center on Homelessness and Poverty, 2015, 6–8.

12. "Housing Not Handcuffs," 22, 24, 25.

13. Rebecca Vallas and Sharon Dietrich, "One Strike and You're Out: How We Can Eliminate Barriers to Economic Security and Mobility for People With Criminal Records," Center for American Progress, December 2014, 7.

14. "Housing Not Handcuffs," 19.

15. John Flynn and Matt Kramer, "Sacramento's $100,000 Homeless Man," *Sacramento News and Review*, February 16, 2017.

16. "No Safe Place," 8.

17. "Housing Not Handcuffs," 11.

18. "Picking Up the Pieces: Policing in America," American Civil Liberties Union, 2015, 15.

19. Ibid.

20. Adam Nagourney, "Aloha, and Welcome, Unless You're Homeless," *New York Times*, June 4, 2016.

21. Justin Jouvenal, "Cities v. the Homeless," *Washington Post*, June 3, 2016.

22. Jennifer Medina, "Los Angeles Puts $100 Million into Helping Homeless," *New York Times*, September 23, 2015.

23. Adam Murray, "Preventing Homelessness," *Los Angeles Daily Journal*, October 1, 2015.

24. Adam Murray, "L.A. Has 46,874 People Who Are Homeless. If We're Not Smart, We'll Have 250,000 More," *Los Angeles Times*, July 14, 2016.

25. Adam Murray, "From the Executive Director," Inner City Law Center 16th Annual Awards Luncheon, 2016.

26. "Housing Not Handcuffs," 7.

9: Taking Criminal Justice Reform Seriously

1. Melissa Kearney and Benjamin Harris, "Ten Facts About Crime and Incarceration in the United States," Hamilton Project, 2014.

2. "We All Benefit from a Clean Slate for Minor Criminal Records," Community Legal Services, Philadelphia, 2016, 1.

3. "We All Benefit."

4. "We All Benefit."

5. Richard A. Oppel Jr., "States Trim Penalties and Prison Cells, Even as Sessions Gets Tough," *New York Times*, May 19, 2017.

6. Danielle Kaeble et al., "Correctional Populations in the United States in 2014," Department of Justice, Bureau of Justice Statistics, 2015, 2.

7. Marc Mauer and Nazgol Ghandnoosh, "Fewer Prisoners, Less Crime: A Tale of Three States," Sentencing Project, 2015, 3.

8. David Segal, "Prison Vendors See Continued Signs of a Captive Market," *New York Times*, August 30, 2015.

9. Ibid.

10. Michele Deitch and Michael Mushlin, "What's Going On in Our Prisons?," *New York Times*, January 4, 2016.

11. James Austin et al., "Ending Mass Incarceration: Charting a New Justice Reinvestment," n.d., 20, available at https://www.aclu.org/files/assets/charting_a_new_justice_reinvestment_final.pdf; Mauer and Ghandnoosh, "Fewer Prisoners, Less Crime," 1.

12. James Austin, Michael P. Jacobson, and Inimai M. Chettiar, "How New York City Reduced Mass Incarceration: A Model for Change?," Brennan Center for Justice, JFA Institute, and Vera Institute of Justice, January 2013, 6–7.

13. Austin et al., "Ending Mass Incarceration."

14. Jim Dwyer, "An Obstacle to Progress in Brownsville," *New York Times*, January 13, 2016.

15. J. David Goodman, "Council Approves Bills to Divert Minor Offenders from Court System," *New York Times*, May 26, 2016.

16. Austin, Jacobson, and Chettiar, "How New York City Reduced Mass Incarceration," 6; Lauren-Brooke Eisen and Inimai Chettiar, "The Reverse Mass Incarceration Act," Brennan Center for Justice, 2013, 5.

17. Austin, Jacobson, and Chettiar, "How New York City Reduced Mass Incarceration," 7.

18. Eisen and Chettiar, "The Reverse Mass Incarceration Act," 10; S.P. Sullivan, "How N.J. Became a Nationwide Leader in Reducing Prison Population," NJ.com, October 31, 2015.

19. Rob Kuznia, "An Unprecedented Experiment in Mass Forgiveness," *Washington Post*, February 9, 2016.

20. Eisen and Chettiar, "The Reverse Mass Incarceration Act," 6.

21. 563 U.S. 493 (2011).

22. Mauer and Ghandnoosh, "Fewer Prisoners, Less Crime."

23. Sasha Abramsky, "How California Voters Got So Smart on Crime," *The Nation*, March 26, 2015; "California's Prison Experiment," editorial, *New York Times*, November 14, 2015.

24. Margaret Dooley-Sammuli, "Changing Gears: California's Shift to Smart Justice," ACLU of California, 2015, 6.

25. Ibid., 4.

26. Ibid., 3, 9–11.

27. Nell Bernstein, "Prop. 47 Is Changing Criminal Justice. Will It Take Root in U.S.?" *Equal Voice News*, September 29, 2015; Abramsky, "How California Voters Got So Smart on Crime," 10.

28. Bernstein, "Prop. 47 Is Changing Criminal Justice."

29. Ben Poston, "ACLU Faults California Law Enforcement Response to Prop. 47," *Los Angeles Times*, November 10, 2015.

30. "California's Prison Experiment."

31. Frank Stoltze, "Violent Crime Up for Second Straight Year in Los Angeles," KPCC, January 6, 2017.

32. Charis E. Kubrin, Carroll Seron, and Joan Petersilia, "The Crime That Wasn't in California," *Washington Post*, March 18, 2016.

33. Robert Greene, "California's Prop. 47 Revolution: Why Are Police Refusing to Make Misdemeanor Arrests?," *Los Angeles Times*, October 28, 2015.

34. Robert Greene, "California's Prop. 47 Revolution: Do Prosecutors Really Need a 'Felony Hammer' to Deal with Drug Offenders?," *Los Angeles Times*, October 27, 2015.

35. Cindy Chang, Joel Rubin, and Ben Poston, "Prop. 47's Effect on Jail Time, Drug Rehabilitation Is Mixed So Far," *Los Angeles Times*, February 21, 2015; Cindy Chang, Joel Rubin, and Ben Poston, "Unintended Consequences of Prop. 47 Pose Challenge for Criminal Justice System," *Los Angeles Times*, November 6, 2015.

36. Chang et al, "Prop. 47's Effect on Jail Time, Drug Rehabilitation Is Mixed So Far"; Chang et al, "Unintended Consequences of Prop. 47 Pose Challenge for Criminal Justice System."

37. "LA County Counted on Prop 47 to Save Money. It Hasn't Yet," *Los Angeles Daily News*, November 15, 2016.

38. Brett Kelman and Cheri Carlson, "Nearly 200,000 Felonies Erased by Prop 47, but Some Felons Don't Know," *Desert Sun*, December 14, 2016.

39. Kuznia, "An Unprecedented Experiment in Mass Forgiveness."

40. Associated Press, "California: Brown Seeks Changes in Sentencing Laws," *New York Times*, January 28, 2016.

41. "California's Prison Experiment."

42. Kuznia, "An Unprecedented Experiment in Mass Forgiveness."

43. Kelman and Carlson, "Nearly 200,000 Felonies Erased."

44. Bernstein, "Prop. 47 Is Changing Criminal Justice," 12–13.

10: Turning the Coin Over

1. Myron Orfield, "Metropolitics: A Regional Agenda for Community and Stability," *Forum for Social Economics* 28 (1999): 33–49.

2. Matthew Desmond, *Evicted* (New York: Crown Publishers, 2016).

3. John Eligon, "Minneapolis Grapples with a Community Being Left Behind," *New York Times*, January 11, 2016.

4. Northside Achievement Zone and Boston Consulting Group, "Business Plan FY 2015–FY 2022," 4, http://northsideachievement.org/wp-content/uploads/NAZ-Business-Plan-11-Web.pdf.

5. "Picking Up the Pieces: Policing in America, a Minneapolis Case Study," Minnesota ACLU, 2015.

6. Jessica Feierman, Naomi Goldstein, Emily Haney-Caron, and Jaymes Fairfax Columbo, "Debtors' Prison for Kids? The High Cost of Fees in the Juvenile System," Juvenile Law Center, Philadelphia, 2016.

7. Name changed to protect anonymity.

8. Dave preferred not to have his real name included here.

9. "2015 Impact Report," Youth Policy Institute, 11–12.

10. Annalise Orleck, "The New War on Poverty," *Talk Poverty*, March 11, 2016.

Index

Publishing in the Public Interest

Thank you for reading this book published by The New Press. The New Press is a nonprofit, public interest publisher. New Press books and authors play a crucial role in sparking conversations about the key political and social issues of our day.

We hope you enjoyed this book and that you will stay in touch with The New Press. Here are a few ways to stay up to date with our books, events, and the issues we cover:

- Sign up at www.thenewpress.com/subscribe to receive updates on New Press authors and issues and to be notified about local events
- Like us on Facebook: www.facebook.com/newpressbooks
- Follow us on Twitter: www.twitter.com/thenewpress

Please consider buying New Press books for yourself; for friends and family; and to donate to schools, libraries, community centers, prison libraries, and other organizations involved with the issues our authors write about.

The New Press is a 501(c)(3) nonprofit organization. You can also support our work with a tax-deductible gift by visiting www.thenewpress.com/donate.

Printed in the USA
CPSIA information can be obtained
at www.ICGtesting.com
JSHW082151140824
68134JS00014B/173

9 781620 975480